GW00645421

The Damascus Events

The Damascus Events

The 1860 Massacre and the
Destruction of the Old Ottoman World

EUGENE ROGAN

ALLEN LANE
an imprint of
PENGUIN BOOKS

ALLEN LANE

UK | USA | Canada | Ireland | Australia
India | New Zealand | South Africa

Allen Lane is part of the Penguin Random House group of companies
whose addresses can be found at global.penguinrandomhouse.com.

First published in the United States of America by Basic Books, an imprint of
Hachette Book Group 2024
First published in Great Britain by Allen Lane 2024

001

Copyright © Eugene Rogan, 2024

The moral right of the author has been asserted

Printed and bound in Great Britain by Clays Ltd, Elcograf S.p.A.

The authorized representative in the EEA is Penguin Random House Ireland,
Morrison Chambers, 32 Nassau Street, Dublin D02 YH68

A CIP catalogue record for this book is available from the British Library

ISBN: 978–0–241–64690–8

This book is dedicated to Ngaire Tui Woods

CONTENTS

LIST OF ILLUSTRATIONS

1. Damascus with the Umayyad Mosque in the centre. Photograph by Bonfils, 1870s. Library of Congress.
2. Damascene houses had humble exteriors but some hid interiors of striking luxury. Photograph by Francis Frith. Metropolitan Museum of Art.
3. The sumptuous interior of the al-Islambuli House. Photograph by Bonfils, 1870s. Library of Congress.
4. A typical courtyard of a fine Damascene house. Photograph by Bonfils, 1870s. Library of Congress.
5. The Barada River entering Damascus. The Takiyya al-Sulaymaniyya mosque complex is on the far bank. American Colony photographers. Library of Congress, G. Eric and Edith Matson Photograph Collection.
6. Customers at a coffeehouse on the banks of the Barada. Photograph by R.E.M. Bain, 1895. Library of Congress.
7. The great Umayyad Mosque. Photograph by Francis Bedford, 29 April 1862. The Royal Collection.
8. In the Umayyad Mosque's colonnades scholars taught classes, worshippers prayed and Damascenes from all levels of society

could rest and meditate. Photograph by Bonfils, 1870s. Library of Congress.

9. The departure of the annual Haj pilgrimage caravan for Mecca. Photographer unknown. Library of Congress.

10. Dr Mikhayil Mishaqa. Photograph by Bonfils, 1870s.

11. The Amir 'Abd al-Qadir al-Jaza'iri. The Royal Collection.

12. Fuad Pasha in the uniform that he refused to wear upon his entry to Damascus in July 1860. Abdullah Frères photographers, Constantinople.

13. A well-armed Druze farmer from Mount Lebanon. Photograph by Trancrède Dumas. Library of Congress.

14. Bashi Bozuk irregulars. This group accompanied the Prince of Wales on his 1862 tour of the Levant as far as Nablus, where they were dismissed. Photograph by Francis Bedford. The Royal Collection.

15. A *kawass* or consular guard carrying a sword and staff as symbols of his office. Photograph by Bonfils. Harvard Semitic Museum.

16. A dragoman in the lavish uniform and an array of weapons that shows he was both an interpreter and a security guard. Harvard Semitic Museum.

17. The gates of the Citadel of Hasbayya. Photograph by Francis Bedford, 1862. The Royal Collection.

18. Rashayya. Photograph by Bonfils. Harvard Semitic Museum.

19. Zahleh. Photograph by Bonfils. Harvard Semitic Museum.

20. Dayr al-Qamar. Photograph by Bonfils. Harvard Semitic Museum.

21. The courtyard of the British consulate where thousands of Christians took refuge. Photograph by Francis Bedford, 1862. The Royal Collection.

22. Another view of the Takiyya al-Sulaymaniyya, used as a detention centre for hundreds of Muslim men. Library of Congress.

23. The Street Called Straight, facing Bab Sharqi (the Eastern Gate), Damascus, 30 April 1862 in near total ruin. One rebuilt house can be seen clearly and another glimpsed to the right of the palm tree. Photograph by Francis Bedford. The Royal Collection.

24. Ruins of the Greek church in the Christian quarters, 30 April 1862. The logs in the foreground were for reconstruction. Photograph by Francis Bedford. The Royal Collection.

25. The new administrative quarter of Marja. This is where the road from Beirut to Damascus entered the city. Photograph by Bonfils. Harvard Semitic Museum.

26. Marja Square, looking south, showing the central jail, the governor's palace or Saray (with curved roofline), and government buildings, 1895. Photograph by R.E.M. Bain. Library of Congress.

27. The Suq al-Arwam. Photography by American Colony. Library of Congress.

28. A pottery shop in Damascus, 1859. In 1863 the governor ordered benches such as this one to be destroyed to widen the streets and allow through wheeled traffic. Photograph by Francis Frith. Middle East Centre Archive.

29. The Citadel of Damascus. Photograph by Bonfils, 1880s. Harvard Semitic Museum.

A NOTE ON TIME, DISTANCE, DATES, EXCHANGE RATES

They say that the past is a foreign land. Nineteenth-century Damascus was a very foreign land indeed. The modern historian continually runs into markers of difference between their time and ours.

Time was measured against the sunrise, not by a twenty-four-hour clock. The day began at dawn. One o'clock in the morning in 1860 Damascus would have been one hour after sunrise. In converting the time as recorded in my documents into times more recognisable to modern readers, I have consulted online almanacs to know when the sun rose on a given day of the year in Damascus. So when Dr Mishaqa reported that the riots broke out in Damascus at eight o'clock in the morning on 9 July 1860, I counted eight hours after sunrise, which in Damascus in July is around 5:30 a.m., which would correspond to about 1:30 p.m. For more on timekeeping in the late

Ottoman Empire, see Avner Wishnitzer, *Reading Clocks, Alla Turca: Time and Society in the Late Ottoman Empire* (Chicago: University of Chicago Press, 2015).

Distance in nineteenth-century Syria was measured in time. Ottoman maps provide a scale demarcated in hours rather than in kilometres or miles. The standard assumption of Ottoman cartographers was that travellers could cover between five and five-and-a-half kilometres in one hour. For more on Ottoman map-making, see Yuval Ben-Bassat and Yossi Ben-Zrtzi, 'Ottoman Maps of the Empire's Arab Provinces, 1850s to the First World War,' *Imago Mundi* 70, no. 2 (2018): 199–211.

Two calendars predominated in the 1860s. Ottoman subjects and officials operated by the lunar Hijri calendar, and Europe and the Western Hemisphere worked by the solar Gregorian calendar. The Ottoman Mali fiscal calendar, though in existence since the 1780s, was not widely used in Ottoman documents in the 1860s and 1870s. In converting between the Hijri and Gregorian calendars, I have relied on the hijri.habibur.com website.

The standard currency of the Ottoman Empire was the piastre (Pt.). The Turkish *lira* or pound (£T) was worth between Pt. 115 and 130, and a 'purse' (*kis* in Arabic and Turkish) was a unit of Pt. 500. However, officials in different cities had the power to alter exchange rates to make ends meet. The government in Damascus devalued the local currency so that piastres from Beirut were up to 10 per-cent more valuable than those from Damascus. This also affected foreign-exchange rates. For most of the period covered in this book, the British pound sterling traded for between Pt. 110 and 130, the US dollar for about Pt. 22–26, and the French franc for Pt. 5–6. See

Charles Issawi, ed., *The Economic History of the Middle East, 1800–1914* (Chicago: University of Chicago Press, 1966), 520–522.

In the nineteenth century, Turks and foreigners alike tended to refer to the Ottoman capital city of Istanbul by its Byzantine name, Constantinople, but the city was known by several other names. Many nineteenth-century Arabic sources refer to the Ottoman capital as al-Istana. In his consular correspondence, Mishaqa called the capital 'Islambul,' another variant of the name. In this book I will use modern Turkish place names—Istanbul rather than Constantinople, Izmir rather than Smyrna—but retain the usage as it appears within my historical sources. I use standard English spellings for the major Arab cities mentioned in the text—thus Beirut rather than Bayrut, Damascus rather than al-Sham, Aleppo rather than Halab. For more, see Bernard Lewis, *Istanbul and the Civilization of the Ottoman Empire* (Norman: University of Oklahoma Press, 1963).

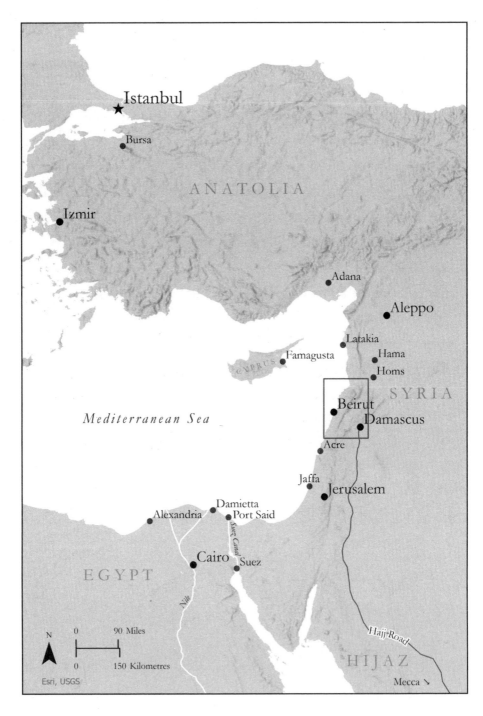

The Ottoman Mediterranean. *Credit: Martin Davis*

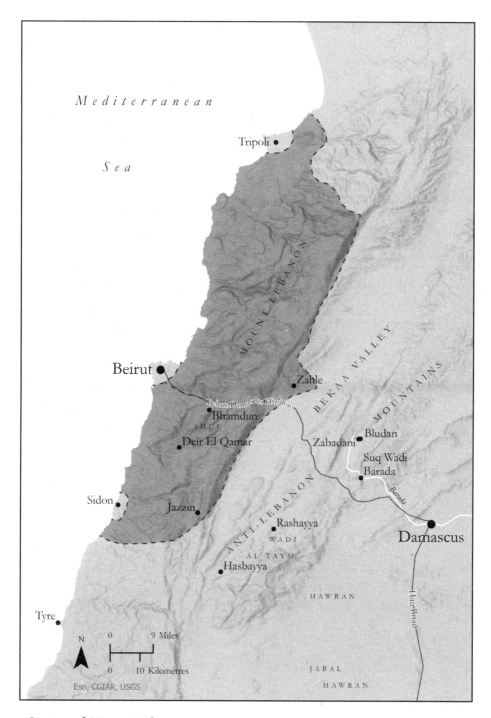

Syria and Mount Lebanon. *Credit: Martin Davis*

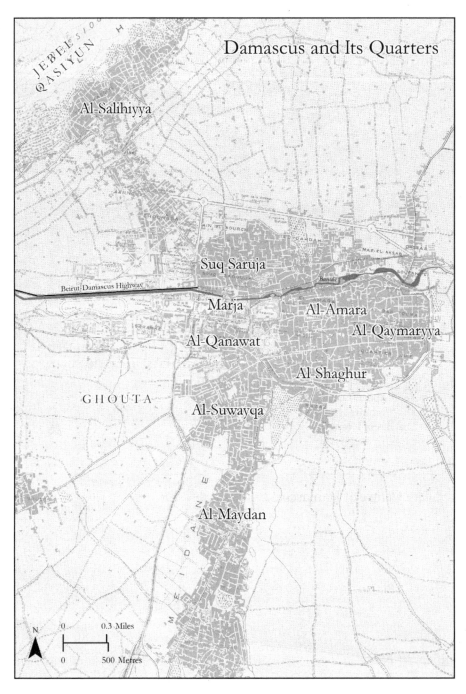

Damascus and Its Quarters. *Credit: Martin Davis*

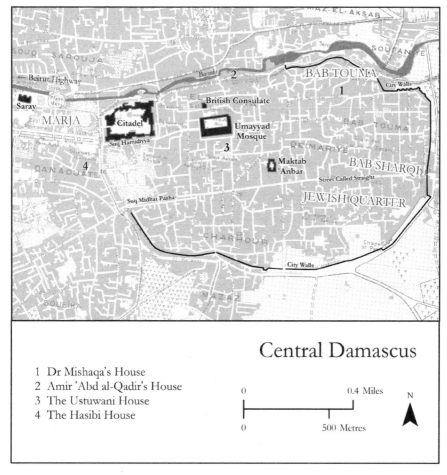

The City Centre of Damascus. *Credit: Martin Davis*

1 Dr Mishaqa's House
2 Amir 'Abd al-Qadir's House
3 The Ustuwani House
4 The Hasibi House

Central Damascus

0   0.4 Miles

0   500 Metres

N

Introduction

Found in the Archives

I had a sense of occasion as I walked up the vast limestone steps into the National Archives in Washington, DC. The classical architecture impresses on the visitor that this is the repository of the memories of a great nation. Inside the broad domed lobby, display cases house copies of the Declaration of Independence, the Constitution, and the Bill of Rights along with other select treasures on display for visitors, capturing the foundations and milestones of the American republic's journey.

On that January morning in 1989, I did not stop to take in the displays but made my way past the guards into the reading room. I had come in search of documentation for my doctoral thesis on Ottoman rule in Transjordan in the second half of the nineteenth century. At that time, Transjordan was a frontier region of the Ottoman province of Syria with its capital in Damascus. The United States opened its first diplomatic mission to Damascus in 1859, and

I wanted to see if there was any material in the US consular archives that related to my research interests.

I was also interested in the first American vice-consul, a man named Mikhayil (Michael in Arabic) Mishaqa. The United States was a small power in 1859 and maintained a modest diplomatic corps overseas. In many jurisdictions, the Foreign Service hired local talent to represent US interests to economise on the number of diplomats posted abroad. But the man they chose for Damascus was one of the most celebrated intellectuals of his day.

Mikhayil Mishaqa (1800–1888) was a true Renaissance man. He served in the courts of the princes of Mount Lebanon and trained as a medical doctor. He published numerous books and tracts on theology, philosophy, and even Arabic musical theory. Yet his best-known work is a history of Syria and Lebanon in the eighteenth and nineteenth centuries. The book was written toward the end of his life, at the suggestion of friends and family who urged him to capture the stories told him by his father and the historic events to which he himself had been an eyewitness, and Mishaqa called it *A Response to the Suggestion of the Loved Ones* (the title works better in Arabic, where it rhymes).

Months before my visit to the National Archives, Mishaqa's book came out in a brilliant English translation by Harvard scholar Wheeler Thackston under the more sensational title *Murder, Mayhem, Pillage, and Plunder*. I had read the book from cover to cover as soon as it came out and, as I settled into my workspace in the archives reading room, was particularly curious to read Mishaqa's consular correspondence. The first two volumes from Damascus, spanning the years 1859–1870, coincided with Mishaqa's term of duty. I ordered the first several volumes of the Damascus records and waited in heightened anticipation as they were called up from the stacks.[1]

When I went to collect my records from the archive's circulation desk, I was disappointed to find the earliest volumes from Damascus missing. The archivist confirmed that no one else was reading them and assured me that there must have been a mistake. I renewed my request for the Mishaqa volumes and took the later correspondence back to my desk to read in the meanwhile. Yet this second request proved no more fruitful than the first. The Damascus records were not often consulted, the archivist explained. Perhaps the early volumes had been mis-shelved. She suggested that I request an appointment to enter the stacks with an archivist and look for myself.

My request to visit the stacks was granted, and later that week, accompanied by a specialist on diplomatic records, I entered the inner sanctum of the National Archives. It was no less impressive than the building's neoclassical exterior. Miles of shelves filled with the US government's standard-issue leather-bound volumes, their crested spines embossed with the city and country of their mission and the dates covered by the volume, gave the stacks an aura of order and authority.

We went straight to the bay holding the volumes from Damascus. As far as I could see, they were in good order. The volumes were in numerical order, and the volume numbers aligned with the dates they covered. A few volumes were missing from the shelf—the ones I had successfully called up earlier in the week and that now graced my workspace in the reading room. But, much to my disappointment, there was no sign of the earliest volumes—the Mishaqa volumes—on any of the shelves.

Not wanting to waste the archivist's time, I was about to give up and return empty-handed to the reading room when I noticed three small notebooks at the end of one of the shelves. The three volumes took up less space than one of the standard-issue State Department registers. Curious, I took the first slender notebook of seventy-eight pages off the shelf and found a paper label glued to the leather cover. Written in Arabic, the label read: 'Register of the Dispatches of the Consulate in Damascus Beginning in July of the Western Calendar, 1859.' The second notebook, only fifty-six pages long, picked up in 1866, where the first volume ended. The third was smaller yet, and it spanned the years 1870–1873, when Mishaqa's son Nasif succeeded him as US vice-consul in Damascus. All three were almost entirely in Arabic, with nothing in English to provide either the location or dates to assist the archivists in shelving these precious first volumes of consular correspondence from Damascus. The archivist shared my delight in locating the missing registers, which until then had been lost in the archives.

I returned to the reading room with the three slender notebooks in hand. I was literally shaking with excitement as I leafed through the pages of the first volume, the first modern researcher to lay eyes on the documents since their deposit in the National Archives. For all I knew, Mishaqa himself might have been the last person to read them. It is always exciting to handle original autograph documents, knowing that their author had turned the same pages. It feels like a virtual handshake across the ages. But I had never experienced the distinctive adrenaline rush of discovering *new* autograph documents that had until then been lost to scholarship.

I knew where I wanted to start. I turned to Mishaqa's reports of July 1860. In that month, Damascus was swept up in a horrific massacre that Mishaqa himself only narrowly survived. We have his account, preserved in his book, written thirteen years after the events. But what did Mishaqa write *at the time*? I found his first entry after the outbreak of the violence on page 35 in a dramatic report drafted to his superior, Consul J. Augustus Johnson in Beirut:

> Your Excellency no doubt has heard of the disaster which befell the Christian residents of this city last Monday morning. The arson and plunder and killing began eight hours after sunrise and continues still. The *Mitawila* [the Syrian Sh'ia community] of our quarter attacked our house and plundered all they found and destroyed what they could. They did not set fire to the house, so as not to bring disaster on their own. They fired shots but did not hit any of us, though I was struck on the head by an axe and my eye was crushed by a club. One of my [Muslim] friends, al-Haj Muhammad al-Sawtari, arrived with a group of North African soldiers and took me from the mob to his house, stripped naked, barefoot and bareheaded as my God created me, where he reunited me with my family. I am now in his house under God's mercy, confined to my bed, my eye swollen shut so that I can't assess the gravity of the injury. One of my arms is injured.[2]

It is almost certainly the earliest Arabic account of the eight-day Christian massacre that is ominously remembered down to the present day as 'the Damascus Events.'

The Damascus Events were part of a broader outbreak of communal violence that devastated Syria and Lebanon in the summer of 1860. In the more than five centuries since its founding, the Ottoman Empire had known its fair share of massacres. Sixteenth-century campaigns led by the Ottomans against the Persian Safavid Empire, and the Mamluk Empire in the Arab lands, were basically imperial expansion by massacre. However, by the mid-sixteenth century, when the pace of conquest slowed, the Ottoman Empire came to be known more for the rule of law than for state violence against its subjects. Sultan Suleyman I (r. 1520–1566), known in the West as 'the Magnificent,' is remembered in Turkey and the Arab world as 'Kanuni,' 'the Lawgiver.' For 250 years following the death of Suleyman, Ottoman Muslims exercised preeminence over Christian and Jewish minority communities in which non-Muslims were protected yet still second-class citizens, and such massacres were all but unheard of.[3]

It was only in the early nineteenth century, with the emergence of separatist nationalist movements, that the Ottoman rule of law collapsed into violence between Muslims and Christians. At that stage, the horror was confined to the Balkans, where, starting with Greece in 1821, Christian separatists and their Muslim neighbours engaged in reciprocal massacres. The impact of the Greek uprising (1821–1829) was felt across the Ottoman Empire. In retribution, the Ottoman government hanged the Greek Orthodox patriarch and many leaders of the Greek community in Istanbul for treason, and mobs swept through the Greek quarters in the southern port city of Izmir, massacring and plundering innocent civilians. Ottoman forces applied scorched-earth methods against Greek resistance in

Crete and the southern Peloponnesian Peninsula in their attempt to quell the uprising. Where Ottoman Christians sought to subvert the sultan's authority, they were seen as an existential threat. Extermination became a reasonable solution.

Images of Turkish violence against Greek civilians captured in the graphic paintings of Eugène Delacroix and the poetry of Lord Byron enflamed European public opinion and provoked calls for military intervention on the side of the Greek insurgents. With foreign assistance, the Greek insurgents prevailed and secured the independence of the Kingdom of Greece from the Ottoman Empire in 1829. The success of Greek Christians inspired other Balkan Christian communities, as nationalist movements emerged to challenge Ottoman rule in Serbia, Bosnia, Bulgaria, and Albania. In each case, nationalist insurgencies gave rise to massacres of both Muslim and Christian civilians.[4]

Although Christian nationalist movements and massacres were confined to the Balkan provinces, communal relations in the Arab lands also came under strain in the first half of the nineteenth century. A series of shocks raised tensions between the Muslim majority and different minority communities in the Arab provinces. In 1831 the forces of Egyptian governor Mehmed Ali Pasha occupied all of Syria, Lebanon, Palestine, and Jordan, disrupting both Ottoman rule and local government for nearly a decade. The European powers assisted the Ottomans in driving the Egyptians out of Syria and back to the Nile Valley, initiating a period of escalating European interference in Ottoman affairs known in diplomatic history as 'the Eastern question.' The Ottoman government sought to contain European intervention through an ambitious reform programme known as the Tanzimat (1839–1876), imposing radical changes on Ottoman society with little warning and less consent from the Muslim majority. The Ottoman economy also faced new challenges—and opportunities—through the rapid expansion of European trade in the eastern Mediterranean. Christians seemed the prime beneficiaries of the opportunities, leaving Ottoman Muslims to grapple with the challenges. This made local Christians increasingly wealthy and assertive, provoking growing hostility from the Muslim majority. Conscious of the Balkan experience of Christian separatism aided by European intervention leading to the fragmentation of Ottoman rule, many in the Arab Muslim community came to see their Christian neighbours as an existential threat to their very way of life. By 1860, this perception gave rise to a genocidal moment, in which the extermination of Syrian Christians seemed a reasonable solution.

The first warning signs came in the northern Syrian city of Aleppo, where Muslim rioters attacked the Christian quarters in October 1850, killing dozens (precise figures are not available, but estimates range from twenty to seventy killed). The Ottoman government was able to restore order in Aleppo but could not eliminate the risk of further violence elsewhere in Syria. Communal tensions in Greater Syria continued to mount across the 1850s, erupting in unprecedented violence in the summer of 1860 that claimed more than ten thousand Christians in Mount Lebanon and five thousand in Damascus—the 1860 Events.[5]

For Syria and Lebanon, two of the keystone states of the modern Middle East, the 1860 Events were a defining moment: a definitive break with the old Ottoman order and a violent entry into the modern age. Before 1860, the Ottomans left Syria and Lebanon to their own devices, with local institutions and factions competing with Ottoman governors for control. After 1860, both Damascus and Mount Lebanon came under far more centralised government, ruled through a bureaucratic state with elected officials, anticipating the statecraft of the twentieth century. Syrians and Lebanese trace the beginning of their fateful relationship with France, their twentieth-century imperial power, to the 1860 Events. Moreover, the Lebanese link the origins of their complex sectarian form of government to the 1860 Events and trace every subsequent civil war back to the 'original sin' of 1860. This is as true for the brief Lebanese civil war of 1958 as it is for the fifteen-year conflict spanning 1975–1990. In many ways, the modern history of Syria and Lebanon begins in 1860.

Unsurprisingly, the Events have commanded the scholarly attention of some of the greatest historians of the modern Middle East. Syria and Lebanon are central in Arab history, and the Events transformed both regions in ways that are still felt today. The violence of 1860 also presaged Armenian massacres in the 1890s and 1909, as well as the genocide of Armenians and Assyrians in World War I. Interest in the subject has only grown in recent years, with major new studies of the 1860 Events in French, English, Arabic, and Japanese. The 1860 Events remain a subject of perennial interest to scholars and policy makers alike. Hence my excitement, in January 1989, when I first discovered Mikhayil Mishaqa's consular reports. I recognised that I had uncovered the most important new source on one of the most momentous events in modern Arab history.[6]

The Mishaqa reports are unique documents, not least because of their celebrated author. A well-documented figure, Dr Mishaqa emerges from the obscurity that cloaks most of his fellow

Damascenes as a three-dimensional character. We have his books and personal history, we have biographical essays by his Syrian contemporaries, and we have reports on him by Protestant missionaries. We even have a photograph of the man, from a time when perhaps fewer than one in ten thousand Syrians would have had their picture taken. Moreover, Mishaqa was the kind of person whose views a historian would most value. He was an eyewitness to remarkable historical events in his own lifetime. He was incredibly well connected. A trained physician, he enjoyed access to the Ottoman ruling elite, to the Muslim notables of Damascus, as well as to the Christian and Jewish communities of the city. He knew everyone, and everyone knew him.[7]

The timing of Dr Mishaqa's appointment as US vice-consul to Damascus was also fortuitous. He took up his post in September 1859. This means that his reports trace the breakdown in order in Syrian society over a nine-month period leading up to the violence of the massacre itself. Perhaps more valuable yet, Dr Mishaqa continued to file reports from Damascus for a full decade after the Events, providing the detail and texture of the social divisions and tensions that bedevilled both the reconstruction of the city and the reintegration of its displaced Christian survivors.

Whereas many survivors of the Events wrote memoirs, they tended to do so five to ten years after the events, with the full benefit of hindsight. The same is true for Mishaqa's own book, written thirteen years after the events. What makes Mishaqa's reports so special is that they reflect the writer's present, with no knowledge of what the future held. As such, they capture the fears and hopes of Damascenes in real time, standing as some of the most detailed accounts of the tortuous path the city followed from the brink of genocide to the restoration of communal balance between the city's Muslim majority and Christian minority.

Although they held little of value for my doctoral research, I recognised the Mishaqa reports for the historian's gold mine they were. I spent the day photocopying all three notebooks, determined to write a book on the Damascus Events.

Over thirty years have passed since I first discovered Mishaqa's reports. My photocopies gathered dust, but they were never forgotten. I first had to complete my doctorate, and I revised my dissertation for publication in 1999. With my first research project behind me, I was free to begin work on Damascus.

I secured a research grant to consult the archives in Damascus in 2001, to help place the Mishaqa reports in context. I had been a frequent visitor to the Syrian capital since my childhood in Beirut in the 1970s, but as part of my preparation for the book, it was important to familiarise myself with the urban landscape in which the events of 1860 transpired. I walked the Christian quarters of Bab Tuma and Bab Sharqi that had been the epicentre of the mob violence. I divided my time between research in the archives during opening hours, walks through the old quarters of the city when the archives were closed, and after-hours research in the rich library of the French Institute in Damascus, where I had taken one of the studio flats reserved for visiting scholars.

My research in Damascus was cut short when, on the eleventh of September, a group of hijackers flew jetliners into New York's World

Trade Center, the Pentagon, and a field in Pennsylvania. Anticipating a crisis after such an unprecedented attack on American soil, I packed my bag and headed straight to the airport. The Damascus airport was surreal on 9/11. There were no crowds in the terminal and practically no international aircraft on the tarmac. The departure boards showed the cancellation of all flights by European carriers to the Syrian capital. I managed to secure a seat on a flight to Tunis that evening and made my way home to Oxford with a suitcase full of photocopied documents from libraries and archives in Damascus.

I continued my research the following year with a visit to the Ottoman Archives in Istanbul in 2002. Working with a research assistant among recently catalogued sources, I managed to photocopy hundreds of pages of Ottoman documents for my project. I next went to Beirut, where I consulted manuscript sources on the 1860 Events from the American University of Beirut's Jafet Library. In the autumn of 2002, I even returned to the US National Archives, since relocated to a new facility in College Park, Maryland, to consult the consular correspondence from Beirut and Damascus. I was beginning to assemble the critical mass of material to put Mishaqa's reports into their proper context and tackle the complex history of the 1860 events in Damascus.

In addition to the materials by Mishaqa, I had collected accounts from several Ottoman and Damascene figures who lived through the Events and their aftermath. Balancing the Christian survivors' accounts, we have important Muslim narratives. There is the young notable, Muhammad Abu al-Sa'ud al-Hasibi, a descendant of the Prophet Muhammad, who suffered a year's imprisonment following the Events and recorded his experiences in a detailed memoir.

Another Muslim notable, Shaykh Muhammad Sa'id al-Ustuwani, was a preacher in the city's ancient Umayyad Mosque. His memoir was published in Damascus in the 1990s and provides vivid detail on the Events and their aftermath. Amir 'Abd al-Qadir, exiled by the French to Ottoman domains from his native Algeria, emerged as one of the most influential figures in the Damascus Events. He left a rich trove of letters and interviews that shed new light on Damascus in 1860 and after. The Ottoman archives hold extensive reports from such key officials as the governor of Damascus, Ahmad Pasha, and the foreign minister, Fuad Pasha, dispatched by the sultan to restore Ottoman control over Damascus and Mount Lebanon in the aftermath of the Events. These eyewitnesses, who will become familiar figures in the course of the narrative, have left such detailed accounts that Damascus emerges as a real city, a metropolis marked by history and culture as well as by deviance and criminality.

The September 11 attacks continued to cast a shadow over my Damascus project. With hindsight, I was beginning to see 9/11 as America's 'Events.' The shock of the unprecedented destruction to the urban fabric of New York and Washington and the magnitude of the loss of life (2,996 people died on 9/11, and thousands more were injured) inflicted a collective trauma on Americans that took years to heal. Living through those years sensitised me to the experiences of the Damascenes, who had suffered proportionally higher losses and material damage that took years to rebuild.

As much as I wanted to work on nineteenth-century Damascus, I believed it more important to challenge the assumptions underlying the post-9/11 American-led war on terror by writing a history of the Arab world for the general reader. I put down the Damascus project and wrote *The Arabs: A History*, which was published in 2009. A book on World War I in the Middle East, timed to coincide with the centenary of the war, further delayed my work on Damascus.

It is only now, after more than thirty years, that I return to the documents that I was so excited to find in 1989, and to the challenge of making sense of both a massacre and the process of reconstruction and reconciliation that followed the Damascus Events. One of the first questions that people ask me when I tell them about the book is why did the Muslims of Damascus massacre the Christians of their city? It is an obvious question but a difficult one to answer. The first four chapters of the book trace the changes that transformed Damascus from the 1830s to the 1850s and gave rise to murderous tensions between Muslims and Christians in the city. Chapter 5 provides a day-by-day account of the Damascus Events, from the outbreak of violence on 9 July 1860 to the massacre's end on 17 July. The last four chapters then trace Ottoman measures to restore the rule of law and bring those responsible for the massacre to justice, to provide for the needs of the destitute Christian survivors, to fund the reconstruction of Christian properties, and to reintegrate the Christians into the social structure of Damascus. The book is thus both a study of one city's descent to the brink of genocide and the road pursued by the Ottoman authorities to bring the city back from that brink.

The context in writing now is shaped less by America's traumas of 9/11 than by Syria's own tragedy of total war between the government and its citizens. In the wake of the peaceful protest movements of the 2011 Arab Spring, Syria has succumbed to a violent civil war that has claimed hundreds of thousands of lives, levelled whole city quarters, and displaced millions from their homes and their homeland. For the first time since 1860, Syria's minority communities have suffered sectarian violence, caught between the brutality of the Baathist government of President Bashar al-Asad and the Sunni Muslim militias aspiring to create an Islamic state. The scale of the horror and destruction across Syria since 2011 is of an entirely different order of magnitude than the events of 1860. According to contemporary figures, the rioters destroyed some 1,500 houses in the Christian quarters of Damascus in 1860. The Syrian Observatory for Human Rights estimated that nearly three million houses were partially or totally destroyed between 2011 and 2018. Yet the history of the Damascus Events and the nineteenth-century reconstruction of the city holds much of relevance to contemporary Syrians as they confront the magnitude of the challenges to end this conflict and rebuild their shattered country and restore their fragmented society. As Syrian historian Sami Moubayed has written, we study this history 'that we might learn from it, in the hope that we never repeat it.' History does not provide a road map for solving contemporary problems, but it does demonstrate what is possible.[8]

1

Dr Mishaqa Opens the US Vice-Consulate in Damascus

The United States consul general in Beirut, J. Augustus John-son, was in a fury. He had long sought access to the Damascus market for American trading companies. Without their own diplomatic mission in Damascus, however, the Americans systematically lost out to better-placed European competitors with consulates in the Syrian capital. Johnson had entrusted US interests in Damascus to the British consul there, Mr James Brant, who had done nothing to open the Damascus market to American traders. When a US company finally brokered its first contract in Damascus in 1859, the treacherous Brant pulled strings to get the Ottoman authorities to obstruct the deal. It was time, Johnson concluded, for the United States to open its own mission in Damascus.

The United States was a minor player in the Ottoman Empire in the mid-nineteenth century. Although its thirty-three states and ten territories spanned the North American continent from the Atlantic to the Pacific, the US was not seen by the Ottoman government as a nation of any political or economic importance—certainly not on a par with European imperial powers such as Britain and France. The first American envoy to the Ottoman Empire presented his credentials to the sultan's government in 1831. The Ottomans saw fit to reciprocate only by waiting thirty-six years to open a legation in Washington in 1867. This meant that US diplomats received far less consideration from the Ottoman authorities than did their European peers. The discrimination piqued American diplomats in the field.

Working with a Beirut-based trading firm called Tabet Brothers and Partners as local agents, Consul Johnson had managed to secure a consignment of Damascene wool for the Boston-based textile manufacturer Dabrey and Cunningham. The Tabet brothers enjoyed American consular protection and expected British consul Brant to uphold their interests, given his role as America's representative in Damascus. Instead, Brant put British interests first. A growing number of steamships were making their way to Beirut with British manufactured goods for the Syrian market, and British consuls helped their captains find raw materials to fill their ships' empty holds to make the return voyage profitable. Brant had no interest in encouraging Americans to compete for the limited stocks of wool on the Syrian market, so he asked the Ottoman governor in Damascus to sequester the American consignment. The Ottoman governor was only too happy to comply and confined the Tabet brothers' wool to a customs warehouse. Johnson did little to hide his outrage in his correspondence with the US ambassador in Istanbul, James Williams.

If they were to stand a chance trading under such treacherous conditions, the Americans needed their own man in Damascus. The name that Consul Johnson proposed to Ambassador Williams was Dr Mikhayil Mishaqa.[1]

It wasn't unusual for a local man to be nominated to the American consular service in Ottoman domains. In line with their limited economic interests in the eastern Mediterranean, the Americans maintained a modest diplomatic presence in Ottoman lands. In addition to the minister resident, or ambassador, in Constantinople (modern Istanbul), a US Foreign Service officer was posted as consul to major port cities such as Smyrna (modern Izmir), Beirut, and Alexandria. These consuls oversaw a network of vice-consulates based in secondary ports and inland cities. Both as an economy measure (it cost less to hire locals than to bring Americans to the field) and to benefit from local knowledge, the American consuls tended to appoint local Christians to serve as vice-consuls in the smaller cities under their jurisdiction. In the 1850s, native Syrian vice-consuls in such lesser entrepots as Latakiya, Tripoli, Sidon, and Haifa reported to the US consul in Beirut. Most filed their reports in Arabic, to be translated by specialists in the consular translation bureau in Beirut for the American consul general's benefit.

Mikhayil Mishaqa was, by general consensus, the best-educated man in Damascus.[2] Born into a Greek Catholic family in the modest Lebanese village of Rishmayya in 1800, he had travelled widely across Egypt and Syria, served in the courts of the princely households of Mount Lebanon, and mastered many trades. A native of Mount Lebanon, Mishaqa settled in Damascus in 1834 and, over the next quarter century, established himself as a leading Christian notable of the city. Yet what most commended Mishaqa to the US consular service was the fact he had left his native church to embrace the Protestant faith in 1848. The American missionaries could hardly believe their good fortune. After years in the field with precious few converts to their credit, they were jubilant to have won to their faith a man they described as 'the most intelligent and best informed Arab' in the region. The missionaries could have recommended no one more highly than Dr Mishaqa to Consul Johnson.

Mishaqa was an eyewitness to many of the historic events that rocked Syria and Lebanon in the first half of the nineteenth century. His life story thus captures the mounting tensions that, by the time of his appointment as US vice-consul in Damascus, were about to explode into unprecedented communal violence. Indeed, his rise to the rank of consular agent of a Western state, with all the influence and economic privileges of such a position, was symptomatic of the changing position of Christian elites, which was then generating dangerous resentments in the Muslim community. No one better captured those resentments than the Ottoman governor in Damascus, Ahmad Pasha, who tried by all means to block Dr Mishaqa's accreditation to the post in 1859, just months before similar, broadly shared resentments would crescendo into the intercommunal violence known as the Damascus Events.

Mikhayil Mishaqa was a remarkable polymath. Aged fifty-nine at the time of his nomination as vice-consul, he had already mastered four professions. He began his working life as an apprentice merchant. At the age of just seventeen, Mishaqa travelled to the Egyptian port of Damietta to learn the principles of commerce from his maternal uncles. He worked alongside his older brother as a clerk in his uncle's merchant house, where he earned a good salary and began to build a nest egg. After three years in Damietta, Mishaqa returned to his family home in Mount Lebanon and put his merchant skills to work, entering the silk trade. Silk was one of the most profitable industries in Mount Lebanon, and in the 1820s Mishaqa made a good living exporting silk to Damascus.

Mishaqa's second career was in politics, which he entered through the courts of the princes of Mount Lebanon. The Shihabi family had reigned in Mount Lebanon since 1697. They ruled over a complex society that was divided into rigid social classes. The princely families, among which the Shihabs were preeminent, were at the pinnacle of power and took the title 'amir,' or 'prince.' Beneath them were the shaykhs or communal leaders, followed by the commoners (peasants, craftsmen, and traders) who made up the overwhelming majority of the population. These social divisions were far more influential in Lebanese society than the differences among the many religious communities that had taken refuge in Mount Lebanon over the centuries: the Maronite Christians, an Eastern church that had submitted to the authority of the Pope; the Druzes, a schism from Shi'a Islam that evolved over the centuries into a distinct religious community; the Sunni and Shi'a Muslims; the Jews; and the Greek Orthodox and the numerous other Christian denominations (including Mishaqa's Greek Catholic community, a schism from the Orthodox Church that, like the Maronites, had submitted to papal authority). Mount Lebanon was one of the most theologically diverse regions of the Ottoman Empire.

From time to time, relations between the different branches of the ruling Shihabi family broke down. In the 1820s, Amir Bashir II (r. 1789–1840), the reigning prince of Mount Lebanon, called on the young Mikhayil Mishaqa to mediate with a dissident cousin who was in league with a Druze rival, Shaykh Bashir Jumblatt. After engaging in fruitless shuttle diplomacy between the princely cousins, Mishaqa admitted to Amir Bashir that he was out of his depth. 'Your servant is expert in knowing how to derive numerical and quantitative unknowns,' Mishaqa explained, 'but my mind is not capable of finding a way to derive the unknown of this political affair.'

'The reason for your inability to solve it is your lack of experience in politics,' Amir Bashir replied with a laugh. 'I will teach you how to discover this unknown.'[3]

There was no subtlety or ideology to the politics of Mount Lebanon in the early nineteenth century—all was realpolitik. When confronted by a superior, like an Ottoman governor with a larger army at his disposal, the prince submitted. However, when dealing with a threat from a peer or subordinate, the prince struck with no mercy. In 1825 Amir Bashir II lashed out at his Druze rival, Shaykh Bashir Jumblatt, and defeated him in pitched battle. The Druze shaykh was captured and dispatched to the Ottoman authorities for execution. The dissident princes of his own family who had been in league with Shaykh Bashir Jumblatt were dealt with no less harshly. The fortunate ones were simply executed. The others had their tongues cut out and eyes blinded, and were sent home on mules to serve as a warning to others of the perils of challenging Bashir's rule. In this way, Amir Bashir II asserted his authority over Mount Lebanon for more than half a century and came to be known as 'Bashir the Great.'

Mikhayil Mishaqa was not deterred by violence from entering politics himself. In the aftermath of the events of 1825, he was taken into the household of the Shihabi prince of the mountain town of Hasbayya, where he served as personal secretary to Amir Sa`d al-Din, a loyal supporter of Amir Bashir II. The ruler of Hasbayya awarded Mishaqa vast agricultural estates in the northern Galilee region (today in northern Israel) to provide for his income and gave him a stately home confiscated from a disgraced Druze shaykh. At that point, Mishaqa closed his silk business and entered his third trade—agriculture. He was just twenty-five.

Five years into his new profession, Mishaqa's life was once again disrupted by regional politics when the ambitious governor of Egypt, Mehmed Ali Pasha, rebelled against his master the Ottoman sultan and invaded Syria. After twenty-five years in office, Mehmed Ali had emerged as a demi-emperor in his own right. He had total control over the revenues of Egypt's agriculture and trade, which gave him unprecedented wealth. He built up a powerful army that had already conquered the Sudan and the Arabian province of the Hijaz, home of Islam's holiest cities, Mecca and Medina. In 1824 the Ottoman sultan ordered Mehmed Ali to dispatch both his army and navy to Greece to assist in suppressing a massive nationalist insurgency, then in its third year. The Egyptian army invaded Crete and the southern half of Greece before the British, French, and Russians intervened in support of Greek independence. In the 1827 Battle of Navarino, European warships destroyed the Egyptian fleet and shipped the stranded Egyptian troops back home. Stripped of his Greek conquests, Mehmed Ali Pasha sought compensation in other Ottoman territory. In November 1831 his son and generalissimo,

Ibrahim Pasha, led an army into Palestine to conquer the Syrian lands.

The Egyptian invasion interjected a whole new complexity to the politics of Mount Lebanon. To preserve his position in power, should Amir Bashir II remain loyal to the Ottoman governors in Syria, or should he side with the invading Egyptians? The principles of real-politik dictated that he should submit to the stronger force. Amir Bashir dispatched Mikhayil Mishaqa to observe Ibrahim Pasha's army in action in the coastal town of Acre, where Egyptian forces were laying siege to the Ottoman governor, who was holed up in the impregnable crusader-era castle.

When Mishaqa reached Acre in late November 1831, the Egyptian siege was in full force. He saw twenty-two battleships 'pounding Acre incessantly, and Acre, which could not even be seen for the smoke of gunpowder, pounding them in return.'[4] He stayed with the Egyptian army for twenty days, assessing its strength and tactics. The defenders were brave and fought valiantly. But the Egyptians had strength in numbers and were digging in for ultimate victory. Mishaqa returned to the Lebanese town of Dayr al-Qamar, Amir Bashir II's capital, to brief the Shihabi princes on the situation and to encourage neutrality until they knew the outcome of the siege of Acre. It took six months before Egyptian forces finally breached Acre's defences to conquer the strategic fortress at the end of May 1832. When he moved from Acre on to Damascus, the Egyptian general Ibrahim Pasha was accompanied by his new ally: the prince of Mount Lebanon, Amir Bashir II, and his entourage.

Egyptian forces dispersed the Ottoman defenders of Damascus after a brief skirmish and occupied the city in early June 1832.

Mishaqa accompanied his patron, Amir Sa'd al-Din, to Damascus, where they joined the Egyptian campaign. Ibrahim Pasha did not tarry in Damascus but pressed his advantage in pursuit of the Ottoman defenders. The Shihabi princes and their retainers served with Egyptian forces as they defeated the Ottoman army near the central Syrian market town of Homs in July. Mishaqa stayed in Homs for a month and a half, practicing his fourth profession—medicine.

Mishaqa had first studied medicine in 1828, when he was confined to home for five months with quartan fever, a form of malaria. He secured some medical texts in Arabic and was 'able to understand the jist' but 'was stumped by the technical terminology taken from foreign languages like French or Greek.' He sought instruction from Amir Bashir II's physician, an Italian doctor named Carlini, and 'began to practice medicine gratis,' his intention being 'to acquire some practical experience.'[5] It was a modest beginning, but Ottoman medicine in the 1820s was a fairly modest science. In the battlefield of Homs in the summer of 1832, even a man of such limited experience as Mishaqa was better than no doctor at all.

After the Egyptian conquest of Syria, Mishaqa settled in Damascus, where he bought a house and got married at the age of thirty-four. His wife, Elizabeth, was the daughter of Mikhayil Faris, a Greek Catholic of Damascus. She was only eleven at the time of their marriage. When later questioned by an American missionary about why he married so young a girl, Mishaqa reportedly claimed that 'in his day, young girls received no training at home, and young men, who wished properly trained wives, had to marry them young, so as to educate them to suit themselves!' Elizabeth gave birth to their first child in 1838, when she was just fifteen. In later years, Mishaqa referred to his wife as Khanum, or 'lady.'[6]

With a family to provide for, Mishaqa applied himself to the medical profession. He seized the opportunity to deepen his training when the Egyptian government sent the head of their medical service, the famous French doctor Clot Bey, to tend to the growing number of sick and wounded soldiers in Damascus. Dr Antoine-Barthélemy Clot was a native of Marseilles who entered the Egyptian medical service in 1825 and was given the honorific title of Bey. His primary concern was the medical needs of the Egyptian army, which suffered higher losses from disease than from battle wounds. Clot Bey persuaded Mehmed Ali Pasha to establish a medical school in Cairo, arguing that the best way to protect the Egyptian army from the ravages of disease 'would be to train local doctors rather than solicit the services of European ones.'[7] The French doctor was thus favourably disposed toward Mishaqa, who came with more knowledge and experience than the average student entering the Egyptian medical school. As Mishaqa later recalled, 'Clot Bey liked me and used to summon me to assist him in his operations. He gave me not only all the medical texts that had been translated into Arabic and printed in Egypt, but surgical implements as well.' In due course, Mishaqa was appointed chief physician of Damascus, although by his own admission he 'was not competent to hold such a post.'[8]

The shift in professions from agriculture and politics to medicine proved felicitous, for in the course of the Egyptian occupation of Syria and Mount Lebanon, Mishaqa was driven to the brink of bankruptcy. He lost his job with the Shihabi prince of Hasbayya and earned no revenues from his estates because of plundering by

Egyptian soldiers, local uprisings against the occupation, and over-taxation by the Egyptian state. Although Mishaqa had practiced medicine for free in the past, by the late 1830s he was forced to charge for his services. In 1847, during a later visit to Egypt, he completed his training under Clot Bey's instruction at the Qasr al-'Ayni medical school in Cairo, where the faculty subjected him to examination and awarded him a medical diploma with the title of doctor. Henceforth, Mikhayil was known as Dr Mishaqa.

The Egyptian occupation destabilised Syria and the Ottoman Empire as a whole. In 1840 the European powers combined forces with the Ottoman government to force the Egyptians to withdraw from Syria. By the end of December 1840, Ibrahim Pasha retreated from Damascus to make the long march back to Egypt. With the Ottoman restoration in Syria and Mount Lebanon came a day of reckoning for the ruling Shihabi princes of Mount Lebanon. Amir Bashir II was deposed in 1840 and sent into exile in Malta. He was replaced by a distant cousin, Bashir III, whose brief and undistinguished reign (r. 1840–1842) marked the end of the Shihabi family's rule in Mount Lebanon. With nothing left in Mount Lebanon to return to, Mishaqa chose to remain in Damascus permanently.

In the course of his scientific inquiry, Dr Mishaqa grew increasingly sceptical of his Greek Catholic faith. At the age of eighteen, he had experienced his first 'religious crisis.' In his words, 'There were dogma I thought I had to believe, yet no sound mind could accept them.' Over the years, Mishaqa's reading of European Enlightenment philosophers in Arabic translation further confused him. Voltaire and Rousseau, drawing on pure reason, rejected all religion, whereas Isaac Newton, 'with all his vast erudition and towering intellect...was the fiercest in clinging to religion and in opposing those who rejected it.' Mishaqa was no atheist. He continued to believe in God and to fear eternal damnation. What Mishaqa sought was a well-reasoned religion that could reconcile faith and intellect. And he found it in the Arabic translation of a Protestant tract published by American missionaries in Lebanon. As he later reflected, 'What the leaders of my church taught and the fables they told had no basis whatsoever in Christianity; it was all an invention of priests, and not only was it unsupported by scripture, but most of it flatly contradicted it. It was simply to enhance the power of the ecclesiastical mantle, to amass the wealth of the people and to enslave them.'9 In 1844 Mishaqa contacted the American missionaries to engage them in theological discussion.

Upon his return from Egypt, perhaps emboldened by his diploma in medicine, Mishaqa made the fateful decision to leave the Greek Catholic Church to embrace Protestantism in 1848. His conversion provoked alarm throughout the Greek Catholic hierarchy, reaching up to Patriarch Maximus Mazlum himself. The patriarch reached out to Mishaqa to try and show him the errors of his ways. When persuasion failed, Mazlum unleashed the full fury of his ecclesiastical powers, pronouncing an anathema against Mishaqa and condemning the apostate in his sermons and his writings. However, the patriarch had met his match. As the American missionaries reported, 'Our friend Mr Meshakah...is probably the most intelligent native layman in the country, and the Patriarch the most learned ecclesiastic.' Their debate was a battle of the titans, attracting 'attention from all quarters...with much interest, to what is going on between them.'10 Between 1852 and 1860, Mishaqa wrote eight books capturing the arguments of his debates with Maximus Mazlum and shredding the teachings of the Greek Catholic Church, all duly published in Arabic by the American missionaries in their bid to spread arguments in favour of Protestantism.

Dr Mishaqa no doubt paid a price for cutting his ties to his ancestral religious community, but being a Protestant opened new doors to him. Though still supporting himself and his family through his medical practice, he was increasingly drawn into the diplomatic world. The long-serving British consul in Damascus, Sir Richard Wood, was outspoken in his admiration of Mishaqa, whom he engaged in 1840 to serve as dragoman, or interpreter, for the British consulate in Damascus.[11] The irony of the appointment was that, for all his erudition, Mishaqa had never learned a foreign language. Writing in 1844, the American missionary Eli Smith marvelled that 'his general information is truly wonderful for one who knows only Arabic.'[12] It seems more likely that Wood (who was himself fluent in Arabic and needed no translator) appointed Mishaqa as dragoman to extend British consular protection to the brilliant doctor. Although his appointment as dragoman preceded his adherence to Protestantism, Mishaqa's conversion would have reinforced his claim to British protégé status, as Britain extended its protection over the tiny Protestant church in Ottoman domains, just as France served as protector of Catholics and Russia of Orthodox Christians.

British and French missions first gained the right to designate their native dragomans as protégés through their seventeenth-century commercial treaties with the Sublime Porte. As foreign protégés, dragomans received a *berat*, or patent, from the Ottoman government that exempted them from the poll tax levied on all Christians and Jews, as well as from all irregular taxes, which were imposed from time to time when the government ran into financial difficulties. The coveted berat also conferred the same advantageous customs tariffs on protégés as European merchants enjoyed, giving them a competitive edge over all other Ottoman merchants (although berat holders were legally barred from engaging in trade, few were restrained by this prohibition). And berat holders benefitted from the same extraterritorial legal status as their European patrons, which meant that dragomans would be subject to the law of their protector state rather than Ottoman law. What started as an Ottoman concession to encourage foreign trade missions evolved over the course of the eighteenth century into a system subject to widespread abuse, with Ottoman Christian merchant houses using their connections to the French and British to secure the preferential trade status conferred through a berat. By the early nineteenth century, 'few of those Ottoman subjects that were protected actually provided any translation services to the foreign consuls.'[13] Thus, in 1840 it was not unusual for Consul Wood to appoint a man like Mikhayil Mishaqa, who didn't speak English, to serve as a dragoman. But such abuses provoked the resentment of many Ottoman officials, who objected to seeing members of religious minority communities exempted from taxes and given such preferential treatment over the Muslim majority. The Muslim notables in Damascus were yet more resentful, seeing local Christians secure legal and economic advantages through their links to European diplomatic missions that were inaccessible to Muslims. Well-connected Christians were growing rich and powerful at the expense of the city's ruling elite. It was an inversion of the natural order.

For US consul Johnson in Beirut, searching for the best person to open an American mission in Damascus in 1859, Dr Mishaqa emerged as a candidate of unrivalled networks and experience. He had the fulsome support of the American Protestant missionary community as well as the endorsement of the troublesome British consul in Damascus, who had raised barriers to American commercial access to the Syrian capital. In a series of letters exchanged with the American ambassador in Istanbul, Johnson secured approval for Mishaqa's appointment. By 1 September, Johnson could write to British consul Brant in Damascus to inform him of Mishaqa's appointment. 'Happy thus to be able to relieve you from the increase of cares which your generous attention to American affairs has added to your official duties,' Johnson concluded with ironic flourish.[14]

Mikhayil Mishaqa assumed his duties as US vice-consul in Damascus on 5 September 1859. Any hopes he might have harboured for a smooth transition were swiftly dispelled. Mishaqa needed to secure American records from the British consulate. Although America's relations with Consul Brant had been strained by the wool sequester, Mishaqa himself had enjoyed nearly two decades of cordial ties to the British since his designation as a British dragoman and protégé in 1840. Mishaqa's very first letter, on his first day at work, was addressed to Brant, thanking him for his help in securing the vice-consular post and offering his full cooperation in upholding

British interests in Damascus. The British consul returned his good wishes, but his clerks claimed they could find no records related to American interests and couldn't find the seals used to certify documents. Mishaqa would have to open his vice-consulate without any records and would have to find his own seals to officiate his correspondence.

Dr Mishaqa met with no more success in securing accreditation from the Ottoman authorities than he did in recovering American records in Damascus from the British. The American ambassador in Istanbul had dispatched the Sublime Porte's formal deed of investiture, or *firman*, naming Mikhayil Mishaqa as American vice-consul in Damascus. Mishaqa submitted the firman to the office of Ahmad Pasha, the governor of Damascus, requesting an appointment to confirm his accreditation. Ahmad Pasha had little sympathy for Ottoman Christian subjects like Dr Mishaqa who eluded Ottoman law and taxation through the protection of foreign powers. Mishaqa's request for an appointment was denied. The governor's office claimed that it required more documentation from Istanbul and specifically requested Mishaqa to submit his berat before the governor would agree to recognise Mishaqa as US vice-consul designate. In fact, Mishaqa's sources related, the governor doubted that he had ever gained official Ottoman recognition as a British subject. As an ordinary Ottoman citizen, Mishaqa would be ineligible to serve as the consular agent of a foreign power. Ahmad Pasha would not receive Mishaqa until he had firm confirmation from the Sublime Porte of Mishaqa's legal status.[15] Until Mishaqa was recognised by the local governor, his appointment would be frozen and his ability to act on behalf of US interests severely constrained.

While he faced obstruction from both the British consulate and the local governor, Dr Mishaqa was under growing pressure from the US consul in Beirut to make progress on the outstanding cases involving American interests. In addition to the Tabet wool sequester, the American consul pressed for justice for an American missionary named William Benton, who had been attacked in the Lebanese mountain town of Zahleh earlier in the year and whose attackers had taken refuge in the province of Damascus. Consul Johnson pressed Mishaqa for quick action on both the Tabet wool sequester and the 'Benton outrage' to uphold America's standing in Syria.

The 'Benton outrage' was a sensitive case. William Benton and his wife, Loanza, had lived twelve years in Lebanon preaching Protestantism. In May 1859 they moved from their home in the mountain village of Bhamdun to expand their work into Zahleh, a large Christian town on the eastern slopes of Mount Lebanon overlooking the Bekaa Valley. They rented a house in the centre of the village, offering medical treatment and religious instruction, and were warmly welcomed by the local people. 'We had never witnessed so much eagerness for religious instruction,' Benton claimed. However, the Greek Catholic bishop of Zahleh was less welcoming of the foreigners, who sought converts from his flock, and he roused the community to action against the American missionaries. After only two days in Zahleh, the Bentons heard a crowd gathering outside their house and shouting for them to leave. Throwing stones and breaking windows, the mob burst into their home, seized the Bentons and their children, and forcibly marched them out of Zahleh to a neighbouring village. The very next day, Benton rode to Beirut to lodge a formal complaint with US consul Johnson, who took him to meet the Ottoman governor in Beirut and demand redress. Two men were identified as ringleaders of the attack on the Bentons' house in Zahleh, and both had now fled Mount Lebanon to take refuge in the neighbouring province of Damascus, outside the jurisdiction of the governor in Beirut. Johnson pressed Mishaqa to meet with the governor in Damascus to secure the men's arrest and extradition to Beirut to face justice. But the governor would not receive Mishaqa because his papers were not in order.[16]

Dr Mishaqa made no more progress on the Tabet wool order than he did on the Benton affair. Johnson drafted a letter for Mishaqa to deliver to Ahmad Pasha, the governor of Damascus. In his letter, Johnson asked Ahmad Pasha to release the wool purchased by the Tabet brothers on behalf of an American firm. Johnson noted that Ahmad Pasha had impounded the wool on the request of the British consul and that the British had no legal right to interfere in American commercial activity. Johnson concluded by warning that should the governor fail to lift the sequester, he would hold Ahmad Pasha personally responsible for any damage to the wool as a result of its seizure. However, Mishaqa was in no position to press Johnson's case in person because the governor refused to grant him an audience. Instead, he had one of his servants deliver Johnson's letter to the governor's office. Ahmad Pasha's office replied that the matter did not concern him but was between the British and Americans. He refused to release the wool until requested to do so by the British consul, further infuriating the American consul in Beirut.[17]

By mid-October, Consul Johnson made no attempt to mask his impatience with Mishaqa's failures. 'Nothing was heard from you by the last post,' Johnson nagged, in reference to the Benton outrage. 'This case being so important it is not right to be loose about it nor is it possible to overlook it.' One week later, Johnson was writing again about the wool sequester: 'This matter is too important to be given up before justice is done. This Consulate will be ready to answer the English Consulate about every question raised concerning its conduct.'[18] With each prod from Beirut, Mishaqa renewed his efforts, but found all official doors closed to him as long as the governor, Ahmad Pasha, refused to recognise his appointment as US vice-consul. It seemed as though Mishaqa was condemned to fail in his new position before he was even given the chance to start.

In repeated dispatches to Beirut, Mishaqa spelled out the problems he faced acting on America's behalf without accreditation by the local government in Damascus. Consul Johnson wrote to the American ambassador in Istanbul for his help in breaking the impasse. James Williams (1796–1869) was a political appointee on his first diplomatic mission. Born and bred in Tennessee, the energetic Williams had run a steamboat company on the Tennessee River, launched a newspaper in Knoxville, and helped establish the first bank in Chattanooga before coming to the attention of the governor of Tennessee, Andrew Johnson (later vice president under Abraham Lincoln and, following Lincoln's assassination, the seventeenth president of the United States). It was Johnson who suggested Williams to President James Buchanan and his secretary of state, Lewis Cass, for a diplomatic post abroad. Williams was named to the post in Constantinople and presented his credentials to the sultan's government on 27 May 1858.

A tall, well-built man with a grey receding hairline, a full brown moustache, and long beard reaching to his chest, Ambassador Williams cut an impressive figure. The Williamses mixed comfortably with European aristocracy, travelling around the Levant with the Anglo-Irish peer Lord Dufferin (later appointed as Britain's delegate to the international commission on Syria in 1860) and the conservative MP and secretary of state for the colonies Lord Bulwer. One of their daughters married an Austrian baron, and their youngest wed an Italian prince. Williams and his wife, Lucy Graham, were well received in the Ottoman capital, their embassy celebrated for 'its southern hospitality.' By all accounts, Ambassador Williams was well suited to work in the diplomatic culture of the Ottoman court.[19]

Alerted by Consul Johnson to the official obstruction in Damascus, the embassy urged the Sublime Porte to confirm that Dr Mishaqa enjoyed British protégé status and was not a regular Ottoman subject. Once the Porte could demonstrate that, as a British subject, Dr Mishaqa was eligible to hold a consular appointment, the embassy could then instruct the governor in Damascus, Ahmad Pasha, to recognise Mishaqa as US vice-consul. Yet the Porte would only confirm receipt of the American embassy's request and did not give any sense of when the matter might be resolved. It was a formula for delay and inaction.

In response, Ambassador Williams took immediate and extraordinary action. With no prior warning to his subordinates in Beirut, Williams and his entire family—wife, three children, and the ambassador's brother, William Williams—boarded the next steamship for the Syrian coast. They arrived in Beirut on 10 November. Consul Johnson sent word by special messenger to Damascus warning Dr Mishaqa of the ambassador's imminent arrival and his request to meet with the governor, Ahmad Pasha. This time the governor was quick to respond, demanding that Mishaqa give him two days' advance notice before the ambassador's visit. Mishaqa was himself at a loss over the ambassador's itinerary and fired off repeated requests to Johnson for more precise details. He also requested that the ambassador honour Mishaqa with a visit to his home. Receiving a dignitary of such high standing would raise Mishaqa's stature in the eyes of the local government and the elite in Damascus alike.

Ambassador Williams, his family, and Consul Johnson set off together from Beirut to Damascus on horseback. Mishaqa sent word to both the local government and the consular corps in Damascus advising that the ambassador of the United States was due to arrive in the Syrian capital on 16 November. The Mishaqa family welcomed the Williams family to their home, where they stayed until 23 November. And that's where Mishaqa's account of the visit ends. Because both Consul Johnson and Ambassador Williams took part in the visit to Damascus, there was no need for Mishaqa to report to his superiors on the outcome of the ambassadorial intervention. What we do know is that, in the immediate aftermath of the ambassador's visit, all official obstructions to Mishaqa's position and work were swiftly resolved. Williams also persuaded Consul Brant to lift his sequester on the order of wool. As Mishaqa noted in a later report, 'But for the honour of the Ambassador's visit to Damascus, there might never have been an end' to the British sequester on the Tabet wool.[20] The missionary William Benton, in a letter dated 5 December, noted that Williams's visit 'led to a pleasant settlement of the difficulty' resulting from his expulsion from Zahleh, and added that 'indeed, all the entanglements of every case, at Jaffa, Damascus, and Zahleh, seemed to disappear at his presence, and the impression of his visit is peace everywhere.'[21]

It is also clear that in the course of his stay, Williams persuaded the governor of Damascus, Ahmad Pasha, to receive Dr Mishaqa as America's vice-consul in Damascus. The fact that the Williams family chose to lodge with Mishaqa would have only enhanced his claims to diplomatic status. In the immediate aftermath of the ambassador's visit, Mishaqa drafted letters to the other members of Damascus's tiny consular corps in English, French, and Arabic (the foreign letters translated by his son Nasif), notifying them of his accreditation: 'I have the honor to inform you that I have received the appointment of Vice Consul of the U.S. of America in Damascus and that in Conformity with the Firman of the Sultan I was recognised in that capacity by the local Authorities.'[22]

Although Ambassador Williams's visit had secured Mishaqa's accreditation and resolved America's outstanding cases in Syria, it did little to address the underlying tensions between the new diplomat and the local government in Damascus. After Williams's departure, the governor in Damascus resumed his efforts to block Mishaqa's appointment. Ahmad Pasha dispatched a letter to the Sublime Porte on 6 January, one month after Williams's visit, raising questions about Mishaqa's legal standing and eligibility to serve as a foreign diplomat. Even after the Sublime Porte responded to Ahmad Pasha with an imperial decree confirming Mishaqa's appointment, the governor continued to obstruct the work of the US vice-consulate.[23]

In a letter dated 9 February 1860, Mishaqa complained to the US consulate in Beirut that 'the local government is still not treating us with due respect.' According to local protocol, new members of the consular corps were expected to visit the governor, the treasurer, and the chief justice, who, as a matter of courtesy, would return the visit to the diplomat's consulate. Mishaqa noted that he had observed the formalities to the letter but that, weeks later, none of the government officials had returned his visits. 'No doubt it is the governor who forbids the others' from reciprocating the visits, 'for the judge had promised that he would call on me,' and it was out of character for the judge not to keep his promise. After all, these were people Mishaqa knew personally after years as chief physician to Damascus and as one of the city's most prominent Christian notables. It wasn't a personal slight, Mishaqa insisted. His concern was that the governor and his officials were making public their disrespect of the United States in a way that was bound to hurt American interests in the future. Mishaqa was already encountering official obstruction to a number of consular issues as a mark of ill will from the governor.[24]

The lapse in protocol was all the more blatant, Mishaqa asserted, given that government officials had recently exchanged visits with the vice-consul of Belgium, the consular agent of Greece, and the vice-consul of Russia. The obvious difference was that virtually all of the diplomats in the Damascus consular corps *except* Dr Mishaqa were foreign nationals: Mr Makeiff of Russia, British consul Brant, the Frenchman M. Outrey, Vice-Consul Pffachfinger of Austria, and Mr Spartali of Greece. It might have been standard practice for local Christians with foreign protégé status to hold consular appointments in other towns and cities in Syria, but Damascus was distinctly more conservative in upholding a stricter segregation between the Muslim majority and the minority communities. As a result, there was something ominous in Ahmad Pasha's hostility toward Mishaqa's appointment that no ambassadorial visit would resolve.

Nor would Ambassador Williams ever return to Syria. By 1860, the United States was growing increasingly divided over the issues of slavery and state rights. James Williams and his wife were, in keeping with the politics of Tennessee at that time, strong supporters of slavery and outspoken critics of abolitionism. With these issues coming to the fore in a presidential election year, Williams spent his free time drafting essays in support of slavery. Upon the outbreak of the US Civil War, Williams resigned from his ambassadorial post with the Union and threw his support behind the Confederate States of America in May 1861. Aside from a brief visit to the post–Civil War United States, following a presidential pardon for treason charges from Andrew Johnson, Williams spent the remainder of his life in Europe, stripped of his property in America and unreconciled to a South without slavery. He seems never to have looked back on Syria or the Ottoman Empire and remained consumed by the divisions raging in the United States.[25]

It was an inauspicious start to Dr Mishaqa's diplomatic career. The governor of Damascus remained hostile to the new US vice-consul even after an extraordinary ambassadorial visit. By the old rules that governed social standing in Damascus, in which non-Muslim minorities were protected but were still second-class citizens, Dr Mishaqa, as a Syrian Christian, had risen above his station in claiming diplomatic status on a par with British, French, and Russian diplomats. The governor simply refused to honour a local Christian with the sort of official visit reserved for foreign representatives of great powers. The hostility that Dr Mishaqa encountered from the governor was not isolated but reflected dangerous tensions turning Muslims against Christians in Damascus as the city entered the fateful year of 1860.

2

Damascus 'the Fragrant' at Mid-Century

By the time Mikhayil Mishaqa was accredited as US vice-consul in Damascus, he had been a resident in that city for a quarter of a century. He bought his house in 1834, when all of Syria and Mount Lebanon were under Egyptian occupation. In the reckoning that followed the Egyptian withdrawal from Syria in 1840, the Ottomans and their European supporters devised a whole new system of government for Mount Lebanon that replaced the Shihabi principality that Mishaqa had served faithfully. With nothing in Mount Lebanon to return to, Mishaqa chose the life of a Christian notable practicing medicine in the wondrous city of Damascus. It was a natural choice. Damascus was the big city, a rich and cosmopolitan power centre, and one of the most important provincial capitals in the Ottoman Empire.

Damascenes rated their city above all others for its beauty, its culture, its history, and its centrality in Islamic civilisation. Nicknamed

'Damascus the Fragrant' (*Dimishq al-Fayha*'), the city is an oasis at the edge of the Syrian Desert. In Ottoman times, its main source of water was the Barada River, which flows from the Anti-Lebanon Mountains to irrigate the farms and orchards of the city's garden suburbs, known as the Ghouta. The river traces its course along the northern walls of the Old City and in that era created open public spaces where the townspeople gathered for promenades or to sit in riverside cafés among blossoming fruit trees and jasmines. In addition to the Barada, Damascus drew on an ancient canal network and aqueducts that channelled water from a variety of springs directly into every quarter of the town. 'Every house and every garden have their sparkling fountains and rivulets of water,' marvelled the American author Samuel Clemens (better known by his pen name: Mark Twain). The omnipresent water and lush gardens were all the more astonishing in a city located at the desert's edge. Even so jaded a traveller as Clemens was openly enchanted by the contrast between the green oasis and its arid surroundings: 'Right in the midst of the desert is spread a billowy expanse of green foliage; and nestling in its heart sits the great white city, like an island of pearls and opals gleaming out of a sea of emeralds.'[1]

Proud Damascenes lay credible claim to theirs being one of the oldest continuously inhabited cities in the world. The Hebrew Bible is peppered with references to Damascus, from Genesis through the books of the Prophets. It was already an ancient city when the Roman Saul was blinded by the light and converted to Christianity on the road to Damascus, nearly two millennia ago. In the seventh century of the current era, the Prophet Muhammad reportedly declined to enter Damascus, with its verdant watered gardens, on the grounds that a man should enter paradise only once. Twenty-nine years after the death of the Prophet, Damascus became the capital of the first Islamic empire, the Umayyad caliphate, in 661 CE. Past civilisations have left their mark on the modern city, with fragments of Roman, Byzantine, and early Islamic structures incorporated into later buildings as part of one continuous urban fabric spanning the millennia.[2]

Dr Mishaqa lived in a grand old house in the northeastern quadrant of the walled city of Damascus. It was a gracious home, parts of which dated back to the seventeenth century, built around a series of interior courtyards with fruit trees and water fountains. As was common in Syrian cities, the modest exterior of the house gave no sense of the beauty within. The rooms were richly decorated in the Damascene style, with painted wood ceilings and elaborate inlaid stonework in geometric patterns. When James Williams and his family visited Damascus in November 1859, it was a home fit to receive an American ambassador.

These old courtyard houses were considered one of the city's most beautiful features. 'The chief glory of Damascus is its private houses,' the Irish missionary and longtime resident in Damascus, Josias Leslie Porter, wrote in 1855. 'No contrast could be greater than that between the exterior and the interior. The mud walls, and rickety projecting chambers, give poor promise of the splendour within.' Indeed, Damascenes gave their homes deceptively humble exteriors, reserving all extravagance for the interior, which was divided into reception areas for guests and the more private domestic quarters reserved for women and family members. Surviving examples from the Ottoman era provide an idea of the splendour of these courtyard houses, with their elaborate stonework, geometric patterns woven in multicoloured pastework, hand-painted tiles, inlaid mother-of-pearl and fine mosaics, and painted murals and ceilings. The sound of running water and sparkling fountains in the central courtyards completed the magical effect.[3]

Behind the façade of timeless beauty, the ancient city of Damascus entered an era of accelerated change in the mid-nineteenth century. Coming out of centuries in which all innovations had either local or Ottoman origins, the nineteenth century marked the advent of European influences in the city. Western diplomats and missionaries took up residence, imposing their values and institutions on Muslim notables who neither sought nor consented to the change. Aided by their diplomats, European manufacturers sent ever more textiles to Damascus, challenging local weavers to adapt to a supply of cheap cloth that surpassed local demand. The development of steam navigation accelerated European commerce in the Levant and competed with the overland caravan trade on which Damascus formerly relied. Although these developments enhanced trade and prosperity in Damascus, change favoured the Syrian Christian elites—people like Dr Mishaqa—over the Muslim notables of the city, as Europeans preferred well-connected Christians to serve as their agents and trade partners. In this way, Christian notables grew wealthy at the expense of the leading Muslim families of Damascus. No city thrives in stasis, but change can be dangerous, particularly when it threatens the interests of the rich and powerful.

Damascus was one of the largest cities in the Arab lands, with a diverse population of Arab, Turkish, Kurdish, and Persian Muslims;

Christians of no fewer than nine different denominations; and a sizeable Jewish community. There are no precise figures for the population of Damascus at mid-century. The Ottoman census served primarily to assess taxes, and officials counted only those who were economically active. This led to underreporting and wide variation in population estimates. Best estimates from both Arab and Western sources suggest a total population of about 150,000 residents at mid-century, with a Muslim majority of roughly 85 percent, a large Christian community of 10–12 percent, and a smaller Jewish community of less than 5 percent.[4]

Unlike cities in the West, which are typically divided into town quarters, central Damascus was organised in 'eighths' (in Arabic, *thumn*), each divided into a number of smaller quarters and neighbourhoods set off by their own city gates, which closed at sundown. Three of the eighths fell inside the walls and counted among the oldest districts of the city. The Mishaqas lived in the northeastern thumn of al-Qaymariyya, a mixed area in which Muslims and Christians cohabited. Two predominantly Christian neighbourhoods of al-Qaymariyya—Bab Tuma and Bab Sharqi—were home to most of the city's ten churches and nine convents and monasteries. Mishaqa's house was on a mixed thoroughfare near Bab Tuma, easily accessible to all of Damascus's residents, which had served him well as he practiced medicine.[5]

The Jewish Quarter (*Harat al-Yahud*) fell within the southern thumn of al-Shaghur, surrounded by Muslim and Christian residential neighbourhoods. The small Jewish community had grown over time to reach an estimated total of between five and twenty thousand residents by 1860. The native community was reinforced by Sephardi immigrants arriving in the sixteenth century (some of whom pre-served Ladino as their spoken language) and, more recently, 'Frank' or European Jews following growing trade opportunities and settling in the Syrian capital.

The place of the Jewish community in Damascene society had been seriously threatened in 1840, when the murder of a Capuchin priest in the Jewish quarter gave rise to a blood libel and unprecedented persecution of the Jewish community by the Egyptian authorities then ruling the city. More than a dozen leading members of the community were arrested by the Egyptian authorities and tortured to force confessions. Four men died under horrendous violence. The case gained extensive press coverage in the West and provoked a humanitarian response in Europe that was led by philanthropist Sir Moses Montefiore and French politician Adolphe Crémieux, who secured the release of the remaining Jewish detainees from Egyptian prisons. Dr Mishaqa was drawn into the case as a forensic expert, to identify human remains believed to be those of the murdered priest and his assistant. With the restoration of Ottoman rule at the end of 1840, the security of the Jewish community was restored. However, the horrors perpetrated by the Egyptian authorities combined with the silence of their Muslim and Christian neighbours undoubtedly undermined the Jewish community's trust in both the government and society of Damascus.[6]

The thumn of al-'Amara was the nerve centre of the old city, combining the Citadel, the main markets and commercial thoroughfares, and the Umayyad Mosque—one of the oldest and most revered places of worship in the Muslim world. The leading Muslim notable families of Damascus were concentrated in al-'Amara, and the area boasted some of the most luxurious mansions in the whole of Damascus.

The Citadel is an ancient and imposing structure enclosing an area the size of six football fields that formerly housed the Janissary corps. With the Egyptian occupation in 1832, new barracks were built to the west of the city walls to accommodate the tens of thousands of soldiers billeted in Damascus. At mid-century the old fortress retained its impressive walls, but its interior was in ruins, the result of a massive 1842 fire in the gunpowder magazine of the fortress that burned for a full day and night before it could be brought under control. As a foreign observer noted, the castle was 'a mere shell' by the 1850s.[7]

The central markets of the city distinguished Damascus as one of the most important commercial hubs in Ottoman Arab lands. An inland city, Damascus was a desert port served by long-distance caravan trade routes. Periodically, long lines of camels, the 'ships of the desert,' entered the ancient walled city through narrow roads designed for animal rather than wheeled traffic. The celebrated French poet Alphonse de Lamartine, who visited Damascus in 1833, witnessed the impressive sight of a string of more than three thousand camels entering Damascus from Baghdad. He joined the feeding frenzy following the caravan's arrival and bought Indian shawls and mocha coffee from the traders. The main commercial arteries ran to the northeast, connecting the city to Baghdad, Persia, and India beyond; to the north, linking Damascus to Aleppo and Turkey; to the southwest, for trade with Palestine and Egypt; and due south to Mecca and Medina. Little from the Mediterranean world made it to Damascus before mid-century. Until then, the trade of Damascus was focused on the Muslim world.[8]

The markets of Damascus reflected the caravan trade that supplied the city's shops. The camel-borne trade tended to favour high-value goods. It simply wasn't cost-effective to transport bulk foodstuffs like grain or raw materials like cotton long-distance by camel, where the value per weight hardly covered the cost of transport. Instead, merchants from Persia or Turkey or Egypt would send consignments that were of high value by weight—coffee and spices, silks and embroidered fabrics, precious carpets and metalwork, gemstones and jewellery. Combined with the quality artisanal production of Damascus, such as inlaid woodwork, fine metalwork, and rich fabrics in wool, silk, linen, and cotton blends, the markets were a rich emporium that dazzled visitors and imparted a sense of luxury to the city. Isabel Burton, who lived for two years in Damascus as the wife of British consul Richard Burton, was captivated by the diversity of the city's markets:

> The Suks (bazars) are all divided into different trades and merchandize. There is the saddlers' bazar, brilliant with holsters, bridles, saddle-cloths and trappings of every colour and blazing with gold; the shoemakers, with those bright toe-pointed, lemon-coloured slippers; the seed bazar; the tailors' bazar; the tobacco bazar; and the silk and thread bazar. The gold and silver smiths' bazar is the most curious place in the world, more like a covered shambles than anything

else.... The marqueterie bazar is very pretty, there you buy clogs or pattens, tables and chests, all inlaid with mother-of-pearl.... There are also the book bazar, the Greek bazar, full of divan stuffs and embroidered jackets; the sweet bazar... the mercers', the spice bazar, the box or trunk bazar....[9]

The markets were also the cleanest part of the city. The paved roads were swept daily, and the main market arteries were covered to protect shoppers from winter's rain and the summer sun. The covered thoroughfares also served as the main access routes to the city's most cherished and important monument: the Umayyad Mosque.

The Umayyad Mosque was the spiritual, cultural, and political centre of Ottoman Damascus. Built between the years 706 and 715 of the current era, on the site of a Roman temple dedicated to Jupiter and a Byzantine basilica in honour of John the Baptist, the Umayyad Mosque is one of the largest and most revered places of worship in the Muslim world. The Umayyad Caliph al-Walid (r. 705–715) spared no expense in securing the most beautiful materials and the finest artisans to embellish a monument designed to distinguish Damascus as the then-capital of Islam. Although the Umayyad empire was toppled in 750 CE and the caliphs of the successor Abbasid dynasty built their capital in Baghdad, the Umayyad Mosque preserved its special place as Sunni Islam's fourth-most-important mosque after those of Mecca, Medina, and al-Aqsa in Jerusalem. The Umayyad Mosque has suffered numerous fires and much restoration over the centuries, yet the beauty of its stonework and mosaics remains exceptional even today.

The Umayyad Mosque was an object of civic pride for all Damascenes, Muslim and non-Muslim alike. Christian chronicler Nu'man al-Qasatli boasted immoderately of this most prominent Damascene monument as 'one of the largest, oldest, most famous and most beautiful of all the Muslims' mosques.' He described the daily rhythms and flows of people through the mosque as if he were himself a regular visitor: 'Each day a great number of 'ulama, teachers, imams, students and speakers meet in the mosque. It has seventy-five muezzins who give the call to prayer from the three minarets with the most beautiful voices. Each night the mosque is lit with thousands of candles, turning night into day.'[10]

The large public space provided by the Umayyad Mosque served first and foremost as the venue for Friday prayers. Here, thousands of Damascene artisans and merchants would converge with the Ottoman governor, his officials, and the Muslim notables of the city: members of the Islamic learned establishment, or 'ulama; leaders of the town's armed factions, or aghawat; and those who claimed descent from the family of the Prophet Muhammad, known as the ashraf. All assembled each Friday at midday to pray together and to listen to the weekly sermon given by the preacher or khatib of the Umayyad Mosque—one of the most prestigious posts in the city. The Friday sermon was always recited in the name of the ruling sultan. Failure to do so—as occasionally happened over the centuries when the Damascenes were at odds with the Ottomans—was seen as an act of rebellion. As such, Friday prayers served to legitimise the sultan's government and to demonstrate the Damascenes' submission to his rule.

The Umayyad Mosque also served for special occasions, such as the prayers for rain after a period of drought. One such service was held in 1845, bringing together the governor of Damascus and his officials, members of the town *Majlis* (ruling council), and an enormous crowd of notables and townsfolk who filled the Umayyad Mosque to capacity. The voices of the faithful 'shook the world' as they beseeched their Creator to favour their city's farmlands with rain.[11]

Finally, the mosque was an important centre of Islamic learning. Some of the most famous scholars of Quranic studies, Hadith (the theological discipline of interpreting the sayings and practices of the Prophet Muhammad), and the different schools of Sharia law taught in the Umayyad Mosque to prepare young men for careers in the religious establishment. In all these ways, the Umayyad Mosque was central to the spiritual, social, pedagogical, and political life of Damascene Muslims.

Over the centuries, Damascus expanded well beyond the confines of the walled city. In Ottoman times, following the conquest in 1516, new quarters were established to the north, west, and south of the city along major trade arteries.

The seat of Ottoman government in Damascus was based in the Marja district, one of the new quarters to the west of the Citadel in the thumn of al-Qanawat. Here, near the banks of the Barada River, stood the office and residence of the *wali*, or provincial governor, known as the *Saray*. Municipal buildings flanked the Saray, as well as the office of the military commander (*Mushir*) and barracks for the local garrison. The courts of justice were in Marja, as well as the prison. Unlike the narrow lanes of central Damascus, which were built for pedestrian and animal traffic, Marja had wide streets to accommodate horse-drawn carriages and soldiers' drills.

In 1860 the governor of Damascus was Ahmad Pasha, who also served as the commander of the province's armed forces, or *mushir*. The other members of the provincial government included the chief financial officer (*muhasibji*) and the chief justice (*qadi*). All were appointed by the central government in Istanbul and were usually Ottoman Turks. To bridge the linguistic and cultural gap dividing Ottoman Turks from the Arab residents of Damascus, the governor relied on the city's notables—members of the 'ulama and the ashraf, the landowning elite, and the paramilitary commanders (agha-wat)—who served as intermediaries between the masses of both urban and rural workers and the Ottoman government. These notables served in a powerful twelve-member advisory council known as the Majlis. Meeting two or three times each week, the Majlis enjoyed wide-ranging powers spanning provincial administration, finance, and justice. The politics of Damascus were largely shaped by the interplay between Ottoman-appointed Turks dispatched from Istanbul to govern the city and its province, and local leaders who filled the ranks of the Majlis. Although Christian and Jewish leaders were in theory eligible for membership of the Majlis, in practice the body was dominated by the Muslim notables of the city and the Ottoman administrative elite.[12]

Two other thumns of Damascus experienced particular growth in the late Ottoman period. The northern suburb of al-Salihiyya served as the reception area for new communities settling in Damascus. Built on the slopes of Jabal Qasiyun, the mountain overshadowing Damascus, al-Salihiyya was home to a large Kurdish community and more recent immigrants such as the Circassians, who took refuge in Ottoman lands from the expansion of the Russian empire. Separated from central Damascus by a fifteen-minute ride by horseback, the quarter was considered rough by Damascene standards. The townspeople used to joke about its name, al-Salihiyya, which means 'the virtuous,' claiming it would be more honest to rename the quarter al-Talihiyya, 'the villainous.'[13]

To the south lay al-Maydan, a commercial and industrial zone linking Damascus to its agricultural breadbasket, the Hawran, and the Bedouin-dominated regions of the Syrian desert. A distinct division of labour within Damascus had al-Maydan receiving and processing raw materials from the countryside—wool, skins, and agricultural products—and then passing them on to the workshops in the centre of the city, where artisans turned out the fine leather and fabrics for which the city was famous. Al-Maydan was also the gateway to the South, through which the pilgrimage caravan to Mecca passed each year in one of the most important rituals in the life of the city.

Each year, thousands of pilgrims descended on Damascus from across the Muslim world to perform the once-in-a-lifetime duty of Hajj, or pilgrimage to Mecca, the birthplace of Islam. The Ottoman sultan staked his legitimacy on the safe passage of the pilgrimage each year, and he delegated responsibility for organising the caravans to two great Arab capital cities: Cairo, to service pilgrims from Africa, and Damascus to provide for those coming from Asia. The Ottoman government placed so much importance on the Syrian pilgrimage that starting in 1708, the governor of Damascus was tasked with leading the caravan himself and was spared the duty of contributing soldiers from the local garrison for the sultan's wars to concentrate his forces on providing for the security of the pilgrims against Bedouin raids.[14]

The annual pilgrimage was an important source of income for the markets of Damascus as well as a highly prestigious religious ritual that anchored the city's place as one of the centres of the Muslim world. One month before the Hajj caravan was due to depart from Damascus, pilgrims began to arrive in the city from across Ottoman and Asian lands. Between mid-Ramadan, the holy month of fasting in the Hijri or Islamic lunar calendar, and mid-Shawwal, when the pilgrims' caravan departed, the markets of Damascus were alive with traders from all parts of the Muslim world trying to cover the expense of their journey and, where possible, to turn a profit. Persian pilgrims carried 'gorgeous carpets, fine embroidery, rich shawls, inlaid caskets, and precious stones, to barter for Damascus silks and cotton fabrics'—items that they would take back to their hometowns and sell for a good price.[15] Travellers from other lands brought equally precious goods to trade. The pious pilgrims also bought the provisions they needed for the arduous march along the Hajj Road through the deserts of Transjordan and the Hijaz—a three- to four-month round-trip journey. Further trading went on in Mecca itself, with pilgrims returning to Damascus with loads of henna, coffee, Indian cloths used for turbans, jewels, ostrich plumes, perfumes, and incense, all of which injected further vitality into the markets of Damascus.[16]

The departure of the pilgrimage caravan was an occasion of great pomp and ceremony. Each year, thousands of hajjis (as those making the hajj are called) gathered in Damascus. The governors and religious authorities of the city assembled in their finery to bless the pilgrims in three days of public rituals. On the first day, artisans accompanied by a military band paraded with monumental candles and vessels filled with the purest olive oil sent to light the mosques of Mecca and Medina. On the second day, an honour guard carried the holy banner of Caliph 'Umar in a gilded box through the streets of the city in preparation for the formal departure of the caravan on the third day.

The final ceremonies for the departure of the pilgrimage caravan drew all the Muslims of Damascus together for a festive event. With military marching bands providing stirring music, brigades of soldiers in dress uniform accompanied by Bedouin tribesmen provided an honour guard for the camel litters carrying the precious tributes to the holy cities of Mecca and Medina. The commander of the pilgrimage had a richly caparisoned litter with mirrors to oversee all that went on ahead of and behind his position. Leading members of the religious establishment marched in their finest robes with colourful turbans to recite prayers for the caravan's safe travels. The procession made its way down the length of the al-Maydan quarter, whose streets were thronged with the men and women of the city. Street vendors added to the noise and colour of the occasion, shouting above one another to sell their wares to passersby. At the southern extremity of the al-Maydan stood the Bawabat Allah, or the Gates of God, marking the start of the Hajj Road to Mecca. Here the caravan was launched with the blessings of the 'ulama onto the road to Islam's holiest city, some 1,500 kilometres away.[17]

The annual Hajj rituals reinforced the centrality of Islam in the culture of Damascus. The city's history as the first capital of the

Islamic caliphate, the glory of the Umayyad Mosque and the scores of other historic mosques scattered across the city, the renown of the Islamic scholars of Damascus, and the pomp and excitement of the pilgrimage combined to make the city's Muslim community very proud of its Islamic heritage—and highly conservative.

To describe the Muslim majority in Damascus as 'conservative' is not to argue that all Damascenes were pious, devout Muslims. Like all big cities, Damascus was fraught with social problems and deviance. The diaries left by mid-nineteenth-century Damascenes record instances of murder and graft. In 1849 the governor convened a committee to examine the financial records of the Umayyad Mosque and discovered that the trustees had been siphoning thousands of piastres from the mosque's endowments in bribes and corruption. In 1854 the provincial administration was wracked by another corruption scandal, in which anonymous pamphleteers posted notices throughout the city accusing Governor 'Arif Pasha of taking bribes. The charges ultimately led to the governor's dismissal. His successor, Salih Pasha, was 'weak and ineffectual.' Under Salih Pasha's rule, the town was disorderly, insurgents blocked the roads, and murders went unpunished. In the al-Maydan quarter, rival gangs erupted into street violence in 1858. The exchange of gunfire left many dead and wounded, and forced the army to intervene to restore order. And Ahmad Pasha, the governor who held up Dr Mishaqa's accreditation, introduced a tax on wine, which, though forbidden by Islamic law, was apparently widely sold and consumed in Damascus in 1859. Clearly, Damascus was a real city with a diverse population of sinners and saints combined.[18]

The conservatism in Damascene society was more apparent in relations between the Muslim majority and non-Muslim communities than in the strict observance of Islamic law and practice. The Muslims of Damascus fully respected the persons and property of Christian and Jewish residents of the city, in keeping with Islamic stricture. Muslims, Christians, and Jews lived in the same neighbourhoods, their shops intermixed in the markets, and members of different religious communities worked together in their professions. However, the Muslim majority held minority communities to strict codes of behaviour and dress that confirmed Christians and Jews as protected but second-class subjects. Starting in the 1830s, when Syria came under Egyptian occupation, Damascus was subject to major political and economic changes that would transform the old social order, provoking new tensions between Muslims and minorities across Syria.[19]

The first change came with the opening of European diplomatic missions in Damascus. All the Western powers had consulates in Mehmed 'Ali's Egypt. Now that Syria was under his control, many looked for new opportunities in Damascus, which had until then been closed to European influence. At first, they found the way barred by the implacable opposition of the Damascene elite. Lamartine, who visited Damascus in March 1833, gave some sense of the local hostility to British efforts to open a consulate in their city: 'The Damascenes alone among the Orientals, nourish more and more religious hatred and horror of the European name and costume. They alone have refused to admit consuls, or even consular agents, for Christian powers. Damascus is a holy, fanatical, and free city—nothing must pollute it.'

The British government had in fact already nominated a consul to open offices in Damascus as early as 1830, but as Lamartine
noted at the time of his visit, 'The people of Damascus have obsti-
nately refused access within the walls to the English consul-general
in Syria. Two terrible seditions have arisen in the city, on the mere
rumour of the consul's approach. If he had not turned back, he
would have been torn in pieces.'[20]

It wasn't until January 1834 that Consul William Farren dared
venture into Damascus under Egyptian protection to take up his
post. The *Times* of London reported the British consul's entry as a
triumph:

> All the streets through which they passed were lined
> with spectators, the windows and roofs of the houses
> were crowded, and the people were even standing two
> and three deep on the ledges of the shops; such a scene,
> in fact, was never, it is said, before seen in Damascus,
> which up to the entrance of Mr Farren, had been kept
> sacred from the dress and habits of the Europeans, and
> being a holy city, no person until then had been allowed
> to enter it on horseback.[21]

The issue of a non-Muslim riding into Damascus on horseback
was particularly sensitive. Among the social conventions imposed on
non-Muslims was the rule that Christians and Jews could ride only
shorter mounts such as donkeys in the city so that they would never
be in the position of looking down upon a mounted Muslim. Europeans never missed an opportunity to challenge such restrictions,

which they saw as an affront to their personal and national honour. The flaunting of local social conventions did little to endear the new consular corps to the Muslims of Damascus. As J. L. Porter noted in his sober assessment of Consul Farren's 1834 entry into Damascus, 'The fanatical citizens indulged their wrath and muttered their curses in private, but made no open demonstration of their hatred.'[22]

The hostile local reaction in 1834 seems to have given other European states pause in opening their own consulates. The French waited until 1839 to send Count Ulysse de Ratti-Menton to open their consulate in Damascus, and by 1840 Austria had followed suit. Other European powers opened consular agencies in the years after the Egyptian withdrawal in December 1840. The Russian government established a new vice-consulate in Damascus in 1846, and the Prussians in April 1849.[23] Greece, the Netherlands, and Persia were the only other countries to establish consular agencies in Damascus before Mikhayil Mishaqa was accredited as US vice-consul in 1859.

The second change was in the commerce of Damascus. The European powers sought entry into Damascus for commercial rather than strictly diplomatic reasons. They saw the Egyptian occupation as an opportunity to circumvent Ottoman restrictions on entering lucrative markets in the Arab East, and Damascus was the largest still closed to Western goods. The *Times*, in its article on Consul Farren's entry into Damascus in 1834, explicitly linked his appointment to the goal of gaining entry to the Damascene market:

The commercial relations of the two countries [Britain and Syria] may now, therefore, be considered as established on a firm basis, and a mine of wealth and enterprise opened by the important position of Syria with reference to the affairs and commerce of the east. Our merchants are too acute not to take advantage of this state of things, though it is said that they are likely to encounter some serious opposition from the jealousy of those who have heretofore enjoyed the monopoly of the Turkey trade.[24]

It did not take long after the first European consuls entered the city for European manufactured goods to find their way into its markets. Great Britain concluded a trade agreement with the Ottoman Empire in 1838 that gave British merchants preferential tariffs for both imports and exports, eliminated long-standing monopolies on the purchase and sale of certain agricultural goods, and dispensed with internal duties on the movement of goods within Ottoman provinces that had served as real barriers to trade. France and Russia were quick to demand the same terms for their trade, with smaller European states following suit.[25]

British trade to Syria experienced a major expansion as a result of these developments. Although volume rose and fell from year to year, the overall trend in the 1830s and 1840s was on the rise. Between 1836 and 1839, the volume of British trade was approximately £120,000 per annum (approximately £16 million in 2023 currency).[26] Trade volume leapt to over £440,000 per annum between 1840 and 1844.[27] By the 1850s, France and Austria had weighed in as major trade partners in Syria, with total European imports through the port of Beirut nearly doubling between 1853 and 1857, rising from £723,000 to £1.3 million. Cheap industrial cotton fabrics made up the lion's share of this trade in 1857 (£578,000), followed by woollen fabrics (£150,000) and silks (£60,000). Over 60 percent of the European goods flooding into Damascus in the 1850s were fabrics that competed directly with the domestic weaving industry. Writing of the markets of Damascus in the early 1850s, Porter noted the 'spacious khans filled with the substantial fabrics of Western Europe.'[28] This was a major change in both the industrial and the commercial life of the city, as Mediterranean trade from Europe overwhelmed overland commerce with the Muslim world.

The sudden influx of cheaper cotton and woollen fabrics in the Damascus market had an immediate impact on the local weaving industry. With more than 77 million yards of British fabrics dumped on the Syrian market in 1842 alone, the sudden glut meant there were four yards of fabric on the local market for every man, woman, and child in Syria: 'Faced with this avalanche of cheap European fabrics, protected by only the most minimal of tariffs, it is not surprising that many Middle Eastern spinners, weavers and dyers were forced out of business.'[29]

Local weavers faced a second pressure, in that European merchants were actively buying raw cotton, wool, and silk to fill the holds of their ships to prevent them returning empty from Beirut. It was this British imperative, to secure valuable raw materials for their merchant ships returning home from Beirut, that most likely led Consul Brant to obstruct the first American wool contract in Damascus in 1859 and would explain the governor's cooperation in imposing the sequester. After all, foreign competition for local fibres drove up the prices for the raw materials upon which Damascene spinners, dyers, and weavers relied. An 1859 French report estimated a 50 percent increase in the price of raw materials for the local weaving industry. The Ottoman governor had no interest in seeing a new foreign competitor like the United States enter the market for Damascene wool. On top of this, local producers faced all the internal tariffs that Britain and the other European powers were now spared. For instance, raw silk was taxed at 12 percent by the customs officials in Damascus. 'Under these conditions,' the report concluded, 'it is easy to understand why many looms are abandoned. This happens daily.'[30]

The third major change in the 1830s was in transport. The British established the first steam-shipping lines to the eastern Mediterranean in 1835, with the French following in 1837 and the Austrians in 1839. By 1841, there were more than seventy-five steamships of different European flags plying the waters of the eastern Mediterranean. These first paddle-wheel steamers had smaller holds than contemporary sailing vessels and charged higher rates for freight. But they took the uncertainty out of sea travel and cut the times for journeys significantly. Over the course of the 1840s and 1850s, steamships grew larger, faster, and more powerful, lowering the cost of freight and the transport of passengers.[31]

These developments increasingly recommended steam transport to Muslims making the annual pilgrimage to Mecca in the 1840s and 1850s. At the start of the nineteenth century, as many as 15,000 to 20,000 pilgrims converged on Damascus each year for the annual

Hajj—with all the commerce that such a large number implied. In the 1840s, with the expansion of steam shipping to the eastern Mediterranean, that number began to fall dramatically. In 1845 only 6,000 pilgrims took part in the Damascus Hajj caravan. Increasingly, hajjis from Turkey chose to travel to the Hijaz by steamship, disembarking in Alexandria, where they boarded the railway to Suez and completed the journey by steamship from Suez to Jidda, bypassing the overland route altogether. Some chose to take the overland route outbound to Mecca and to return home by steamer. By the 1850s, French consul Henri Guys reported that the outbound caravan from Damascus to Mecca numbered only 2,300 pilgrims and that the returning caravan was reduced to 1,500 hajjis, the other 800 returning home by sea either via Egypt or the Persian Gulf.[32] The commercial significance of the Hajj pilgrimage would have been similarly undermined. Given the centrality of the Hajj caravan in the culture and economy of Damascus, these were grave developments indeed.

The growing power of the local minority communities represented another major transformation in the society and economy of Damascus, starting in the 1830s. When occupying Syria in 1832, the Egyptians introduced notions of legal equality between Muslims and non-Muslims that had already been implemented in Egypt but were alien to Damascus. Mehmed Ali Pasha had introduced the changes in Egypt more to impose the standard fiscal and military responsibilities on minorities and Muslims alike rather than as a human-rights gesture. The same measures, when introduced to Damascus, provoked resistance from the Muslim majority. As

Lamartine observed in 1833, the Muslims of Damascus were 'exasperated at the equality which Ibrahim Pasha has established between them and the Christians. Some of the latter abuse the toleration they enjoy, and insult their enemies by an open violation of their usages, which embitters [the Muslims'] fanaticism.'[33]

The expansion of legal rights gained by Syrian Christians and Jews was enhanced by the growing economic opportunities that minority communities enjoyed through their ties to European merchants. Although Damascus was now accessible to European merchants, few, if any, sought to open offices in the city. Five British merchant houses opened offices in Damascus in 1842, and by 1849 all had closed. Guys, who served as French consul in Beirut, noted how, twenty years after the French had opened their consulate in Damascus, not a single French trading house had established offices in the city.[34] Most preferred to keep their offices in Beirut and to rely on local agents to advance their commercial interests in Damascus. Local Christians, and to a lesser extent local Jews, were thus the prime beneficiaries as middlemen for the expansion of European trade into Damascus. For, in addition to securing commissions on the bulk of European goods flooding Damascene markets, many of those working for European trading houses gained European legal protection as well.

In keeping with ancient privileges first bestowed on the European powers by the powerful Ottoman sultans in the sixteenth century, foreign diplomats and merchants enjoyed extraterritorial rights within the Ottoman Empire established by treaty right. These treaties, known as the Capitulations, protected foreign nationals from local justice. If an Englishman or a Russian were to break the law, they would be judged by their own consuls according to the law of their own countries, not by Ottoman courts. Moreover, foreign powers benefitted from preferential terms of trade and taxation that had originally been designed to encourage weaker European states of the early modern period to ply their trade in Ottoman lands. By the nineteenth century, the European states were no longer the weaker party, and they upheld these old and established privileges to secure unfair advantages in Ottoman trade.

Moreover, the Capitulations permitted foreign powers to extend these favourable terms to local Christians or Jews who entered the service of a European consulate or trading house. Thus, even before taking up his American consular post, Dr Mishaqa had already been a British protégé since the time Richard Wood had him appointed dragoman in 1840. His case was not uncommon: Western consulates engaged ever more local staff in an increasingly corrupt system. As one contemporary European observer wrote, 'Contrary to the treaties and the capitulations, a consular agent will have as many as four dragomans, four or five cavasses,' and other employees, 'each of whom buys for a fine price the right to elude the direct rule of the Sublime Porte.' Once they held a *berat,* a legal document confirming foreign-subject status, local Christians could extend extraterritorial rights to their own relations: 'Each of these consular staff in turn rent out their protection to associates, brothers, or friends to offset the price they themselves paid to gain an office that conferred protection.... Everywhere you find consulates, consular agents or the agents of these agents in Syria, the number of protégés is unlimited.'

Foreign merchants could also extend privileges to their local agents. Each European merchant enjoyed an unwritten right to hire up to fifty employees, each of whom enjoyed consular protection.[35]

Damascene Muslims were incensed by the privileges enjoyed— and abused—by certain Christians and Jews. As one Damascene Muslim notable wrote in his diary,

> Every member of a Christian sect had a relative under the protection of a foreign power, most of them under the French. Any [Christian] with a claim on a Muslim would transfer the case to someone who was a foreign subject. If there was a quarrel between a Christian and a Muslim of any rank, [the Christian] would say 'I am a subject of such-and-such a state' even when it wasn't true and that it was one of his relatives or loved ones who was a protégé.

The Christian would then draw on the influence of the friend or relative to have the Muslim arrested and tried in 'their' consulate's court, where invariably the judge decided in favour of the Christian and 'the Muslim was sentenced to a longer term than the offense for which he was convicted. If the law called for ten days' imprisonment, he would be sentenced to twenty from lack of mutual support.'[36]

The system of foreign protection made for an ever-expanding web that was subject to widespread abuse and gave members of the minority communities unfair access to lucrative privileges coming from the growing European diplomatic and commercial presence in Syria.

The period of the Egyptian occupation of Syria (1831–1840) introduced a series of changes that continued to transform Damascus two decades after the Egyptian withdrawal. The introduction of European consuls, the opening of Damascus's markets to Mediterranean trade, the advent of steam navigation, and the changing social relations between Muslims and minorities placed Damascene society under tremendous pressure. Increasingly, it seemed as though all the challenges of the nineteenth century came from outside of Damascus and worked to the disadvantage of the city's traditional elites.

Against this background of transformational changes in the politics, economy, and society of Damascus, we can begin to appreciate the resistance to Dr Mishaqa's appointment as US vice-consul. As a Syrian Christian, his appointment reflected the increasing powers that local Christians enjoyed through their connection to foreign powers. He enjoyed immunity from Ottoman law and avoided the taxes that Ottoman citizens had to pay. He was one of the few who benefitted from the transformative changes of the 1840s and 1850s, when so many in Damascus saw their social and economic position undermined. In his reports to US consul Johnson in Beirut, Mishaqa frequently reported on the growing hostility shown him by Ottoman officials. All the evidence would suggest that he wasn't imagining things.

An important provincial capital of the Ottoman Empire, Damascus might have looked to the sultan and his government for solutions. But in the age of Ottoman reforms, the beleaguered notables of Damascus found that the central government was only making matters worse. Far from reversing the harmful measures introduced by the Egyptians, the government in Istanbul codified the legal equality between Muslims and non-Muslims, and conceded to European demands for greater access to Syrian markets. The Muslim notables of Damascus viewed with mounting hostility both the changes imposed by government fiat and the minority communities that seemed to be the main beneficiaries of the reforms.

3

Resistance to Ottoman Reforms

It is easy to understand the objections of the Muslim notables of Damascus to the rapid pace of change they witnessed in the middle decades of the nineteenth century. They found the growing European presence after the 1830s an affront to their city's Islamic culture and traditions. Overland trade routes that they had long controlled were in retreat before the aggressive spread of steam travel. By the 1850s, even the cherished pilgrimage caravan to Mecca was yielding to the power of steam. And the beneficiaries of these changes were the minority communities, the protégés of the European powers, who gained in wealth and social power at the expense of the Muslim elites. The Muslim notables looked to the sultan and his government to stand up for their rights and interests. The sultan's representative in Damascus was the governor, Ahmad Pasha. Judging from contemporary accounts, the townspeople of Damascus were none too certain of the governor's intentions toward them or toward the reforms being imposed by the central government.

Ahmad Pasha is an enigmatic figure. He earned a ten-page biography in the Damascene equivalent of *Who's Who*, a biographical dictionary compiled by the Muslim religious scholar 'Abd al-Rizaq al-Bitar (1837–1917). Al-Bitar was a contemporary of the governor and would have been in his twenties when Ahmad Pasha was appointed. In his biographical essay, al-Bitar extolled the governor's virtues in rhymed Arabic prose: 'The great minister, the governor and commander of the army, who dazzled by his good management and solicitude, who appeared among the people as a full moon at night, he pursued the highest course of piety and worship, and in the course of his days he was beyond comparison for his refinement, pure beliefs, and elevated thought.' It is clear that al-Bitar held Ahmad Pasha in the highest regard, although the reader searches in vain through the rest of the essay for such basic biographical facts as the governor's place or date of birth, or career record prior to assuming his post in Damascus. We know that he first came to Damascus in 1858 as *mushir*, or commander of the Army of Arabistan (the Ottoman term for the Syrian provinces), and rose to *wali*, or governor, the following year. The only personal detail that Bitar shared was that Ahmad Pasha practiced Islamic mysticism and was a member of the Khalwati Sufi order.[1]

The Muslim notables of Damascus did not all share al-Bitar's glowing assessment of Ahmad Pasha's rule. The illustrious preacher of the Umayyad Mosque, Shaykh Muhammad Sa'id al-Ustuwani, was critical of the governor's record. Already as mushir, Ahmad Pasha had antagonised some of the leading notables of Damascus.

When rival gangs broke into armed conflict on the streets of the southern suburb of al-Maydan in 1858, Ahmad Pasha responded with an iron fist. As Shaykh al-Ustuwani recorded in his diary, 'They arrested men at random until the jails were full,' including a number of influential members of the *aghawat*, the traditional militia leaders of Damascus. More than one hundred of those detained were exiled with little or no due process, some to the fortress of Acre, others to the island of Cyprus. 'He wants to cleanse the city [of its crime], though he acts with unbounded harshness,' al-Ustuwani concluded of Ahmad Pasha's conduct as mushir.

Nor did al-Ustuwani credit Ahmad Pasha's methods when he was promoted to governor in 1859: 'He wanted to make the condition of the people more orderly. However, he was unable to do this. He mandated innovations for which he will bear responsibility until the Day of Judgement.' Among these 'innovations' was a series of tax levies to refill the provincial government's depleted coffers. He imposed land registration, raised the 10 percent tithe on harvests by a quarter to 12.5 percent, and introduced a head tax on livestock. It was Ahmad Pasha who began to tax wine, 'as the drinking of wine was widespread,' despite its being forbidden. More to the point, Ahmad Pasha was raising taxes, which is something all conservatives object to—hence the ominous reference to the Judgement Day.[2]

The members of the consular corps in Damascus were divided in their views of the governor. In his memoirs, Dr Mishaqa gave a favourable initial assessment of Ahmad Pasha, claiming that 'he got along very well with everyone' when first appointed. British consul James Brant enjoyed a cordial relationship with the governor, commending Ahmad Pasha's energy and competence. Brant knew the governor well enough to record something of his domestic life, noting that Ahmad Pasha was a widower who lived in Damascus with his mother and two sons. French consul Michel Lanusse was deeply mistrustful of the governor, drawing on intelligence from his agents in Damascus. The rest of the consular corps ranged from agnostic to hostile toward the new governor.[3] But in the course of his consular duties, Mishaqa seemed to go further than any of the other Western diplomats in Damascus in antagonising the governor.

Following his appointment as US vice-consul, Dr Mishaqa began to take advantage of his new diplomatic status. The post of vice-consul came with no salary but provided tax exemptions and other benefits that might enable a resourceful person to thrive. Mishaqa expanded his financial and commercial dealings, and extended consular protection to those working for both American and his personal interests. These were the kinds of practices that provoked the indignation of the governor and the Muslim elites of Damascus as an abuse of consular privilege—privileges deemed all the more egregious when exercised by a Syrian Christian like Mishaqa, rather than a bona fide foreign diplomat like Brant or Lanusse.

For example, Dr Mishaqa made a loan of Pt. 47,000 (worth around £425 or $2,100, a substantial sum at the time) to a group of thirty-five farmers from the village of Suq Wadi Barada, in the Anti-Lebanon Mountains to the northwest of Damascus. The villagers requested this vast sum to enable them to clear a preexisting debt, presumably on extortionate terms, to a powerful Jewish notable of Damascus named Ya'qub al-Islambuli. According to a contemporary Damascene source, Ya'qub al-Islambuli was 'the wealthiest member of the Jewish community of Damascus' and made much of his money from such loans to farmers.

Many merchants loaned money to local farmers as a form of debt bondage, the loan secured against a share of the borrower's future harvests at discounted prices. Lenders had no interest in seeing such loans actually repaid so long as they were assured a steady supply of cheap grain. Alternately, lenders reaped profits by charging annual interest rates ranging from 36 to 50 percent. Judging by the size of the loan—Pt. 47,000—al-Islambuli must have secured either a major position in the village's agricultural yields or massive interest payments. By buying out the peasants' debt, Dr Mishaqa was effectively cutting Islambuli's revenues from a prosperous village—and no doubt securing a share of the harvest of Suq Wadi Barada for himself on terms more favourable to the villagers. It was a bold move, for Mishaqa was taking on a very powerful and well-connected adversary.[4]

Like Dr Mishaqa, al-Islambuli enjoyed British protégé status, with all the legal and tax benefits conferred by great-power protection. But al-Islambuli was far better connected to the ruling elites of Damascus than was the US vice-consul. As insurance for his high-yield loans, al-Islambuli gave lavish gifts to powerful and influential figures like the governor and the notables on the Majlis (ruling council). He was particularly close to Ahmad Pasha. Remarkably, the governor who refused to return Mishaqa's courtesy call accepted a lunch invitation to al-Islambuli's sumptuous mansion. 'Never before has a governor of Damascus accepted to take lunch in the home of a non-Muslim,' a Damascene chronicler recorded.[5]

No sooner did Dr Mishaqa conclude his loan to the villagers of Suq Wadi Barada than al-Islambuli went on the offensive to protect his position. Al-Islambuli retained the services of Mustafa Bey al-Hawasli, one of the Kurdish aghawat, to protect his interests by the credible threat of violence. Many of the Muslim notables of Damascus viewed the Kurdish agha as a thug, one going so far as to describe Mustafa Bey as 'very stupid and hateful to the people of Damascus.' A hateful thug was just the man to check Mishaqa's efforts in Suq Wadi Barada.[6]

Given that the US vice-consul enjoyed extraterritorial legal rights, al-Hawasli went after the villagers of Suq Wadi Barada instead. He took the case to the Majlis, claiming that the villagers had broken the law by contracting a debt with a 'foreigner': Dr Mishaqa. Al-Hawasli no doubt expected a favourable hearing from the Majlis, given his patron Ya'qub al-Islambuli's record of generosity to Majlis members and his ties to Ahmad Pasha. The influential notables on the Majlis didn't disappoint him.

The Majlis summoned the villagers to Damascus to answer the charge. The thirty-five men were subjected to a torrent of abuse for contracting a loan with a foreigner. When the villagers tried to speak in their defense, the session turned violent, with eyewitnesses confirming that the mufti of Damascus struck the villagers and the political attaché kicked them 'with both legs' before casting all thirty-five men into debtors' prison for twelve days. While they were in detention, al-Hawasli had the villagers clapped in chains and forced to sweep the streets of Damascus to further humiliate them. In a complaint to the governor, Dr Mishaqa stressed the outrage of honourable farmers being forced to sweep the streets 'like common criminals.' The governor never replied, but his political attaché warned Mishaqa against interfering in matters between the government and its subjects. In the end, Mishaqa was forced to cancel his loan to the villagers of Suq Wadi Barada so that the unfortunate farmers, once again indebted to Islambuli, could be released from their ordeal. Mishaqa clearly suspected Governor Ahmad Pasha and the notables in the Majlis of closing ranks to prevent him from benefiting from his consular privileges. Further setbacks would only reinforce this belief.[7]

Like other wealthy elites of Damascus, Dr Mishaqa held agricultural property in rural Syria. He owned a home and several properties in the village of Bludan in the Anti-Lebanon Mountains to the northwest of the city. The Majlis, perhaps to discourage Mishaqa from exploiting his diplomatic immunity for personal gain, began to threaten his interests in Bludan. The Majlis summoned Mishaqa's superintendent from Bludan to Damascus, where they had him imprisoned on what Mishaqa deemed to be spurious charges. Mishaqa sent his son Nasif to Bludan to investigate, and the village bailiff (*kethuda*) physically attacked him and threw him to the ground. Again, Mishaqa wrote to Governor Ahmad Pasha, this time to protest the assault on his own son. The governor convened a meeting of the Majlis to consider the matter. Mishaqa brought witnesses from Bludan, but the Majlis dismissed the case before Mishaqa's witnesses even got to testify. Moreover, the Majlis undermined Mishaqa's revenues from Bludan by forcing one of the farmers in his section of the village to take out a loan from a Muslim lender. It looked like retribution for Mishaqa's loan in Suq Wadi Barada. This was getting personal.[8]

In May 1860, Dr Mishaqa had a surprise visitor to his home: Surur Agha, former captain of the police and once a leading member of the *aghawat*, the militia commanders, who were an integral part of the Damascene elite. The preacher of the Umayyad Mosque, Shaykh al-Ustuwani, described Surur Agha in his diary as 'the pride of al-Shaghur,' that ancient quarter inside the Damascus city walls. In the aftermath of the 1858 shootout between rival gangs in the al-Maydan quarter, Surur Agha was one of the scores of notables arrested and exiled by Ahmad Pasha with little or no due process during his days as military commander. Surur Agha was sent first to the fortress of Acre and, after a year's imprisonment, was sentenced to indefinite exile on the island of Cyprus. The government sold his property and sent his wife and children to join him in Cyprus. For a proud notable of Damascus, a lifetime in exile was an unbearable punishment. Six months later, Surur Agha fled the island to Mount Lebanon and made his way to Damascus in the hope of clearing his name and securing permission to return to his hometown.[9]

It was strange that Surur Agha should have chosen Dr Mishaqa's consulate to seek asylum. Perhaps he knew Mishaqa from his days as a medical practitioner; perhaps he felt more confident turning to an Arabic speaker with diplomatic immunity. Either way, he wanted Mishaqa's protection. Surur Agha claimed that he had been wrongly sentenced without a proper legal hearing or due process. He sought sanctuary in the US vice-consulate and requested Mishaqa's intercession with the governor. Mishaqa was no doubt flattered to have a prominent Muslim notable request his protection and, in accepting Surur Agha's request, was bound by strict social conventions to ensure the safety of a stranger seeking protection under his roof.

It was Dr Mishaqa's misfortune that his first asylum seeker should be a man whom the governor himself had arrested and exiled. Relations between Mishaqa and Ahmad Pasha were already strained, and he was concerned how the governor would react when he learned that he was harbouring Surur Agha in his consulate. He chose to notify Ahmad Pasha in secret through one of the government clerks 'so that, if His Excellency felt sympathy for this unfortunate man and would treat him with compassion I might send Surur Agha to him, and if this weren't possible, that he should inform me so that I could send Surur away in peace, just as he had entered my home.' The governor was not inclined to compassion. He sent an adjutant with an official letter of protest to demand that Mishaqa surrender Surur Agha immediately. As a precaution, the governor posted police around Mishaqa's house to prevent the fugitive from taking flight. Mishaqa sent the adjutant back to the governor to advise that he would need to take instructions from his superiors in the US consulate in Beirut. The police remained in position, guarding every door and window of Mishaqa's house.[10]

The standoff went on for three days while Dr Mishaqa awaited a response from Beirut. In the meanwhile, he drafted a holding letter to Ahmad Pasha, claiming insufficient knowledge to judge the merits of Surur Agha's case and reassuring the governor that he was in no way party to Surur Agha's decision to flee Cyprus or seek refuge in the US vice-consulate. He also expressed his concern at the police presence surrounding his house night and day. Exasperated, the governor returned Mishaqa's letter unanswered and instructed his courier to inform the vice-consul that he thought it 'unnecessary to prolong such a contrived correspondence' by a written reply.

Mishaqa responded in anger, criticising Ahmad Pasha for 'returning an official letter in such a censorious manner' and insisting that he, in return, could not accept Ahmad Pasha's formal complaint until he had instructions from his superior in Beirut. Relations between the two men were fraying to the breaking point.

After three days under siege, Dr Mishaqa received a reply from Beirut. The consul-general was sympathetic but advised Mishaqa that, in keeping with Article Five of the treaty establishing diplomatic relations between the United States and the Sublime Porte (the Ottoman government), he had no right to intervene in a dispute between the government and its subjects. 'I never thought we had the right to offer protection to an Ottoman subject from their sovereign rulers,' Mishaqa responded, 'but I also never thought we would have to deliver a man seeking refuge in this consulate, after being denied a fair legal hearing, into the hands of his oppressor.' However, Mishaqa recognised that he could not offer further asylum to Surur Agha, and he told his guest as much. Under cover of darkness, Surur Agha managed to escape from Mishaqa's house undetected. Mishaqa had the bitter satisfaction of writing to the governor the next morning to confirm 'that Surur Agha left the Consulate of his own free will, as he had entered the premises.' He had discharged his duties to social conventions about protecting those taking refuge in his house, but at a high cost. Mishaqa's role in the Surur Agha affair only served to deepen the governor's antagonism toward the US vice-consul.

Reflecting on his collisions with the governor and the notables in the Damascus city council, Dr Mishaqa wrote his superiors in Beirut: 'I am convinced that the failure to resolve these issues is not the fault of the governor [Ahmad Pasha] alone but reflects the opposition of

the Majlis to the work of foreigners. I have no doubt that their opposition stems from the prejudices of the men in the Majlis and their
hatred of Christians in general and foreigners in particular.'[11] This
hatred was something relatively new that had developed over the
past twenty years alongside resentments provoked by the growing
European diplomatic presence and the empowerment of their Christian protégés. For if the Muslim elites of Damascus looked to the
Ottoman government to preserve their status and prosperity, they
found the sultan's government only furthering the empowerment of
the Christian and Jewish minority communities through a new age
of reform in the Ottoman Empire known as the Tanzimat.

In the course of the nineteenth century, Ottoman statesmen confronted new challenges for which their institutions of state and economy proved inadequate. Declining tax revenues left the treasury
depleted, and underfunded Ottoman armies lost wars against both
assertive European neighbours and domestic insurgents, as in the
Greek War of Independence (1821–1829) and the Egyptian invasion
of Syria (1831–1840). Ottoman statesmen increasingly recognised
that their empire would not long survive without a root-and-branch
reorganisation—in Turkish, 'Tanzimat.'[12]

The Ottomans' first experiments with reform date back to the
last quarter of the eighteenth century and focused on modernising the military. It soon became apparent that the Ottomans could
not afford to upgrade the military without significant new funding.
However, to increase tax revenues required a new system of land registration and detailed census records. The education system needed

to go beyond literacy to embrace maths, the sciences, and foreign languages if the government was to recruit civil servants capable of bringing the empire into line with those threatening it. In short, Ottoman reformers recognised that they had to make changes in many sectors, not just in the military. This is what distinguished the Tanzimat from previous attempts at reform.

The Tanzimat was launched in 1839 with the Gülhane Reform Decree. It was a moment of particular vulnerability for the Ottoman Empire. The forces of the rebellious Egyptian governor Mehmed Ali had just defeated the Ottoman army in northern Syria, taking the grand vizier (the Ottoman prime minister) prisoner. The experienced sultan Mahmud II (r. 1808–1839) suddenly died of tuberculosis before news of his army's defeat reached the imperial capital, Istanbul. His son and successor, Abdülmecid I, was only sixteen at the time. The Ottoman navy took stock of the situation—with Mehmed Ali's forces once again storming deep into Turkish territory and the accession of a teenage sultan—and mutinied, pledging its allegiance to the Egyptian viceroy. Britain, France, and Russia were all manoeuvring to prevent their rivals from taking advantage of this moment of supreme Ottoman weakness.

Never had the Ottoman government been more dependent on Europe's goodwill than it was in 1839. To secure guarantees of its territory and sovereignty against the Egyptian threat, the Ottoman government believed that it needed to demonstrate to the European powers that it could adhere to European norms of statecraft. Moreover, the reformers who had worked under Mahmud II were determined to consolidate the changes already undertaken under the late sultan's reign and to commit his youthful successor to the reforms he had initiated. The architect of those reforms was the Ottoman foreign minister, Mustafa Reshid Pasha, and he took the lead in drafting the reform decree. On 3 November 1839, the foreign minister read the decree on Sultan Abdülmecid's behalf before a mixed audience of foreign diplomats and Ottoman statesmen. It was the beginning of a new era of reform that would transform the Ottoman Empire from an absolute to a constitutional monarchy in just thirty-seven years.

The reform decree of 1839 set out a modest, three-point reform agenda: to ensure 'perfect security for life, honour, and prosperity' for all Ottoman subjects; to establish 'a regular system of assessing taxes'; and to reform the terms of military service by regular conscription and fixed terms of service.[13] However, little progress was made over the ensuing years to achieve these goals, and by 1856 the Ottoman government doubled down to provide a more detailed and ambitious programme.

The 1856 decree reiterated the reforms set out in 1839 and expanded on the process to address reforms in the courts and penal system. Corporal punishment was to be curbed, and torture abolished. The decree sought to regularise the finances of the empire through annual budgets that would be open to public scrutiny. The decree also called for the modernisation of imperial finances and the establishment of a modern banking system 'to create funds to be employed in augmenting the sources of wealth' in the empire through such public works as roads and canals. 'To accomplish these objects,' the decree concluded, 'means shall be sought to profit by the science, the art, and the funds of Europe, and thus gradually to execute them.'[14]

So long as the reforms applied to the higher echelons of government, the subjects of the Ottoman Empire took little interest in the Tanzimat. In the course of the 1850s and 1860s, however, the reforms began to touch the lives of individuals. Ever fearful of taxation and conscription, Ottoman subjects resisted all state efforts to inscribe their names in the government's registers. Townsmen avoided census officials, and farmers avoided land registration for as long as they could. Ahmad Pasha's attempts to raise taxes in Damascus, and the objections raised by Muslim notables, illustrate such popular resistance.[15]

There are dangers inherent in any major reform programme, particularly when foreign ideas are involved. Conservative Ottoman Muslims denounced the Tanzimat for introducing un-Islamic innovations into state and society. No issue proved more explosive than the changes to the legal status of Christians and Jews introduced by the 1856 reform decree.

Over the course of the nineteenth century, the European powers increasingly used minority rights as a pretext to intervene in Ottoman affairs. Russia extended its protection to the Greek Orthodox Church, the largest Ottoman Christian community. France had long enjoyed a special relationship with the Maronite Church in Mount Lebanon and in the nineteenth century extended formal patronage to all Ottoman Catholic communities. The British had no historical ties to any church in the region. Nonetheless, Britain represented the interests of the Jews, the Druzes, and the tiny communities of converts that gathered around Protestant missionaries in the Arab world. As long as the Ottoman Empire straddled areas of strategic importance, the European powers would exploit any means to meddle in Ottoman affairs. Issues of minority rights provided the powers with ample opportunity to impose their will on the Ottomans—sometimes with disastrous consequences for Europeans and Ottomans alike.[16]

The 'Holy Places Dispute' of 1851–1852 demonstrated the dangers of great-power protection of Ottoman Christians. Differences arose between Catholic and Greek Orthodox monks over their respective rights of worship and custody over specific Christian holy places in Jerusalem, Nazareth, and Bethlehem. France and Russia responded by putting pressure on Istanbul to confer privileges on their respective client communities. The Ottomans first conceded to French pressures, giving the keys to the Church of the Nativity in Bethlehem to the Catholics. The Russians were determined to secure a bigger trophy for the Greek Orthodox Church so as not to lose face to the French. But after the Ottomans made similar concessions to the Russians, the French emperor, Napoleon III, threatened to bombard Ottoman positions in North Africa if the Porte did not rescind the concessions to Russia's Orthodox clients. When the Ottomans conceded to French demands, the Russians declared war and sank a number of ships in the Ottoman Black Sea fleet. The Western European powers mobilised against Russia to prevent the Tsarist empire from exploiting Ottoman weakness to extend its influence into the Mediterranean. What began as an Ottoman-Russian war in the autumn of 1853 erupted into the Crimean War of 1854–1855, pitting Britain and France against Tsarist Russia in a conflict that claimed more than 300,000 lives. The consequences of European intervention on behalf of Ottoman minority communities were too serious for the Porte to allow the practice to continue.[17]

The Ottomans had made a halfhearted attempt to reclaim the initiative over non-Muslim minority communities in the 1839 Reform Decree. 'The Muslim and non-Muslim subjects of our lofty Sultanate shall, without exception, enjoy our imperial concessions,' the sultan declared in his firman, or decree. Clearly, he and his administrators needed to make a stronger statement of equality between Muslims and non-Muslims if they were to persuade the European powers that their interventions were no longer needed to ensure the welfare of Christians and Jews in the Ottoman Empire. The challenge for the Ottoman government was to gain the consent of its own Muslim majority for a policy of equality between different faiths. The Qur'an draws clear distinctions between Muslims and the other two monotheistic faiths, and these distinctions had been enshrined in Islamic law. For the Ottoman government to disregard such distinctions would, in the view of many believers, go against God's book and God's law.

In the aftermath of the Crimean War, the Ottoman government decided to risk public outrage at home to prevent further European interventions on behalf of the non-Muslim minority communities of the empire. The 1856 Reform Decree was timed to coincide with the Peace of Paris, concluding the Crimean War. Most of the provisions of the 1856 Reform Decree were concerned with the rights and responsibilities of Ottoman Christians and Jews. The decree established for the first time complete equality of all Ottoman subjects regardless of their religion: 'Every distinction or designation tending to make any class whatever of the subjects of my empire inferior to another class, on account of their religion, language, or race, shall be forever effaced from administrative protocol.' The decree went on to promise all Ottoman subjects access to schools and government jobs, as well as to military conscription, without distinction by religion or nationality.

The reform process had already been controversial for its European leanings. But nothing in the reforms prior to the 1856 Decree had directly contravened the Qur'an, revered by Muslims as the literal and eternal Word of God. To contradict the Qur'an was to contradict God, and not surprisingly the decree provoked severe consternation among pious Muslims when it was read in the cities of the empire—beginning in the imperial capital, Istanbul.

On 18 February 1856, the new reform decree was read before Ottoman ministers, Muslim notables, the Greek and Armenian patriarchs, and the grand rabbi, all gathered at the Sublime Porte in Istanbul. The stunned audience listened in silence as a slate of new reform proposals were read out conferring full legal equality to Muslims and non-Muslims. 'When the reading of the edict finished, the customary invocation of God's blessing was offered by a preacher well known in the mosques of Istanbul,' a modern historian of the Tanzimat related. '[H]is prayer contained no mention at all of reforms, of non-Muslims, or of equality. "O God," he beseeched, "have mercy on the people of Muhammad. O God, preserve the people of Muhammad." A chill fell on the assemblage.'[18]

The new reform decree received its public reading in Damascus one month after the event at the Sublime Porte. Shaykh Muhammad Sa`id al-Ustuwani, the preacher of the Umayyad Mosque, was there. He recorded his impressions in his diary in language that spoke for the Muslim notables of Damascus as a whole in their disenchantment with the government's reforms and their adverse consequences for 'the people of Muhammad.'

Muhammad Sa'id al-Ustuwani (1822–1888) was one of the leading religious scholars of Damascus and scion of an ancient family that traced its origins in the city back to the Crusades. In 1167 his forebears fled their village near Nablus in Palestine to escape from Christian Crusader rule and settled in the al-Salihiyya quarter to the north of Damascus. After the Ottoman conquest of Syria in 1516, the Ustuwanis moved inside the city walls to a house near the Umayyad Mosque, as family members entered the clerical profession—the *'ulama*. Three centuries later, Muhammad Sa'id preserved family tradition and pursued an education in Islamic theology. He trained with some of the most illustrious religious scholars of his day in Quranic exegesis (*tafsir*), the analysis of sayings and practices of the Prophet Muhammad (*hadith*), and the fundamentals of Islamic jurisprudence (*fiqh* and *usul al-fiqh*). He gained early recognition for his brilliance in theology, and at the young age of eighteen was appointed preacher (*khatib*) of the Umayyad Mosque—one of the most important religious posts in the city—in the final year of the Egyptian occupation in 1840.[19]

When he took up his appointment as preacher, al-Ustuwani did something extraordinary for a Damascene of his day and age: he began a diary of key personal and public events. Given the low levels of literacy at the time, and no real tradition of diary keeping in Ottoman society, such books are rare. It is an idiosyncratic record, but it gives some insight into the man. He was proud of his job and the distinction it conferred on him. For instance, he recorded when newly appointed Ottoman officials honoured him with the gift of an imperial cloak: a new chief justice in 1844, a provincial treasurer who dressed him in a pistachio-coloured robe in 1846, a new governor draping him in dark grey in 1848. Such gifts were a show of respect from powerful men to al-Ustuwani for the office he held in one of the most venerated mosques in Islam.

As a prominent dignitary of Damascus, al-Ustuwani placed a high premium on respect for authority. As previously mentioned, he took part in a special service in the Umayyad Mosque to pray for rain after a period of drought in 1845. The service brought together the governor and his officials along with the notables, merchants, and artisans of Damascus—thousands of worshippers in all. Following the service, a group of young men retired to a notable's house for an all-night social in which they tried to outdo each other in ridiculing the Damascene officials. They seized upon the governor's long, wagging chin, which they likened to a zucchini; they made fun of the mufti's stutter; they compared the laugh of one of the leading religious scholars to a donkey's bray; and they picked on another's limp. It was classic schoolyard bullying by a group of privileged young men, and had they shown more discretion, it would have gone no further. But the young wits shared their best barbs with anyone who would listen, and in no time a summary of the night's excesses reached not only al-Ustuwani but the authorities in the governor's office as well. The governor, with his zucchini-shaped chin, was not amused, and he ordered all those who took part to be arrested. It was only when a member of the Majlis—the 'lame shaykh'—intervened that the young men were released with a warning. Al-Ustuwani related these events with a light pen—he apparently wasn't a target of the mockery himself, and he reproduced the rude nicknames in Damascene colloquial Arabic with relish. But he clearly related the account as a cautionary tale on the importance of respect for authority.[20]

Al-Ustuwani emerges from the pages of his diary as a well-travelled and well-rounded man. He made two pilgrimages to Jerusalem between 1846 and 1850, one in the company of fellow theologians and a second with his mother and brother. His travels took him to such Lebanese coastal towns as Beirut, Tyre, and Tripoli, as well as Jaffa, Hebron, and Jerusalem in Palestine. He mourned the passing of family members as well as of his teachers, many of whom were swept away by the terrible cholera outbreak of 1848. He showed compassion for the victims of natural disasters, like the fires that burned down whole city blocks or the house collapses that followed intense periods of snow and rain. He loved his work, was devoted to the Umayyad Mosque, and was a Damascene through and through.

Not surprisingly, given his profession, al-Ustuwani saw Damascus first and foremost as a Muslim city. Christians and Jews were marginal in al-Ustuwani's city and seldom found their way into the anecdotes and events recounted in the pages of his diary. He did relate one account that captured the changing power of minorities under consular protection and revealed his discomfort with the changes taking place in the age of Ottoman reforms.

In 1852 the governor of Damascus was a man named Said Pasha. That year, a Jewish landowner was beaten to death by a bailiff of the Sharia Court. The landowner had had a violent dispute with one of the Muslim sharecroppers who worked his land. The Jewish landholder had accused the sharecropper of attempted robbery and had beaten the Muslim with a stick, causing him personal injury. The

Muslim sharecropper denied robbery and claimed that the landowner had tried to kill him. The judge took the Muslim's side and ordered the bailiff to beat the Jewish landowner with a stick. In pre-Tanzimat times, non-Muslims were expressly forbidden from laying a hand on Muslims, and the judge no doubt was offended by the Jewish landowner's presumption. But in executing the court's order, the bailiff clearly used excessive force and killed the Jewish landowner, who was a protégé of the Prussian state. The Prussian consul in Damascus was quick to lodge a protest against what he saw as the unlawful killing of a Prussian subject.

These events took place during the annual pilgrimage season, while the governor was preparing to lead the Damascene Hajj caravan to Mecca, and Said Pasha did not pause to address the consul's complaint. 'Because of his religious values,' al-Ustuwani noted approvingly, 'Said Pasha wasn't one to yield to pressure from consuls or patriarchs, and he went on pilgrimage instead, referring the Prussian consul to the Sublime Porte.' Al-Ustuwani praised the governor's leadership of the pilgrimage caravan: 'He fed the poor and supported the weak and was generous to the Damascenes in the caravan.' The governor reportedly spent thousands of piastres from his own pocket to help pay for some of the poorer pilgrims, 'for love of God and his Prophet.' For reasons beyond his control, the pilgrimage in 1852 suffered high casualties, with heavy rains, cold weather, and an outbreak of cholera claiming the lives of many pilgrims. The governor returned with a heavy heart after burying so many pilgrims along the way.

While the governor was away, the Prussian consul pursued justice for the Jewish landowner through the Sublime Porte. The government in Istanbul convened a special tribunal to review the case. The tribunal held numerous sessions to gather evidence before reaching a verdict. They found both the judge and the bailiff guilty of the wrongful killing of the Jewish landowner. The judge was dispatched for detention in a castle in Syria, and the bailiff was sent to prison in Istanbul. And eight days after he returned from the pilgrimage, Said Pasha was stripped of his post and exiled to the Anatolian city of Konia for his failure to address the case.[21] Al-Ustuwani noted these decisions without passing any explicit judgement of his own. However, his language suggests more sympathy for Said Pasha, who held his 'religious values' higher than 'pressure from consuls or patriarchs,' than for the Jewish landowner, who was beaten to death.

This anecdote suggests that al-Ustuwani held to a strict social order that had prevailed across the Islamic centuries, in which Muslims were at the top of the hierarchy, with non-Muslim minorities in a subaltern position: protected but still second-class subjects. It was a social structure that was reinforced by religious belief as much as by tradition and convention. This order had come under attack since the Egyptian occupation and the transformations in society and economy that had followed, and had advanced Christians and Jews in ways that undermined the traditional Muslim-dominated social order. If Muslim notables looked to the sultan and the Sublime Porte to set things right, they were to be disappointed. If anything, the Tanzimat served to confirm and advance the interests of Jews and Christians at the expense of Muslims. It was, they believed, an inversion of the natural order. As the preacher intoned after the reading of the 1856 Reform Decree in Istanbul, 'O God, preserve the people of Muhammad!'

Al-Ustuwani recorded his reactions on the day that the 1856 Reform Decree was proclaimed in Damascus:

> Tuesday morning, the fifth of *Rajab* 1272 [12 March 1856], the *firman* of comprehensive instructions relating to the Christians was read in the Majlis of Damascus, in the presence of Mahmud Pasha [the governor] and...the other members of the Majlis, conferring equality and freedom and other [provisions] that clash with the pure Sharia [Islamic law]. The *firman* bears the Sultan's imperial command. It was ashes upon all Muslims. We ask Him [i.e., God] to glorify the religion and bring victory to the Muslims. There is no power and no strength but in God Almighty.[22]

How could the sultan impose his imperial command on a measure that 'clashed with the pure Sharia' by privileging Christians over Muslims? For the preacher of the Umayyad Mosque, it was inconceivable that his sovereign would dare to contradict God's book and God's law. It is this inversion of the natural order that was cause for mourning and shame, or 'ashes upon all Muslims.'

It was difficult enough for the Muslim establishment to come to terms with the 1856 Reform Decree and the new rights and privileges that the Ottoman government was extending to non-Muslims. What made matters worse was the reaction of the non-Muslim community—particularly the Damascene Christians—to the Tanzimat legislation. There was a new assertiveness that accompanied the rise of Christian notables to newfound wealth through their ties to Europe's expanding trade with the city, and the protection that many leading Christians enjoyed as protégés of foreign powers.[23]

Another Muslim notable of Damascus captured this resentment against the assertive Christians of Tanzimat-era Damascus in his own writings. Muhammad Abu al-Sa'ud al-Hasibi claimed notable status as a *sharif* (plural: *ashraf*), a descendant of the Prophet Muhammad. His family came from modest roots, moving to Damascus in the seventeenth century from a village in the hill country between the capital and Homs. It was only in the eighteenth century that they secured recognition of their claim to be descended from the family of the Prophet and entered the ranks of the Ashraf and thus members of the Muslim elite of Damascus. It was his father, Ahmad Efendi al-Hasibi (1792–1876), who raised the family's standing to count among the leading families in Damascus. As his wealth and position in Damascene society rose, Ahmad Efendi moved to a prominent house in the al-Qanawat district of Damascus to the west of the city walls, where his son Muhammad grew up.

Like al-Ustuwani, al-Hasibi kept a notebook in which he recorded his impressions, current affairs, and popular proverbs. We don't know his age for certain, but he was an adult in 1860 and, given that he died in 1914, he was probably in his twenties when the 1856 Reform Decree was first read. He certainly knew al-Ustuwani and wrote deferentially of the preacher of the Umayyad Mosque. But judging from his egregious spelling and heavily colloquial Arabic, al-Hasibi lacked the scholarly refinement of the preacher. As the editor of his notebook wrote a century later, the book 'reveals a young man of leisurely habits who enjoyed going around town or sitting in the Beylik coffeehouse at the eastern end of al-Qanawat and talking politics with the men of the neighborhood.'[24]

Clearly, one of the recurring topics of conversation among Muslims in the coffeehouse was the Tanzimat reforms and their impact on the Christians, who, encouraged by foreign consuls, were exceeding the bounds of decency:

> The Europeans entered the Syrian lands and impressed on the Christians that the Tanzimat made the Muslim and the Christian the same, all God's creatures, so why shouldn't a Christian wear the same clothes as a Muslim and so on. If a Christian quarrelled with a Muslim, whatever the Muslim said to him the Christian would say the same and more. If they complained to the government, it would take the side of the Christian.[25]

It wasn't just the Muslims of Damascus who noticed the change. Reflecting back on the years after 1856 in his memoirs, Dr Mishaqa as a Christian notable had a similar reflection:

> As the Empire began to implement reforms and equality among its subjects regardless of their religious affiliation, the ignorant Christians went too far in their interpretation of equality and thought that the small did not have to submit to the great, and the low did not have to respect the high. Indeed they thought that humble Christians were on a par with exalted Muslims.

They did not want to understand that, just as equality was based on regulations and legal rights, the people of stature had to maintain their proper dignity before whatever community, especially when it came to Christians vis-à-vis Muslims.[26]

For all his confrontations with the governor, Ahmad Pasha, and the members of the Majlis, Dr Mishaqa was respectful of the social hierarchy. In a sense, he felt more connected to the Muslim notables of the city, whom he saw as his peers in wealth, education, and social standing, than to lower-class Christians. The speed with which the average Damascene Christian acted upon their new equality did not allow the Muslims of the city enough time to adapt to such major changes. Instead, it was provoking a dangerous reaction, as Mishaqa reported in early 1860, from 'the prejudices of the men in the Majlis and their hatred of Christians in general.'

The years since the Egyptian occupation of Syria in 1832 had proved to be a period of unprecedented change in Damascus. The city came to be linked to the Mediterranean world through the activities of European consuls and foreign merchants. Steamships brought European fabrics and took home Syrian fibres, putting local artisans under double pressure, competing with cheaper European goods in the local market and facing higher prices for wool, cotton, and silk because of European competition. The overland trade suffered, and the pilgrimage caravan shrank perceptibly. These changes from abroad were compounded by reforms at home that promoted minority rights over time-honoured conventions that preserved the ascendancy of the city's Muslim community. The fact that the reforms were introduced by the sultan's government, the guarantors of the empire's Islamic values, made them all the more intolerable to the Muslim notables of Damascus.

The main beneficiaries of these changes in Syrian society were the minorities, as protégés of foreign consuls and agents of European merchants. The Jewish community of Damascus, perhaps still scarred from the atrocity of the 1840 blood libel, seems not to have pushed the boundaries of their newfound freedoms. By all accounts, the Christians did. As they grew wealthier, and took advantage of the legal and commercial benefits of European protégé status, the Christians of Damascus grew ever more assertive. Their rise came at the expense of the Muslim elites, who found themselves tightening their belts because of the same measures that granted Christians new prosperity. Rumours of a 'great replacement' gained ground, of Christians displacing the Muslim notables as the ruling elite in Syria. This perception expanded into an existential threat, generating antagonisms that grew year on year after the 1856 decree. By 1860, it took only a spark to turn that hostility to violence. The explosion of communal violence in Mount Lebanon in the summer of 1860 was to prove such a spark.

4

Rivers of Blood in Mount Lebanon

In late November 1855, the French frigate *Tage* sailed into the familiar waters of the port of Beirut, carrying the world's most famous Arab into exile. For fifteen years, Amir ʿAbd al-Qadir had sustained a guerrilla war against the French occupation of his homeland, Algeria. The international press followed his exploits closely, seeing a national leader rallying his people to repulse imperial invaders. The *New York Times* compared ʿAbd al-Qadir to the North African king Jugurtha, defeated by the Romans in 105 BCE, and to the Haitian revolutionary Toussaint Louverture (1743–1803), 'who stood up stiffly for the independence of his native Hayti' against Napoleonic France.[1] By the time of his surrender to the French in 1847, ʿAbd al-Qadir enjoyed global name recognition.

ʿAbd al-Qadir ibn Muhyi al-Din al-Jazaʾiri (1808–1883) was born and raised near the town of Mascara in western Algeria. Son of a religious scholar and a descendant of the Prophet Muhammad,

'Abd al-Qadir was raised among Islamic mystics of the Qadiriyya Sufi order. He memorised the entire text of the Qur'an by the age of fourteen and accompanied his father on pilgrimage to Mecca at seventeen. Father and son took advantage of their long overland journey to Arabia to visit leading centres of Islamic learning, from Tunis to Cairo en route to Mecca, and Damascus and Baghdad after completing their pilgrimage. In each city they met the leading scholars of the age, deepening 'Abd al-Qadir's religious training. He returned home with his father in 1828 fully prepared for a career in Islamic theology and mysticism.[2]

No one could have foreseen the turn of events that would propel 'Abd al-Qadir from small-town obscurity to global celebrity. In July 1830 a French campaign force invaded Algiers, marking the start of a 132-year occupation. The reasons for the invasion were as obscure to the Algerians as to the French themselves: an argument between the ruler of Algiers and the French consul over grain shipments to France that had gone unpaid since the early 1800s. The French consul claimed that the ruler of Algiers had struck him with a fly whisk and demanded that his government redeem national honour by making a demonstration of force. The deeply unpopular government of the Bourbon King Charles X hoped to rally domestic support through a foreign adventure and seized on the 'Fly Whisk Incident' to justify a full-scale invasion.[3]

The French faced popular resistance almost from the start of their occupation. Tribal leaders mobilised across the different regions of Algeria as the French extended their conquests from Algiers westward toward the city of Oran. The city surrendered in December 1830, bringing the French occupation to 'Abd al-Qadir's doorstep. In November 1832, tribesmen turned to `Abd al-Qadir's father, Muhyi al-Din, to lead their resistance against the French. He declined and entrusted this duty to his twenty-four-year-old son instead. The tribesmen were quick to pledge their allegiance to `Abd al-Qadir, declaring him their 'commander of the faithful'—in Arabic, *Amir al-Mu'minin* (`Abd al-Qadir went by the briefer title *amir*, meaning 'prince' or 'commander'). For the next fifteen years he rallied tribesmen from across Algeria to wage a relentless war against the French occupation. By December 1847, however, superior French forces and resources ultimately prevailed, forcing `Abd al-Qadir to surrender.

In defeat, the Algerian leader only grew in stature. The French government lionised `Abd al-Qadir as a Saladin figure, a noble adversary of brilliance and refinement, to inflate the significance of their victory over him. The British had a hard time masking their appreciation of the Arab insurgent who wore down the French army and treasury for fifteen years. The Americans saw `Abd al-Qadir as a scourge against imperialism as a whole. And in the Arab world, the amir was celebrated for redeeming Muslim honour against Christian Europe through repeated victories on the battlefield.

Following his surrender, Amir `Abd al-Qadir was detained in a series of French prisons for five years. In October 1852, Louis Napoleon (elected president in 1848, subsequently crowned Emperor Napoleon III, r. 1852–1870) restored the amir's freedom in return for his vow never to return to his native Algeria or to renew hostilities against the French empire. `Abd al-Qadir pledged his firm friendship to France and Louis Napoleon, and asked to be exiled to the Ottoman Empire. Supported by a generous French pension, he first moved to the Turkish city of Bursa, near Istanbul, where he lived for two years with his family and a large group of retainers.

The Algerians did not speak Turkish and felt isolated in Bursa. Following a devastating earthquake in 1854 that levelled whole parts of the city, 'Abd al-Qadir petitioned the French government for permission to move to Damascus, where he could speak his native Arabic language. Napoleon III provided him with the three-masted sailing ship that carried the amir and his 110-person entourage from Istanbul to Beirut, where they disembarked on 24 November 1855.

After a brief stay in Mount Lebanon, where he was hosted by the British officer and consular official Colonel Charles Henry Churchill, the amir and his entourage set off for Damascus. They found their way blocked by a group of Druze mountaineers—'a compact and splendidly attired cavalcade'—who fired off a volley of gunshots in salute. As they approached, the Druzes dismounted to show their respect and invited 'Abd al-Qadir to pass the night with them. He accepted with pleasure, glad to be 'once more amongst the Arabs.'[4]

No doubt the Druzes questioned the amir about his campaigns against the French, which they had followed for years, fascinated by his many victories over a great European imperial power. No doubt 'Abd al-Qadir took the opportunity to question his hosts about the state of affairs in Syria and Lebanon. The Druze shaykhs could only report that, for the past twenty-five years, the Egyptians, the European powers, and their Maronite Christian neighbours had conspired to strip the Druzes of every vestige of social standing and political power in their own homeland. Their backs were against the wall.

The Druzes had emerged as a distinct religious community in eleventh-century Egypt. Within a few years the new sect was proscribed by the ruling Fatimid caliphate, and its persecuted members fled Egypt to take refuge in the mountainous highlands of southern Lebanon and northern Palestine. Here they enjoyed the freedom to practice their faith and to shape their own political order. By the time the Ottomans conquered Syria and Lebanon in 1516, the Druzes secured recognition of their autonomy in Mount Lebanon—the highlands dominating the coastal cities from Sidon and Tyre in the South to Beirut and Tripoli in the North—in return for the payment of an annual tribute to the sultan.

The Druzes crafted a unique social and political order in Mount Lebanon that they called 'the Principality' (in Arabic, *Imara*). At the top of a rigid hierarchy were three princely families whose male members took the title 'amir.' Until the end of the seventeenth century, the Druze Ma'n family ruled over Mount Lebanon. When the last of the Ma'n princes died without heir, leadership passed to their Sunni Muslim cousins of the Shihab princely family, who reigned over Mount Lebanon until the 1840s.[5]

Next in the hierarchy came the 'great shaykhs,' who owed their loyalty to the reigning amir and ruled over hereditary estates like feudal barons in medieval Europe. Each notable family (amirs and great shaykhs alike) was awarded one of the districts of Mount Lebanon, with dozens of villages and their agricultural lands, as their family domain. Within their district, the ruling shaykhs wielded vast powers. They collected all taxes, remitting a share to the ruling amir and keeping the rest for themselves. They adjudicated all disputes, having the power to arrest, judge, and punish the people of their district up to but not including the death penalty, which remained the prerogative of the ruling amir. The shaykhs imposed heavily on the farmers and workers in their villages, demanding gifts on special occasions and free labour when needed. In times of war, the shaykhs could summon village men to arms to fight for the ruling amir. At all times, commoners were expected to defer to the shaykhs, to kiss the ring, to do as they were told. There were eight shaykhly families by the eighteenth century. Some of these seigneurial households grew powerful enough to rival the princely families, such as the Jumblatts, whose descendants continue to exercise leadership in the Druze community of Lebanon to the present day. On occasion, the great shaykhs might challenge a ruling prince's authority, but in general all accepted the absolute power of the reigning amir.

The amirs and the great shaykhs represented a tiny fraction of the total population of Mount Lebanon. The vast majority were commoners who farmed the lands and raised the livestock and silk-worms that were the source of wealth in Mount Lebanon. The system was incredibly rigid. Very occasionally, a ruling prince might promote a family for exceptional service. In 1711, for example, the Druze Abu'l-Lama family was elevated to princely status as a reward for its courage in battle, but you could count such promotions on the fingers of one hand. And there was no social mobility through intermarriage between the ranks. Yet the system did not discriminate between religious communities. Maronite Christian families were admitted to all levels of the Druze-led hierarchy on an equal footing.[6]

The Maronite Christians had broken with the Eastern Orthodox Church in Byzantine times over doctrinal differences. Persecuted as schismatics, the Maronites fled Byzantium for the safety of the northern highlands of Mount Lebanon in the tenth and eleventh centuries, settling at much the same time, for much the same reasons, as the Druzes in the southern reaches of Mount Lebanon. During the Crusades, the Maronite Church recognised the authority of the Vatican, becoming a 'uniate' Catholic church while preserving its own distinct rites. By the seventeenth century, the Maronites gained French protection as an Eastern Catholic community, strengthening their position in Ottoman domains and Mount Lebanon alike. Franco-Maronite relations grew stronger in the nineteenth century as French trade and imperial interests developed in the eastern Mediterranean.

Over the course of the centuries, a growing number of Maronite Christian households migrated southward to the Druze districts. This gave rise to mixed towns such as Dayr al-Qamar in the Druze heartlands. Maronite-dominated territories in the north of Mount Lebanon federated with the Druze principality, and their ruling shaykhs gained recognition within the Druze system. By the eighteenth century, the Maronites grew to outnumber the Druzes, not just in their own northern districts but in the southern Druze heartland as well. In recognition of the growing demographic and political weight of the Maronites, with their special relations with France, the ruling Shihabi prince Amir Bashir II (r. 1789–1840) and several of his family members did the unthinkable and converted from their Sunni Muslim faith to embrace Maronite Christianity. Anywhere else in the Ottoman Empire, such an act would have been condemned as apostasy and the converts swiftly put to death. Not so in Mount Lebanon. As long as all parties upheld the social and political conventions of the Druze-crafted principality, it didn't matter what religion individuals chose.

The Egyptian occupation of Syria and Lebanon in the 1830s dealt a fatal blow to the principality as both a social and a political order. The Egyptians had the greatest army in the Ottoman Empire. The sultan's own soldiers could not contain them. Faced with such a powerful invader, the ruling Amir Bashir II saw no alternative but to submit to the Egyptians and offer their commander, Ibrahim Pasha, his total support. The treachery of Bashir II was that he used the Egyptian occupation to undermine the Druze notability in order to advance his personal power and that of his adoptive Maronite community. So when the Egyptians demanded Lebanese conscripts for their army, Bashir II secured an exemption for the Christians and called on the Druzes to fulfil the quota. When the Egyptians called for general disarmament, Bashir II urged his subjects to comply. The very idea of disarmament was inconceivable to the Druzes. They lived in a dangerous land where guns were their only means of self-defence. Compliance would put their lives and freedom in mortal danger.

Rather than surrender their arms, many of the Druzes abandoned their lands and property in Mount Lebanon to take refuge in the highlands of Jabal Hawran, to the southeast of Damascus. In 1838 the Druzes rose in rebellion against renewed Egyptian efforts to conscript and disarm their ranks. The revolt drove a wedge between the Maronites and the Druzes because the Egyptian commander Ibrahim Pasha demanded reinforcements from Mount Lebanon to quell the uprising. Amir Bashir sent his own son at the head of a force of four thousand Christians to assist the Egyptians against the Druzes. It was the first time the Maronites engaged in direct hostilities against their Druze neighbours. When forced to surrender, the Druzes' thirst for revenge ensured that this would not be the last conflict between the two communities.

The Druzes bided their time. In the summer of 1840, they even made common cause with the Maronites, rising in rebellion against Ibrahim Pasha and his ally Bashir II for trying to conscript more Lebanese to the Egyptian army. The European powers encouraged the turmoil and intervened to drive Egyptian forces out of Syria. By the end of 1840, the British had exiled Amir Bashir II to Malta, and the Egyptians were in full retreat. When the Druze notables returned to Mount Lebanon to reclaim their abandoned property and former privileges, the new ruling prince, Amir Bashir III, refused all such requests. Instead, he threw several Druze shaykhs in prison for disturbing his peace. This latest injustice was added to the growing list of Druze grievances against the Maronites.

In the disorder following the Egyptian withdrawal from Syria and Lebanon, the Maronites and the Druzes pursued incompatible goals for Mount Lebanon. The Druzes wanted to restore a Druze-dominated principality similar to the one that had existed before the Egyptian occupation. The Maronites, led by their patriarch and clergy, sought to establish a new Christian-dominated order under a Maronite prince and to drive the Druzes from Mount Lebanon altogether. Inevitably, the conflict gave way to violence. In the mixed town of Dayr al-Qamar, more than 250 Maronites and Druzes were killed in sectarian fighting in October and November 1841. The troubles led yet again to Ottoman and European intervention. When the Sublime Porte deposed Bashir III in January 1842, Shihab family rule and the ancient principality of Mount Lebanon fell with him.[7]

A new political order, crafted by the Ottomans and the European powers, was imposed on Mount Lebanon on New Year's Day, 1843. Instead of seeking to resolve the differences between the Druzes and the Maronites, the powers used their divisions as a pretext for partition. Mount Lebanon was broken into two administrative units along the Beirut-Damascus Road, which crossed Mount Lebanon from west to east, with a Maronite-ruled district to the north and a Druze-ruled district to the south. This partition plan was impractical because the two communities had grown intermixed over the centuries. There were many Druze villages in the northern parts of Mount Lebanon, and the Maronites significantly outnumbered the Druzes in the southern district. It was a formula for further confrontation between the two communities.

By 1845, these arrangements led to renewed conflict between Druzes and Maronites. The European powers intervened with the Ottoman government once again to fine-tune the dysfunctional new administrative order in Mount Lebanon. To provide representation for the different communities in the northern and southern districts, the Ottomans established twelve-man councils to advise the district governors, with representatives from Sunni and Shi`i Muslim communities; the Maronite, Greek Orthodox, and Greek Catholic churches; and the Druzes. For the old notable families, Druze and Maronite alike, this new system of sectarian representation seemed designed to strip them of their traditional powers. The councils assumed responsibility for tax collection and the application of justice, depriving the shaykhs of their revenues and power over commoners.

(Top) Damascus with the Umayyad Mosque in the centre. (Bottom) Damascene houses had humble exteriors but some hid interiors of striking luxury.

(Top) The sumptuous interior of the al-Islambuli House. (Bottom) A typical courtyard of a fine Damascene house.

(Top) The Barada River entering Damascus. The Takiyya al-Sulaymaniyya mosque complex is on the far bank. (Bottom) Customers at a coffeehouse on the banks of the Barada.

(Top) The great Umayyad Mosque. (Left) In the Umayyad Mosque's colonnades scholars taught classes, worshippers prayed and Damascenes from all levels of society could rest and meditate.

هذا محمل الشريف يا مثلاً

(Top) The departure
of the annual Haj
pilgrimage caravan
for Mecca. (Left)
Dr Mikhayil Mishaqa.

(Top) The Amir 'Abd al-Qadir al-Jaza'iri. (Bottom) Fuad Pasha in the uniform that he refused to wear upon his entry to Damascus in July 1860.

(Left) A well-armed Druze farmer from Mount Lebanon. (Below) Bashi Bozuk irregulars. This group accompanied the Prince of Wales on his 1862 tour of the Levant as far as Nablus, where they were dismissed.

(Top) A *kawass* or consular guard carrying a sword and staff as symbols of his office. (Bottom) A dragoman in the lavish uniform and an array of weapons that shows he was both an interpreter and a security guard.

The shaykhly families did their best to undermine the new system of government. In the northern Kisrawan region, the Maronite Khazin shaykhs refused to allow the election of representatives to the council and preserved their family rule in defiance of the new system. In the South, where Druze lords ruled over a majority-Christian population, the shaykhly families retained their positions as lords over their districts but allowed the election of two representatives from each district, one Maronite and one Druze, to advise the council. The old elites faced new challenges in rapidly changing times. The commoners in Lebanese society—the vast majority of the population who for centuries had endured the excesses and extractions of the lords of Mount Lebanon—saw an opportunity to strip the amirs and shaykhs of their privileges and run the administration themselves. It was a recipe for social revolution—and civil war.

Much of this the Algerian amir 'Abd al-Qadir would already have known. No doubt the British agent Colonel Churchill had briefed the amir on the local political situation while hosting him in his village home in Huwara in Mount Lebanon. But 'Abd al-Qadir's visit with the Druzes allowed him to hear their views on the crisis brewing in Mount Lebanon for himself. Druze hopes for a restoration of the privileges they enjoyed under the principality had collapsed in the face of insurmountable opposition. The Maronites had grown demographically to dominate the population of the whole of Mount Lebanon. Figures from a tax register in 1851, which recorded only taxable males, gives some sense of the order of magnitude, with

80,353 Christians and 17,457 Druze and Muslim men of working age registered.[8] Even allowing for underreporting and fiddling the books to avoid taxation, the Druzes had been reduced to a compact minority in their own homeland.

Furthermore, the Druzes had no patrons to match the intensity of French support for the Maronites. The Ottomans and the British often took the side of the Druzes, but they were unreliable allies. The Ottomans were happy to use the Druzes to advance their influence in autonomous Mount Lebanon but never respected their religion, which they saw as a heresy. For the British, the Druzes were useful in countering French influence, but the British were always capable of letting the Druzes down when higher interests prevailed. Outnumbered and short on allies, the Druzes undoubtedly related to 'Abd al-Qadir's experiences in Algeria—and took the opportunity to learn from their illustrious visitor how to fight and win against superior numbers.

When 'Abd al-Qadir took his leave to complete the journey to Damascus, his Druze hosts accompanied the Algerian to the limits of their territory. According to Churchill, 'After thanking them for their courtesy and attention, Abdel Kader parted from them with the words, "God grant we may ever remain one!" and the Druzes replied, "God grant it! May we soon meet again." '[9]

As he entered Damascus, 'Abd al-Qadir received a hero's welcome. Townspeople lined the route into the city for a mile from the city's gates. 'Preceded by a detachment of Turkish troops and a band of military music, Abdel Kader passed, almost like a conqueror, through the crowd,' Churchill recorded. 'No such Arab had entered Damascus since the days of Saladin.'[10]

Once settled in Damascus, 'Abd al-Qadir led multiple lives. He became one of the Muslim notables of Damascus and gained a seat on the Majlis (ruling council). At the same time, he seized the opportunity to practice the theological career long denied him by the French occupation of Algeria. He wrote several books and gave lessons on the Qur'an and Hadith in the Umayyad Mosque, where he would have encountered the mosque's preacher, Muhammad Sa'id al-Ustuwani. Finally, 'Abd al-Qadir served as an agent for the French in Damascus. He seems to have been sincere in his gratitude toward Napoleon III for restoring his liberty and was dependent on the French for the financial support that funded him and his large group of Algerian veterans in the city. In addition to the 180 men who accompanied the amir from Bursa to Damascus, he found another group of 500 Algerians, led by one of his former commanders, already settled there, like him exiles from the French occupation of their homeland. Their presence in Damascus attracted further veterans from Algeria. By 1860, 'Abd al-Qadir was believed to have up to 1,200 armed Algerians on his payroll in Damascus.[11] Those retainers gave 'Abd al-Qadir a loyal militia and a vast network for intelligence gathering that proved invaluable to French diplomats as politics in Syria and Lebanon descended into crisis.

By the late 1850s, Lebanese commoners seemed to ask themselves a simple question: If, following the collapse of the principality in Mount Lebanon, the great shaykhs who once ruled their lands no longer exercised any formal power, why should the common people continue to submit to their authority? Under the new system of government, the former distinctions between shaykhs and commoners no longer applied. And in 1856 the Ottoman sultan had decreed a new age of equality among citizens through the Tanzimat reforms. Mikhayil Mishaqa, born and raised in Mount Lebanon, observed the changes resulting from the new political order after 1843: 'The [nobility] had formerly been autonomous in their regions, but they began gradually to decline from their former estate until they reached the level of commoners. Emirs, shaykhs and guildsmen are all alike. Whatever distinction the nobility of the Lebanon had has been wiped out.'[12] Yet the notable families continued to force the peasants to pay most of the taxes and maintained their right to claim free labour and 'gifts' from the peasants, the majority of whom lived on the edge of poverty. The feudal barons had degenerated into robber barons, and the commoners had had enough.

The Greek Catholics of Zahleh led the way. This fiercely autonomous community declared its independence from the government of Mount Lebanon. The townspeople chose their own leader and gave him the oxymoronic title of 'shaykh shabab' or 'elder of the young men' (the word *shaykh* means both 'elder' and 'leader') to head an elected town council of eight. The Mount Lebanon Christians collectively held their breath to see what consequences the people of Zahleh would suffer for their presumption—and in the wake of the subsequent resounding silence, others were quick to follow suit. In the Kisrawan district, ruled by the Maronite Khazin shaykhs, commoners began to meet and discuss their grievances. Villagers chose a shaykh shabab and council to represent them and advised the Khazin shaykhs that they would no longer live by the old rules in the new age of Ottoman reforms.[13]

The Khazins were, by all accounts, absolute tyrants. Even the French consul in Beirut, who systematically took the side of the Maronites, described Khazin rule as 'la tyrannie.'[14] They rejected the Ottoman-appointed governor of the Christian northern district of Mount Lebanon, coveting that title for themselves, and refused to cede control of the Kisrawan region to the northern district governor, preserving their stranglehold over the Kisrawan and its people. In December 1858 a group of villagers sent a list of demands to their shaykhs that gives a good sense of how oppressive Khazin rule was. The commoners requested tax reforms 'so that even the Shaikhs shall be obliged to pay what is apportioned to them'; a ban on 'all irregular levies,' forced labour, and demands for 'presents and marriage taxes' imposed by the shaykhs on the villagers; the abolition of such humiliating practices as kissing the hand of the shaykh; and an adherence to Tanzimat notions of 'universal equality and complete freedom.'[15]

The Khazins' first reaction, rather than address the legitimate demands of the downtrodden commoners, was to reach out to the other Maronite and Druze shaykhs to make common cause against the peasantry. Their appeal fell on deaf ears. Other Christian shaykhs sought to distance themselves from the Khazins; they faced challenges from commoners in their own districts. And the Druze shaykhs had lost all trust in the Maronites after twenty years of hostilities and calls to drive the Druzes from Mount Lebanon to establish a Christian principality. The Khazins were left to face the growing assertiveness of the peasants of Kisrawan on their own.

At the end of 1858, the villages of Kisrawan elected a leader for the district as a whole. He was a powerfully built forty-three-year-old blacksmith named Tanyus Shahin (1815–1895). The Christians commoners, in the words of a contemporary chronicler, saw Tanyus 'as a redeemer, bringing forth all that they required.' They referred to him respectfully as Tanyus Bey (an Ottoman honorific title) and extended full honours when he visited their villages, 'as if it were the visit of a ruler to his subjects.' European diplomats were less impressed. The British commissioner, Lord Dufferin, described him as 'a ruffian of the most despicable character…and one of the chief promoters of the late disturbances.'[16]

In January 1859, Tanyus Shahin led the Christian commoners in a popular uprising to drive the Khazins from their villages. The shaykhs were caught by surprise by the defiance of commoners who 'since birth had trembled before them.' The insurgents broke into the grand homes of the Khazins and rough-handled the shaykhs and their families, forcing them onto the road to seek refuge in Beirut. The Khazin estates were then robbed, and their property distributed among the villagers as compensation for property unjustly seized by the shaykhs. Once again, the commoners waited to see if the authorities would intervene, and when they didn't, the uprising spread across Kisrawan. By the summer of 1859, armed peasants had driven some five hundred Khazin family members from their homes and lands in the district they once ruled. The Khazins complained to the government, 'claiming that the people of Kisrawan had stolen their money and property unrightfully.' Yet the Ottoman government chose not to intervene because the uprising against the Maronite shaykhs 'was in accord with the inclination of the government.' The Ottomans hoped to use the disorders in Mount Lebanon to advance their claim to bring the autonomous region under Istanbul's direct rule.[17]

The uprising in Kisrawan was nothing less than a social revolution. Tanyus Shahin headed an elected council of a hundred members, more than half of whom were small landholders or landless peasants. They mobilised a militia of a thousand men. They collected taxes and provided services and justice through what contemporary sources referred to as a 'republican government'—the people's republic of Kisrawan. Yet the months of revolt were also a time of hardship for all. As one contemporary Christian chronicler recorded, 'Poverty became general, both among the shaikhs because of the seizure of their properties and…among the people, because of the lack of work by which they could support themselves and because of their resort to evil deeds. Extreme privation prevailed.' Misery compounded the political disorders following the expulsion of the shaykhs from Kisrawan.[18]

The shock waves set off by the Kisrawan revolt reverberated across Mount Lebanon, the tensions between commoners and shaykhs provoking hostilities between Christians and Druzes. The Christian chronicler Antun Dahir al-'Aqiqi recorded the following:

> As hatred continued to grow between the shaikhs and the people, eventually at the beginning of the year 1860 differences arose between the Christians and the Druses in the area of al-Shuf. The reason for this was that some of the population of that region wished to rid themselves of…Druse and Christian shaikhs, and

so they embarked on a course of evil deeds. The Druse shaikhs learned of this and resorted to oppressing the people by deceitful means and promoting disturbances between the two sects.[19]

The Druze shaykhs persuaded Druze commoners to preserve communal solidarity. They pointed to Maronite hostilities against the Druzes from the late 1830s through recent fighting in 1859. They recalled appeals by the Maronite patriarch to gain European support for a Christian state in Mount Lebanon that would exclude the Druzes. They warned that unless the Druzes remained united, the Maronites would drive them from their homes and lands just as they had expelled the Khazin shaykhs. The Druze peasants chose to side with their leadership, abandoning plans for a social revolution of commoners against the shaykhs in favour of a sectarian war, Druzes against Christians.

Tensions between Druzes and Christians led to random acts of violence along the roads and in the countryside of southern Lebanon in the spring of 1860. Christian villagers in the Druze-dominated Shuf region wrote to Tanyus Shahin to see if the Christians of Kisrawan would come to their assistance. Shahin boasted that he could raise a force of fifty thousand armed Christians who would overwhelm the Druzes. The Lebanese historian Kamal Salibi captured the bellicose mood among Christian commoners: 'In the predominantly Christian villages and towns young Christians organized themselves in armed bands, each led by a shaykh shabab, and adopted a special uniform; they roamed from one place to the other displaying their weapons and boasting of their determination to exterminate the Druze.' Druze leaders in the Shuf responded by reaching out to their brethren in the hill country of Jabal Hawran, to the south of Damascus, and in the valleys of Wadi al-Taym, to the south of the Bekaa Valley. They met in secret, and they planned carefully. They knew they were outnumbered—an estimated twelve thousand Druze fighters confronting Shahin's fifty thousand armed Christians. Their very survival at stake, the Druzes could not afford to lose a single battle. To win, they needed the element of surprise and the will to exterminate their enemy—or else face certain extermination themselves.[20]

In May 1860 the Druzes took the offensive to villages in the northern Christian district of Mount Lebanon. They burned every village they overran and killed any men they found in their path. The sudden violence of the attacks rattled the Maronites, who fled more vulnerable outposts without a fight for Christian strongholds like Zahleh.[21] These opening skirmishes demonstrated that despite their strength of numbers, the Christians were disorganised and lacked experienced leaders. The conflicts between shaykhs and commoners had divided Christian ranks. This only compounded the differences between the many Christian denominations in Mount Lebanon. As one contemporary chronicler noted, 'Divisions between the Christians are great, as one will say "I am a Maronite and don't concern myself with the Orthodox," and another will say he doesn't concern himself with the Greek Catholics and so on.' There was no unifying Christian identity in Lebanon. The Druzes might have presented a smaller armed force overall, but they operated in lockstep. 'We saw the Druze united in one voice for love of the honour of their religion which gave them the advantage,' one Christian chronicler reflected.

The shaykhs retained the loyalty of Druze commoners and could count on fellow Druzes from across Syria and Lebanon to rally to their support.[22]

Encouraged by their initial successes in the northern district of Mount Lebanon, the Druzes turned next to the mixed towns and villages in the Druze-dominated regions of southern Lebanon. Here, Druze shaykhs continued to dominate the same regions they had ruled under the principality before the Egyptian occupation in 1832. Although Christians represented an outright majority of the population in the southern district, they had no leadership. As al-'Aqiqi recorded, 'The Christians in the Shuf... were arming themselves, but this was of no use, because they lacked a leader.' This left the Christian communities particularly vulnerable to Druze surprise attacks, in towns where Mikhayil Mishaqa had spent the first thirty-four years of his life.

At the end of May 1860, Druze forces imposed a blockade on Dayr al-Qamar, where Dr Mishaqa grew up. The town served as the seat of government for Mount Lebanon and had a mixed population, with one of the largest Christian communities in the Shuf region. The Christians had earlier concluded a pact with the Druzes of the town to preserve the peace and were caught by surprise by the sudden hostilities. They managed to mount barricades and withstood Druze attacks on 1 and 2 June before an Ottoman force arrived from Beirut on 3 June to secure the town. As Druze fighters withdrew, they torched 130 houses. Casualties were relatively low in this first attack on Dayr al-Qamar.

The town of Jazzin, in the southern reaches of the Shuf, was not so fortunate. As in Dayr al-Qamar, the Druzes had promised to preserve the peace with the large Maronite community. The promise served to give the Druzes the element of surprise. On 1 June, two thousand Druze fighters descended on the villages around Jazzin, where they engaged with small and disorganised bands of Maronites. By the end of the day, hundreds of Christians were killed—by some accounts as many as fifteen hundred—and their villages set afire. News of the atrocity, the first of the Lebanese Civil War, moved slower than Druze forces advancing on their next targets in southern Lebanon, preserving their advantage of surprise.[23]

The Druzes proceeded next to the town of Hasbayya in the Wadi al-Taym, to the south of the Bekaa Valley. Dr Mishaqa had lived in Hasbayya for more than seven years (1825–1832) when he served as personal secretary to the local ruler, Amir Sa`d al-Din Shihab. Even after moving to Damascus, Mishaqa stayed close to the amir. Upon the amir's retirement, leaving one of his sons to rule over Hasbayya, he moved to Damascus himself, where the two men met regularly. They followed the breakdown in civil order in Mount Lebanon and Wadi al-Taym with mounting concern for their friends and family.

Wadi al-Taym was part of the province of Damascus, so it fell outside of the Druze-ruled southern district of Mount Lebanon. Wadi al-Taym was nonetheless an area with a large Druze community. The towns of Hasbayya and Rashayya were ruled by members of the Shihab princely family who had retained their Sunni Muslin faith, unlike Bashir II and Bashir III, who had converted to Maronite Christianity. The fact that the amirs of Hasbayya and Rashayya were Sunni Muslims did not endear them to their Druze neighbours. The most powerful Druze shaykh of Mount Lebanon, Sa`id Bey Jumblatt, harboured resentments against Amir Sa`d al-Din for cooperating with the Ottomans in suppressing a Druze revolt and saw the Shihabs as aligned with the Maronites against them. The Jumblatts wanted to displace the Shihab amirs and rule the main towns of Wadi al-Taym themselves.

Knowing the regional politics intimately, Dr Mishaqa was appalled when the governor of Damascus, Ahmad Pasha, called Amir Sa'd al-Din out of retirement to lead a tax-collecting mission to Hasbayya in May 1860. The amir called upon his old friend Mishaqa for his advice on this unexpected commission: 'This is not a good time either for [you] to leave Damascus or for the outstanding taxes to be collected,' Mishaqa observed, 'since all that remains is owed by the Druze and their Shaykhs. Most likely there will be an uprising against you, particularly during this time of insurrection in the Lebanon and [given the] dispute between your house and Sa'id Bey Jumblat.'

Dr Mishaqa advised the amir to give his excuses and decline the commission. But the governor of Damascus would not take no for an answer and ordered the prince to Hasbayya, sending a detachment of soldiers to accompany him. 'It did not occur to me that a trap was being laid for him,' Mishaqa later recalled.[24]

Events in Mount Lebanon made a dangerous impression on politics and society in Damascus. Dr Mishaqa and his colleagues in the consular corps were convinced that the Ottoman authorities in Damascus were actively assisting the Druzes in their hostilities with the Christians in Mount Lebanon. He observed how the government allowed the Druzes to buy all the arms and gunpowder they needed from the markets in Damascus before imposing an embargo on gun sales. The embargo was applied with particular vigour to

Syrian Christians, and those found carrying guns were disarmed by Ottoman soldiers. Christian villagers from the rural Hawran complained that it would not be safe for them to return home from Damascus unarmed, but their complaints fell on deaf ears. Yet more worrying was the impact of the conflict in Mount Lebanon on Damascene society. 'The Muslims of Damascus are demonstrating joy at the activities of the Druze,' Mishaqa reported. The Muslim resentment toward Syrian Christians that had been building over the past decade found an outlet in Druze attacks on Lebanese Christians. It was nothing short of a bloodlust that subsequent events would only enflame.[25]

As predicted, Amir Sa'd al-Din's mission to Hasbayya provoked a confrontation with the Druzes, who refused to pay back taxes and summoned Druzes in neighbouring regions for support. As bands of Druze horsemen arrived from the Shuf and Jabal Hawran, they fired their rifles and sang war songs. They were dangerous men, coming from Dayr al-Qamar and Jazzin, where they had shed blood and burned villages. They openly called for Amir Sa'd al-Din's death.

On 3 June, Amir Sa'd al-Din invited the Christians of Hasbayya to take refuge in his palace. The Christians brought their belongings and livestock with them. The Ottoman soldiers stood outside the palace gates, ostensibly protecting those within. In fact, they had made common cause with the Druzes. After a week's confinement in the amir's palace, as water and provisions ran low, the commander of the Ottoman soldiers called on the Christians to surrender their arms in return for their evacuation to Damascus. 'I cannot get the Druze away from you unless you hand over your weapons,' the officer claimed. Desperate, the besieged Christians complied. The Ottoman officer loaded all their weapons onto five donkeys as if to transport them to Damascus. Once the little caravan was outside Hasbayya, the Druzes seized all the Christians' weapons. At that point, Druze fighters entered Hasbayya and advanced to the gates of the amir's palace. The Ottoman soldiers, not wanting to engage the heavily armed men, stood aside as the Druzes broke into the palace and killed every man and boy inside. According to Dr Mishaqa's sources, they killed between 900 and 1,100 men in all. Amir Sa'd al-Din was cut down along with 16 other members of his household, and the amir's head was sent to Sa'id Bey Jumblatt as a trophy. Aside from the women and young children, only a handful of Christians survived by hiding under piles of bodies while the Druzes roamed ankle-deep in blood in search of more victims.[26]

After the sack of Hasbayya, Druze forces moved on to the nearby town of Rashayya. Their numbers had now swollen to more than 5,000 fighters, and the Druzes had momentum going for them. As they moved northward, terrified Christian villagers sought refuge in Rashayya, swelling the numbers in the town. As in Hasbayya, the Christians sought refuge in the palace of the local ruler, Amir 'Ali Shihab. Once a majority of the town's Christians were concentrated in the palace, the Druzes broke in and killed the amir and all the men and boys. We have no firm estimates of casualties from Rashayya, but hundreds were believed to have been killed. In all, an estimated 2,500 males were killed in Hasbayya, Rashayya, and the villages of Wadi al-Taym.[27]

The Druze-Maronite conflict in Mount Lebanon was from the outset a war of extermination. 'The country is ours or theirs,' the

Druzes maintained. Once they embarked down the path of annihilation, however, there was no turning back. Even after the shocking violence of their victories, the Druzes remained a clear minority in their native land. Tanyus Shahin was still claiming he could muster fifty thousand Christian fighters from the northern district of Mount Lebanon, and Christian calls for revenge for the dead in Jazzin, Hasbayya, Rashayya, and countless surrounding villages echoed across the land. In order to secure their bloody gains, the Druzes would need to continue the butchery. They turned their gaze next toward the Christian stronghold of Zahleh.

Zahleh was a notoriously independent and assertive Christian town on the eastern slopes of Mount Lebanon, overlooking the Bekaa Valley. Its mostly Greek Catholic population had physically expelled American Protestant missionaries in 1859 in one of Consul Mishaqa's first cases (the 'Benton outrage,' discussed in Chapter 1), and it was the first town in Mount Lebanon to declare its independence from the district government. The Christians of Zahleh took the equality promised by the Tanzimat reforms to heart and actively provoked conservative Muslims. Muhammad Abu al-Sa'ud al-Hasibi, the young Muslim notable of Damascus, recorded in his diary his outrage at the behaviour of the Zahleh Christians:

> If a Muslim entered Zahleh on horseback they made him dismount, and if he didn't dismount they would throw him from the horse's back to the ground and insult his prophet. Among [other] oppressions, they would name their dogs for the prophets and their companions. A Muslim would turn when he heard his name called, like

Umar or Ali or the like, and the Christian would deny calling the man but claimed he was calling his dog, may God strike them dead for their wicked acts.[28]

The Muslims of Damascus were electrified by the idea of the Druzes sacking Zahleh and dealing its 'wicked' residents exemplary punishment.

The Druzes had grudging respect for the Christians of Zahleh, who had twice beat them in battle in 1841. Perhaps there was a score to settle there. More importantly, Zahleh represented the largest concentration of Christian fighters in Mount Lebanon. The Druzes believed they would not be secure until they had eliminated the threat of Zahleh.

Word of the bloodletting in Wadi al-Taym had reached Zahleh, whose townspeople prepared for war. They built defences to protect their town from attack. They appealed to Christians from other parts of the northern district to come to their assistance. Perhaps they still believed that Tanyus Shahin could muster fifty thousand fighters in Kisrawan. Perhaps they thought that the Maronites and the Greek Orthodox would make common cause with the Greek Catholics of Zahleh in seeing off the Druze threat. Assuming that the Christians of the rest of Mount Lebanon had their backs, the fighters of Zahleh set off from their town on 14 June to engage the Druzes as they massed in the Bekaa Valley. For two days, the Druzes drove back the men of Zahleh and inflicted heavy losses on the Christians, who fell back on their town and waited from behind their defences for the Druzes to attack.

The Druzes stormed Zahleh on 18 June. The promised rein-forcements from other Christian districts had yet to arrive. The four thousand defenders faced an assault by some eight thousand Druzes, Bedouin, and Shi`ite Muslims combined. The fighting was fierce, with the Druzes pressing the defenders on three sides. After four hours, a cheer went up from inside Zahleh. Horsemen carrying Christian banners had appeared at the hilltop overlooking the town, singing Christian war songs. But the celebrations were short-lived as the horsemen turned out to be Druze fighters carrying banners they had taken from Christian militias they had defeated. Their defences breached, with the enemy inside their town, the men of Zahleh gath-ered their families in a desperate bid to escape from a side road out of town. In this way, most of the population of Zahleh was able to flee total massacre—although hundreds were killed in the fighting. But they lost their city, which was put to flames by the victorious Druzes.

After the fall of Zahleh, the Druzes no longer feared that the Christians might drive them from their homeland in the south-ern reaches of Mount Lebanon. The final assault of the Lebanese civil war of 1860 was thus an act of gratuitous violence. The city of Dayr al-Qamar had already surrendered to Druze forces at the start of June, and its Christian inhabitants posed no threat to the Druzes of the region. As fighters returned from the sack of Zahleh, they unleashed unspeakable violence on the Christian population of Dayr al-Qamar. Ottoman officials made no attempt to interfere. The carnage went on for three days while the Druzes killed every Christian man and boy they found 'until blood flowed in rivers.' In total, the conflict had claimed eleven thousand Christian lives and left nearly one hundred thousand homeless.[29]

The fall of Zahleh electrified the Muslims of Damascus. Dr Mishaqa reported to Consul Johnson in Beirut:

> On Wednesday afternoon news arrived that the Druze had taken Zahleh. The Muslims became very agitated and set about decorating the streets and lighting lanterns in the suqs. It was necessary to send orders to the notables of the city for each to prevent the people in their quarter from disturbing the peace and ordering lanterns to be extinguished. That same evening my house was stoned.

Less a carnival atmosphere, more a danse macabre, the overriding emotion in Damascus was fear. Fear spread from Governor Ahmad Pasha and the Ottoman administration, which seemed paralysed in the face of the mounting mob violence, and worked its way through the society of Damascus. The Muslim majority of Damascus was whipped into a frenzy by incredible rumours. 'Just yesterday one of my friends asked me if it was true that there were 100 Christian houses [in Damascus] each hiding 1,000 armed men [to rise up and kill the Muslims],' Dr Mishaqa reported. 'I explained to him how this information was a lie and how such a thing was impossible.' Mishaqa might have set his friend straight, but he could not stifle the rumours among all of Damascus's Muslims, who grew ever more hysterical. Most of all, terror descended thick and heavy on the Christians of Damascus, who feared that they might face the same fate as Hasbayya or Dayr al-Qamar as armed Druzes circulated around the city actively provoking violence.[30]

The only person who seemed to know how to respond in a crisis was the Algerian amir ʿAbd al-Qadir. His fifteen-year war with France had sharpened the amir's wits and his nerves. He also saw the bigger picture, of how the imperial powers might respond to sectarian violence in Syria. It took only the 'fly whisk incident' to provoke the French occupation of his native Algeria. It didn't take much imagination to see how a Christian massacre could lead to the colonisation of Syria.

When ʿAbd al-Qadir saw the governor of Damascus unable to restore law and order, he rode out to meet with the Druzes himself. He clearly had preserved his links to the Druze shaykhs from his night as their guest in 1855. According to Dr Mishaqa, the amir 'warned them and advised them of their responsibility and said that he would be their enemy were—God forbid!—anything to happen' against the Christians of Damascus. And, with financial support from the French consulate in Damascus, the amir secured arms and provisions for a rapid reaction force composed of his Algerian fighters and mobile troops loyal to him. Never relenting, ʿAbd al-Qadir 'circulated daily reminding the urban notables of their responsibilities and warning of the reprisals that would follow an attack on the Christians.'[31]

Rumours enflamed passions in Damascus faster than reasonable men like Dr Mishaqa and Amir ʿAbd al-Qadir could tamp them out. On 25 June, Mishaqa recorded wild accounts of alleged massacres in Jerusalem, where the Christians were said to have killed defenceless Muslims while at their Friday prayers. That same week, another rumour gained traction: the Christians of the northern Syrian town of Hums had slaughtered Muslims performing their prayers in the city's mosques. The Druzes reportedly claimed that their shaykh Sa'id Jumblatt had documentary proof of a pact between the Christians of Zahleh and Damascus to attack the Damascene Muslims while they were at Eid prayers just five days hence—on 30 June. These accounts provoked panic and anger among the Muslims of Damascus. 'Thus lies intended to enflame the rage of the Muslims are confirmed quickly,' Mishaqa concluded.[32]

Formally known as the Eid al-Adha, or the Feast of the Sacrifice, the holiday commemorates the Prophet Ibrahim's willingness to sacrifice his beloved son Isma'il out of devotion to God, and God's mercy in letting his faithful servant slaughter a lamb instead (as in the story of Abraham and Isaac in the Hebrew Bible). Those families with sufficient means slaughter a lamb each year to commemorate Ibrahim's submission to God's will. In normal years, the slaughter of lambs would be unremarkable in a mostly Muslim city. But in 1860, spilled blood took on particular resonance. Thousands of Christians in Mount Lebanon had recently been slaughtered. Would the Christians of Damascus take their revenge while their Muslim neighbours were at prayer? The fear wasn't rational. The Christians were less than 15 percent of the total population, had been largely disarmed by the authorities, and were themselves living in terror. But by late June 1860, Damascus had succumbed to a mass hysteria in which rationality had no place.

As the Eid drew closer, fear gripped all communities in Damascus. Christians did not dare leave their homes, faced with open hostility from their Muslim neighbours. Muslims dreaded the arrival of the holiday, fearing revenge attacks by the Christians for the massacres in Mount Lebanon. In a stormy meeting of the town council, Amir 'Abd al-Qadir pressed for firm measures preventing the Druzes from entering the city and forbidding all townspeople from carrying arms until after the Eid. These measures no doubt contributed to security in Damascus but did little to assuage the growing fear. As if to confirm the worst, Governor Ahmad Pasha sent soldiers to surround the city's mosques on the eve of the Eid, 'swords unsheathed and ready to strike.' What should have been a holiday atmosphere succumbed instead to an imaginary state of siege.[33]

When the Eid finally arrived, the mosques were nearly empty. Even the governor failed to put in an appearance at prayers, confirming most Damascenes' fears that it just wasn't safe to go to the mosque. In the Umayyad Mosque, where thousands would normally have gathered to worship on the holiday, Shaykh Muhammad Sa'id al-Ustuwani claimed that there were only two rows of men at prayer: 'This news spread deep anxiety among the Muslims who called for the killing of the Christians.'[34]

In the end, the four days of the Eid passed without incident. Soldiers patrolled the city, reassuring the townspeople. Amir 'Abd al-Qadir continued to meet with the Muslim notables of Damascus and the Druze shaykhs circling outside the city, impressing on them the need to prevent any outbreak of violence against the city's Christians. Following the end of the four-day holiday, the governor sent a town crier through the streets of Damascus, calling for a return to normal life: 'I speak on behalf of our Efendi Ahmad Pasha, Governor of Damascus, who assures you that there is security and safety. Let no one fear anything. Let everyone return to their work and open their shops to resume trading. Let no one carry weapons.'[35]

With these assurances, the townspeople of Damascus began to recover from their recent anxieties, eager to resume their lives. Muslims and Christians alike were relieved that the holiday had passed without any violence. However, the underlying tensions would take more than a long weekend to dispel. After the very different ways they experienced the horrors of Mount Lebanon, Muslims and Christians did not look at each other in the same way. In the calm following the Eid, communal relations in Damascus remained on edge. In such an atmosphere, combining the bloodlust awakened by the massacre of Lebanese Christians with the rumours and anxieties sweeping the city, the slightest provocation could unleash primal violence.

5

Plunder, Kill, and Burn

The Ottoman governor of Damascus, Ahmad Pasha, had been behaving erratically ever since the crisis in Mount Lebanon overflowed into the province of Syria in June 1860. Muslims and Christians, notables and commoners alike, were left perplexed. The governor alternated between decisive, counterproductive actions and utter passivity. His mood swings emboldened the violent bands ravaging the Damascene countryside and deepened the panic among the Christians in Syria. Far from calming the situation, he was making matters much worse.

The governor's orders since the start of the crisis were incomprehensible. Who in their right mind would send a tax party to collect dues in the middle of a tense civil war, as Ahmad Pasha did when he sent Amir Sa`d al-Din Shihab on his doomed mission to Hasbayya? Or respond to baseless rumours of Christian attacks on Muslim worshippers by sending armed soldiers to stand guard at mosques with their sabres drawn, as if to lend credence to the threat? Yet when pressed by the foreign consular corps or the notables in the city council to take measures to calm the situation, the governor wouldn't follow through on his promises, seemingly paralysed in the face of massive human suffering unfolding in Syria and Lebanon—suffering for which he, as governor, would certainly be held responsible.

Survivors from Mount Lebanon and Wadi al-Taym seeking refuge in Damascus brought horrific accounts of violence to the agitated city. Each faith community looked after its own. Muhammad Abu al-Sa'ud al-Hasibi recorded how his father opened the family home to receive the distraught widows of the Shihab amirs of Rashayya and Hasbayya. The Algerian amir 'Abd al-Qadir contributed four thousand piastres to help the widows and their children make ends meet. Dr Mishaqa gave refuge to a Protestant widow from Hasbayya and her daughter. The churches and monasteries in the city centre opened their doors to terrified peasants from villages in a fifty-mile radius of Damascus attacked by Druze raiders. The clergy tried to settle the Christian villagers temporarily among Damascene households, but the flood of refugees overflowed available housing and filled the narrow streets and alleys of the Christian quarters of Bab Touma and Bab Sharqi. The refugees radiated fear and horror of the violence they had witnessed, escaped, and survived.[1]

The people of Damascus looked in vain to Ahmad Pasha for decisive measures to calm the tensions and restore order. Bizarrely, the governor chose this moment of civil disorder to begin renovation works on the Citadel, 'some of which were necessary and some of which were not,' the bemused al-Hasibi observed in his diary. Inside the Citadel, the governor ordered the city's old cannons to be recon-ditioned and had them fired to see how far the shots would reach. The sudden cannon reports after years of silence did nothing to calm nerves in the jittery town. The garrison was depleted, with most of the Army of Arabistan, normally headquartered in Damascus, dis-patched to fight the sultan's wars in Bosnia and Herzegovina, and the remainder sent to escort the Muslim pilgrimage to Mecca. To replace his regular soldiers, the governor recruited police (*zaptiye*) and irregular military (*bashi bozuk*) units from the roughest neigh-bourhoods of Damascus, thus putting weapons in the hands of some of the most disreputable thugs in town. He appointed Mustafa Bey al-Hawasli, the Kurdish agha who persecuted the villagers of Suq Wadi Barada for taking a loan from Dr Mishaqa, to command the local police, entrusting security to a man described by a Muslim notable as 'very stupid and hateful to the people of Damascus.'[2]

In response to repeated demands from the members of the for-eign consular corps and the notables in the city council, Ahmad Pasha finally took measures to secure the Christian neighbour-hoods. He ordered leaders in the city quarters to organise patrols to make the rounds in their quarters day and night. He dispatched irregular soldiers and mobile cannons to secure the entrances to the Christian quarters and made the Christians pay for the extra secu-rity. Yet these steps did little to ease Christian nerves. They all had heard stories from survivors of previous massacres of how Otto-man irregulars had gathered and disarmed Christians in Hasbayya, Rashayya, and Dayr al-Qamar, only to stand by when the Druzes attacked. The irregular troops did little to hide their admiration for the Druzes and their hostility toward the Christians. Such soldiers did not enhance the sense of security in the Christian quarters of Damascus.[3]

Every measure that Ahmad Pasha took, if indeed intended to reassure and restore calm, seemed to achieve the very opposite. At the height of summer, when long, hot days made tempers short, Christian fears were heightened to panic, while Muslim hostility was emboldened.

On 7 July, young men went through the Christian quarters of Damascus drawing crosses on the paving stones in the streets, this despite the fact that 'the quarter was protected by soldiers, for whom the Christians had paid a lot of money,' as Muhammad Sa`id al-Ustuwani, the preacher in the Umayyad Mosque, observed in his diary. He saw the crosses for himself while passing by the Greek Orthodox church on 8 July: 'This was upsetting to the Christians,' who walked around the crosses, not wanting to profane the symbol of their faith. In some streets, however, hooligans forced the Christians to step on the crosses, rough-handling anyone who tried to avoid them. A group of indignant Christian notables stormed into the governor's palace to complain. They had paid good money for additional security only for their 'guards' to watch idly as Christians were abused and their religion insulted. It was nothing less than corruption, and they demanded action. Cooler minds might have framed the complaint differently, but everyone was on edge in Damascus in early July. The complaint clearly irritated the governor, who was himself by all evidence a nervous wreck. The Christians wanted action? He'd show them action. He dispatched his chief of police to arrest any youths suspected of drawing crosses on the streets in the Christian quarter.[4]

The police went through the Christian quarters and arrested a group of young Muslim men. Accounts vary on how many were detained—as few as two, as many as fifteen. They were taken back to the governor's palace and placed in jail. Anxious relatives descended upon the governor's offices to petition for their sons' release but were turned away and sent home. The young men spent the night in jail. Their families, friends, and neighbours fumed. Because of the heightened antagonism of the Muslim community, the governor's intervention left the Christians feeling more vulnerable than before.

The next day, Monday, 9 July, the governor ordered an exemplary punishment for the young hooligans. The jailors slapped ankle chains on each of the detainees and put a broom in their hands. The sad party made its way through the main city markets as a chain gang condemned to sweep the offending crosses from the streets of the Christian quarters. Although the punishment may sound mild to us today, it is worth recalling Dr Mishaqa's outrage when the local governor forced the villagers of Suq Wadi Barada to sweep the streets 'like common criminals' for having contracted a loan with him. Sweeping the streets in chains was a grave humiliation made all the more intolerable in the febrile atmosphere of 1860 Damascus by being imposed on Muslims at the behest of Christians.

As they shuffled from the prison through the main commercial thoroughfare heading eastward toward the Christian quarters, the sight of the detainees sparked outrage among the Muslims as they passed. 'Oh Muslims! Oh community of Muhammad! The Muslims are sweeping the Christian quarter! Close your shops in protest!' they shouted.

'There is no Islam! There are no Muslims while they take us to the Christian quarter to sweep the monastery,' the youths in the chain gang replied.[5]

When the detainees passed near their families' shops, their indignant relatives overwhelmed the police escort to reclaim their sons. They shattered the chains and set the young men free as the policemen retreated from the hostile crowd. The emancipation of the young men did little to calm the furious crowd that set off toward the Christian quarters with bloody intentions. As the mob passed through the commercial centre, shopkeepers shuttered their stores to protect their wares and then joined the riot.

It was about 2:00 p.m. on Monday, 9 July, the hottest time of the day at the hottest time of the year, when Damascus erupted in violence. News of the uprising spread quickly. One contemporary marvelled that within two hours, word had spread across a city that was an hour and a half's walk from north to south and an hour from east to west (in Ottoman times, distance was measured in hours rather than metres).[6]

Muhammad Abu al-Sa'ud al-Hasibi started the morning in the main markets, where the chain gang first passed. Sensing trouble, he retired to his own neighbourhood of al-Qanawat, west of the city walls. He sat with friends in the Baylik Coffeehouse, discussing the tensions brewing in their city. Others joined the party in a state of excitement, some carrying arms. 'If they had a weapon, we took it from them and placed it in the coffeehouse,' al-Hasibi recalled. The young men were excited. It wasn't normal to walk the city streets carrying arms, and they were eager to use them. A passing merchant soon gave them the excuse. 'Woe to you, people of al-Qanawat! Over forty Muslims have been killed and you are still sitting here,' the merchant berated al-Hasibi's group.

The young hotheads didn't bother to confirm the story. They leapt up, recovered their weapons, and made for the city centre. Al-Hasibi wanted nothing to do with mob violence and headed home instead. There he was accosted by a Christian clerk who worked for his family. The clerk had heard rumours and feared for his son, who was working in the city centre. As a Christian, the clerk couldn't face a Muslim mob. Al-Hasibi was a respected Muslim notable—he could enter the city safely to escort the Christian clerk's son home. 'When he saw me, he began to weep and kiss my hands and feet on behalf of his son,' al-Hasibi recalled. In a life-or-death situation, the young Muslim notable felt he had no choice. He grabbed a weapon and set off for the city centre in search of the clerk's son.

Inside the city walls, al-Hasibi raced down the main thoroughfare that Europeans, borrowing from the New Testament, referred to as the 'Street Called Straight.' At a central intersection he encountered an angry crowd massing in front of a group of soldiers who refused to let them pass. When asked, the soldiers explained to al-Hasibi that the mob had already attacked them once, injuring one man and killing others. Elsewhere in the city, soldiers had fired upon the crowds that threatened their barriers—by one report, ten Muslims were killed by gunfire at the barricades. While al-Hasibi watched, a rioter forced his way through the picket, followed by dozens more before the soldiers could re-form their lines. The rioters broke into nearby houses and began looting while the soldiers struggled in vain to hold the rest of the crowd back. Already the situation felt too dangerous, even for a Muslim notable, to navigate the city streets through such a frenzied crowd. Al-Hasibi abandoned his search for the clerk's son and retreated home to al-Qanawat, where he was to remain for the duration of the 'Damascus Events.'[7]

Dr Mishaqa was home with his family on Monday, 9 July. His *kawass*, or consular guard, had gone to the governor's offices on official business. When the kawass heard of the breakdown in order, he raced back to warn Mishaqa of the approaching danger. 'It was then that the insurrection reached our quarter, and I could not go out of my house alone,' Mishaqa recalled. He sent his kawass to the Algerian amir 'Abd al-Qadir to ask for a detachment of his men to escort Mishaqa to safety. The amir was quick to oblige, but the four men he sent were unarmed and could not get through.

The bold kawass forced his way back to the Mishaqa house by himself through a large and growing mob on the verge of violence. 'I then locked the doors of the house,' Mishaqa recalled. 'I only had time to put some money in my pocket when the door was broken, and many ruffians rushed into the house.' He noted that the first across his threshold were Kurdish irregular soldiers.

The crowd that broke through the front door immediately set about robbing the Mishaqas' richly furnished house. This bought the family a bit of time to escape through a rear door into the narrow back alleys of his quarter. Mishaqa sought refuge with Muslim neighbours, banging desperately on their doors, but none opened to let him in. He knew that he would be safe only if he could reach 'Abd al-Qadir's house, but that was more than five hundred metres away. He took his young son and daughter by the hand and set off toward the amir's house by the back lanes. They didn't get far before running into a mob. Mishaqa grabbed a fistful of coins and threw them into the crowd to distract them, racing back toward the street leading to Bab Tuma, where soldiers had been posted. Before he reached the soldiers, he met another group of marauders: 'I threw money as I did before and went by a third way' past the front entrance of his house. Here he ran into a heavily armed mob. Not a mob. His neighbours. He could identify eight of them by name. But their intentions toward the Mishaqas were anything but neighbourly.[8]

The Mishaqa family implored the crowd to spare their lives. Mishaqa's wife, Khanum (Elizabeth), prostrated herself, kissing feet and begging for mercy. The doctor must have been mortified to see his wife so abased, for he never mentioned her desperate pleas in his own reports. His children tried to shield their father. 'Kill us and save our father—we cannot live without him,' they cried. It all fell on deaf ears. One man struck Mishaqa's daughter, Salma, with an axe, wounding her. Mishaqa threw his last fistful of money to distract the crowd from attacking his children, but they kept coming. To his horror, Mishaqa realised that his neighbours were determined to kill him. His kawass stood by him, deflecting as many blows as he could, but he could not stop them all. As his assailants fell upon him, Mishaqa suffered a serious axe wound to the head, was blinded in one eye by a blow from a club, and had his right arm slashed repeatedly by a sword as he tried to ward off the blows. 'Many blows of clubs and poles fell all over my body,' he reported drily. In the end, Mishaqa survived only by paying the ringleaders a fortune—fourteen thousand piastres (about £130)—while the mob carted off 'every description of furniture and valuables' through his front door.[9]

With the assistance of his kawass, Dr Mishaqa limped toward the irregular police standing guard near Bab Tuma. Here he met their commander: none other than Mustafa Bey al-Hawasli, Mishaqa's nemesis in the Suq Wadi Barada loan. Mishaqa had no reason to hope for assistance from such a man. The commander refused to shelter Mishaqa in his own home nearby, insisting that the grievously wounded US vice-consul go instead to the home of 'a notable ruffian' who lived on the same street. Although he feared that he was entering a trap, Mishaqa had no choice but to take refuge in the disreputable house to escape the crowd. His kavass settled Mishaqa into a relatively sheltered spot, promising to return with armed men to take him to safety. Watching from the windows, Mishaqa saw 'people breaking into the Christian houses, plundering and massacring the inmates,' with al-Hawasli's men active among the robbers. Mishaqa knew it was only a matter of time before the murderers came for him.

The Reverend Smiley Robson first came to Damascus in the early 1840s to open a mission for the Irish Presbyterian Church. He had lived eighteen years in a Muslim neighbourhood on the road between the southern al-Maydan and al-Shaghur quarters, which he described as 'the two worst districts in the city.' But at least he wasn't living in the Christian quarters targeted by the growing mob. Fluent in Arabic, Robson listened intently as an excited crowd of Muslim men, women, and boys gathered in his street, 'crying out that all should go to the Christian quarter to plunder, burn and massacre and threatening not to leave a house [standing] or a Christian [alive].' Incredibly, Robson went into the street to try and reason with the agitated crowd: 'It grew rapidly worse. Everyone was calling to others not to come without arms, and the women were violently exciting the men.' Upon his neighbours' urging, Robson retreated to his house for his own safety and followed developments from behind closed doors:

> Soon after I went into my house the ruffians began to return from the Christian quarter with bundles of plunder, while the numbers running towards it were increasing. There were threats, imprecations and yells enough. Every sort and size of thing was carried past my house—mares and goats, gold and old iron nails, silks and cottons, large chests and small ones, tables, chairs, books and every imaginable article.

The plunder went on until well after sunset.[10]

The crowd grew to number in the thousands, attacking the Christian quarters 'to rob, to kill and to burn.' They were, for the most part, from the poorer quarters of the city or were rural bandits drawn by the chance to rob rich Christian households. Al-Hasibi described the crowd as a heterogeneous group of 'Druzes, Nusayris, Jews, Mitwalis, Rafidis, wanderers, worshippers of the sun and moon, Yazidis, Arabs, and people of every community known in Syria and accustomed to misdeeds...joined by the rabble of Damascus.' For al-Ustuwani, the rioters were 'soldiers, Druze, Bedouin, peasants, aghawat, Kurds, and Egyptians—the marginal people of town.' What the descendant of the Prophet Muhammad and the preacher of the Umayyad Mosque tried to stress was that the respectable Muslims of Damascus played no role, or almost no role, in the horrors that followed.[11]

The mob targeted the churches and monasteries of the different Christian communities in Damascus. Many of the churches were filled with survivors of previous massacres in Hasbayya, Rashayya, and villages near Damascus, facing mass murder for a second time. 'Convert to Islam to save your life,' the attackers warned the terrified Christians. Some converted, only to be killed all the same. Monks and priests were slaughtered, church treasuries plundered, and the buildings set afire. Not a single church or monastery inside the city walls survived the carnage of the first day.[12]

Desperate Christians, alerted by screams and gunfire, fled their homes in search of safe refuge. Dimitri Dabbas, a Greek Orthodox Christian aged just twenty-one at the time, hid in a *khan* (commercial building) with four other men, watching as hundreds of townspeople rushed into the Christian quarters bearing guns and clubs: 'We wept blood, fearing the mob would attack us in the khan and kill us.' Some climbed over rooftops in the hope of reaching a sympathetic Muslim neighbour's house. Those with foreign connections tried to make their way to the British, French, or Russian consulates. Others, too fearful of encountering the mob in the street, hid in household cellars and wells in the hope of evading detection. The lucky ones crossed paths with Amir 'Abd al-Qadir and his Algerian fighters, who fanned out across the city's quarters calling out to the Christians with the promise of safe conduct.[13]

The amir had anticipated violence. With funds from the French consul in Damascus, he had armed his Algerian veterans and had a force of some eleven hundred men under his command. When he first received word of the outbreak, 'Abd al-Qadir escorted French consul Michel Lanusse from his consulate to the amir's house, where they ran up the French tricolour, asserting diplomatic immunity. He also posted a detachment of Algerian soldiers to guard the British consulate, which was in the Muslim al-'Amara quarter, near the Umayyad Mosque. Both 'Abd al-Qadir's house and the British consulate became safe havens for the Christians of Damascus. Throughout the afternoon, the amir and his Algerian veterans sent out rescue parties to ferry Christians back to the amir's house, which soon filled to overflowing.

As the sun set over the burning city, Dr Mishaqa grew ever more fearful for his life. His whole body ached. Wounds immobilised his right arm, he had lost a lot of blood, and his clubbed eye had swollen shut, restricting his vision. His kawass had yet to return, and given the violence in the streets, it was reasonable to fear that the mob had injured or killed him. Nor did Mishaqa feel safe in the ruffian's house where his kawass had left him. Throughout the afternoon, he watched as robbers deposited their loot in the same house. They had blood on their hands. Mishaqa had no reason to believe they wouldn't kill him themselves, or hand him over to the bloodthirsty crowd. He waited for darkness to fall and planned to move to the house of Mustafa Bey al-Hawasli, the commander of the local police. Although al-Hawasli had refused him refuge on first request, Mishaqa reasoned that 'they could not murder me openly' in the commander's house.

Before he could make his move, armed men arrived and pounded on the door. They demanded that Dr Mishaqa be delivered to them. 'I thought they intended to kill me,' Mishaqa recalled, 'but ascertained that they were some of the people of Emir Abd-el-Kader.' He was saved. 'They took me to the house of His Highness ['Abd al-Qadir], where I was received very kindly.' At this stage, the amir's house was full, and Mishaqa gratefully accepted the invitation from his friend Muhammad al-Sawtari, a respected Muslim notable, to take refuge in his home. Here Mishaqa was reunited with his wife and children, all of whom had survived against the odds. He and his family would stay with al-Sawtari for the next month while Mishaqa recovered from his wounds, with financial support from another Muslim notable, Shaykh Salim Efendi al-'Attar, who provided clothes and money to the destitute Mishaqa family. Al-'Attar reportedly sheltered more than a hundred Christians in his own home to protect them from violence.[14]

The night sky over Damascus was lit by the fires raging in hundreds of Christian houses. On a normal summer's evening, the quiet would be disturbed only by the croaking of frogs in the town's many streams and the barking of countless stray dogs. On that night, the frogs and dogs were silenced by 'an unceasing tumult of cries, of the fire, of breaking open houses,' and the collapse of buildings. Reverend Robson observed the carnage from the security of his rooftop. 'The flames and smoke presented a sight as grand almost as it was awful,' he wrote. 'During the first half of the night the flames [formed] an unbroken arc of a circle of more than 70 degrees extending from a little south of Bab Sherkey [Sharqi] to the extreme northern point of the Christian quarter.' Small bands of men continued to kill and rob throughout the night, the feverish city seemingly unable to sleep after the first day of violence.

The sun rose on Tuesday, 10 July, through a pall of smoke as the violence resumed with new vigour. The mob had robbed and torched nearly all the Christian houses in Bab Tuma and Bab Sharqi. They took care not to set fire to houses abutting Muslim properties, such as Dr Mishaqa's, but stripped those homes of every moveable good, leaving vacant shells between the Muslim houses. Windows and doors were pulled from their frames and decorative wood panels stripped from painted ceilings. Witnesses reported seeing young men carrying off the very nails and beams of plundered Christian houses. After the rich harvest of the previous day, the stripped and burned houses of the Christian quarters yielded little plunder on the second day of violence. So the mob turned instead to attack Christian-owned shops, warehouses, and workshops in the main city markets.

The city markets remained closed and shuttered as a precaution against the mob. But shopkeepers knew which units were owned by Christians and which by Muslims. The rioters broke into Christian-owned commercial properties and made off with all their holdings. Once again, witnesses saw men and women racing through the streets of Damascus carrying bags of cash, bolts of cloth, jewellery, furniture, machinery, raw materials—basically, anything of value.

The size of the mob grew through the day, as the smoke over Damascus attracted opportunists from neighbouring villages to join in the free-for-all, robbing and killing the Christians with total impunity.

The few regular soldiers in Damascus remained confined to their barracks in the Citadel by order of the governor, law and order yielding to the forces of disorder. There is no doubt that a forceful intervention by well-led soldiers could have put a stop to the riot. From his house in the Muslim quarters, Robson could hear the rioters on the second day as they paused to catch their breath: 'I can affirm that from the first and all through [the rioters] have had the greatest dread of the interference of the soldiers, and constantly ask one another as they meet whether the soldiers in such and such a direction are stopping the murderers or opposing them, and this although during seventeen hours the soldiers have been perfectly passive. I believe firmly that...200 soldiers...could have put down the insurrection at the worst moment.'[15]

The consular corps was united in outrage against Governor Ahmad Pasha for his inaction. However, the consulates of France, Russia, Greece, and of course the United States had been pillaged in the first day's violence, and most of the consuls were confined to Amir 'Abd al-Qadir's home. Only British consul Brant enjoyed freedom of movement. His house was secure in the Muslim al-'Amara quarter, near the Umayyad Mosque, far from the mob that targeted the Christian quarters and protected by a large contingent of 'Abd al-Qadir's Algerian veterans. On the second day, Brant made his way to the governor's Saray (headquarters) under armed guard to demand that Ahmad Pasha take decisive action to restore order to the wounded city. Ahmad Pasha explained that he had withdrawn his soldiers from the city quarters because, as undisciplined irregulars, he feared they might add to the violence rather than prevent it (which in fact proved to be the case). He regretted that the Ottoman government had deployed the larger part of his regular garrison to Bosnia and Herzegovina, and that he could not call on more-reliable soldiers to intervene. Nonetheless, he promised the British consul to do what he could to restore order. Brant did not want to prolong the meeting, mindful of the dangers he faced returning to his consulate through the violent streets of Damascus. At dawn that same day, the mob had lynched Reverend William Graham, a Protestant missionary, mistaking him for a hated European consul. Consul Brant thanked the Ottoman governor and withdrew to regain the relative safety of his consulate, crowded with hundreds of Christian refugees.

Consul Brant's visit to the governor was in vain. Ahmad Pasha took no action. The violence continued unabated on the second day.

The mob prowled the streets in search of Christians to kill. They called for the extermination of all the Christians as if it were a social necessity. The dead lay in piles in the street, but the horror, rather than inhibiting the rioters, seemed only to feed an intense bloodlust—in Robson's words, 'hellish ruffians thirsting and crying for blood.' Everyone had seen 'Abd al-Qadir and his men rescuing Christians and escorting them back to the amir's home. A crowd gathered outside his residence demanding that the amir surrender the Christians he was sheltering. As the crowd gathered, the tone grew more menacing. The amir, confident of his high standing among the Muslims of Damascus, went out unarmed to address the rioters: 'Brothers, this is no way to behave. Have you reached the point where you believe you have the right to kill? How low have you fallen? I see men stained with the blood of women and children.' He quoted the Qur'an to the mob, invoking verses condemning murder as acts against religion.

'Oh soldier of jihad!' the crowd jeered in response. 'We haven't come for your advice. Who gave you the right to meddle in our affairs? And who are you to oppose us? You who killed so many Christians yourself [in the Algerian wars against France]?'

'The Christians are my guests. As long as one of these Algerian soldiers is left standing, you won't get to them. Should you try to take them, you will see how the soldiers of 'Abd al-Qadir can make gunpowder speak.' Furious at the impertinence of the crowd, 'Abd al-Qadir turned to one of his officers and called for his weapons and his horse. Seeing their leader preparing for battle, the Algerian soldiers erupted into cheers that shattered the bravado of the mob. They slunk away without further threat to the Christians sheltering in Amir 'Abd al-Qadir's house.[16]

Hundreds of other Christians still hiding in their quarters were not so fortunate. Robson reported that the killing was yet more extensive on the second day than it had been on the first, as marauders went through the ruined houses in search of victims in basements, wells, and attics. He claimed that Tuesday witnessed the 'greatest butchery' yet, with between one and two thousand Christians killed on the second day. Robson began to worry that one of his Muslim neighbours might denounce him to the mob and asked Consul Brant to send guards to accompany him to safety in the British consulate.

Houses were still burning as the sun set on the second day of violence. The horror went on through the night without respite.

On the third day, fires began to spread out of control toward the Muslim quarters. One of Damascus's leading Islamic scholars, Shaykh ʿAbdullah al-Halabi, dispatched his son Khalil to the northern suburb of al-Salihiyya to call on the men of that quarter to assist in putting out the flames. Built on the slopes of Mount Qasiyun, overlooking the city of Damascus, al-Salihiyya and its residents had remained insulated from the horrors taking place in the city centre, and its men had played no part in the violence. Shaykh Khalil approached the headman of the al-Salihiyya quarter to ask for his help in recruiting firefighters. He sent a crier up the minaret of the central mosque of al-Salihiyya to dramatise the appeal, broadcasting that the flames threatened the Umayyad Mosque itself and that Damascus needed volunteers to save the Muslim quarters. Five hundred men volunteered and set off toward the smoke and flames inside the city walls. The sudden appearance of five hundred men coming from the rough al-Salihiyya quarter must have spread terror among Christian survivors who remained trapped in their charred and plundered houses, mistaking them for another wave of marauders coming to exterminate the Christians. As the men of al-Salihiyya set to work on the burning buildings, a shot rang out. Some say that a fire volunteer was wounded in the leg, others that he was killed outright. Either way, the shooting turned the benevolent volunteers into marauders as the men of al-Salihiyya abandoned their firefighting to seek their revenge 'and renewed the violence against the Christians, killing as many as had been killed on the first day.'[17]

To understand the shot that triggered this renewed wave of violence, one has to imagine the mental anguish of the surviving Christians of Damascus:

> By my life, no pen and no tongue can adequately describe the position of the tragic Christians of Damascus, their anguish and pain. One cannot even imagine it without having witnessed it personally. We saw men running barefoot and naked, desperate to escape, without finding a refuge, crying and wailing like children. They were like drunks who had lost all reason, as if blind, with no idea of where to go to evade their enemies. Some of them were hidden and their nerves trembled constantly while their hearts beat inside them night and day in terror. Their tongues were dry in their mouths, their eyes glazed and their faces as colourless as the dead. With the passing of time, they were overwhelmed with floods of premonitions of death from the voices of their enemies and their repeated attacks. They feared the whistle of the wind and the barking of the dogs.[18]

Amir 'Abd al-Qadir and his men continued to patrol the Christian quarters in search of survivors. They found men and women who had spent more than forty-eight hours hiding in wells or in basements, where they heard the mob ransack their homes and the fire burning over their heads. It was a leap of faith to respond to the calls of the amir's North African fighters, and many feared that the calls were a ruse to lure them to their deaths. But hundreds took the risk, swelling the numbers taking refuge in the amir's home and those of other leading notables. By the third day of violence, 'Abd al-Qadir had some four thousand refugees under his roof and in the homes of his family and lieutenants. They needed a larger venue to protect the thousands of Christian survivors from the growing mob determined to exterminate the Christians altogether.

The amir and the foreign consuls he hosted discussed the situation. They decided to send a delegation under armed guard to Governor Ahmad Pasha, to force him to take responsibility for the Christian refugees or be answerable to their governments for his failings. The governor conceded to their demands and offered the Citadel, which was certainly large enough to hold the thousands of homeless Christians. However, he asked the amir to take responsibility for their security by posting North African guards there, not trusting his irregular Ottoman forces with the job. In that, Ahmad Pasha was not alone. The Christians as well as 'Abd al-Qadir and his Algerians had seen irregular soldiers taking part in the violence. Moreover, everyone had heard of the fate of the Christians of Hasbayya, Rashayya, and Dayr al-Qamar who, having taking refuge in the citadels of those towns, had been delivered by their Ottoman irregular 'guards' to their enemies and massacred. 'Abd al-Qadir agreed to post a large contingent of his troops to secure the Citadel and went home to prepare his protégés for the move.

The Christians sheltering in 'Abd al-Qadir's home were terrified at the thought of moving from the safety of his house to what they imagined to be the killing zone of the Damascus Citadel. They received the news like a death sentence. 'Kill us yourself rather than deliver us to our executioners. You at least would not make us suffer. Don't deliver our wives and daughters to their brutality. Kill us yourself, for pity's sake!' they cried.[19]

'Abd al-Qadir, recounting the story to a French officer months later, was still moved by the fears of the Christian survivors, who thought him capable of delivering them to their killers. The amir understood their fears all too well. He acknowledged that he had his own reservations about their safety in the Citadel. But the situation in his home was untenable, as more survivors were rescued from the flames. The amir and his men had to use force to press the first group to leave his home and set off for the Citadel. The Russian consul accompanied the group to reassure the Orthodox survivors, who looked upon Russia as their patron. Once the first contingent had been settled safely in the Citadel, the others reluctantly agreed to follow. They moved in groups under a massive armed guard, from 'Abd al-Qadir's house and the overcrowded houses of some of the Muslim notables to the gates of the Citadel. By the end of the day, several thousand Christians were sheltered in the relative safety of the Citadel—with no bedding or clothing, limited food and water, and almost no sanitation. Dimitri Dabbas, who reluctantly took refuge among the thousands of survivors in the Citadel, saw women lamenting those left behind and crying in terror, and wounded men shrieking in pain: 'ah, sights that would make a stone weep.'[20]

His house emptied of refugees, 'Abd al-Qadir continued to search for Christian survivors. He sent his men among the crowd and offered a bounty of fifty piastres for every Christian man, woman, or child delivered to his house alive. He received these latest survivors and paid the bounty from his living room. When the number of new arrivals grew large enough, they were accompanied by armed guard to the Citadel to join the other survivors. This work went on throughout the third day, with the Christians caught between the outraged firefighters of al-Salihiyya and the bounty hunters searching for Christians who were suddenly more valuable to them alive than dead.

An angry glow hung over the city at sunset as countless fires, reduced in intensity, continued to burn. The living, hungry and thirsty after days in hiding, didn't dare to leave their hiding places. Corpses lay in piles in the houses and streets. The deepening silence over the Christian quarters was ominous, the silence of a charnel house. The wild dogs, attracted by the sickly smell of blood and decay, returned to the Christian quarter to consume the dead.

The crisis entered its fourth day on Thursday, 12 July, still with no end in sight. It was inconceivable to the foreign diplomats in Damascus that the local governor had yet to take effective measures to restore order. Consul Brant resolved to pay a second visit to Ahmad Pasha. He was accompanied by Robson, who had abandoned his home in the working-class al-Shaghur quarter to take refuge in the British consulate the previous day. The governor received them in his office and listened impassively as Consul Brant made his demands. Firstly, he wanted the governor to provide tents, food, and water to the ten thousand Christian refugees in the Citadel. He requested the governor to send soldiers to bring all remaining survivors from their places of hiding to the safety of the Citadel. He demanded that the government bury the dead as a matter of public health and basic decency. The smell of the dead hung over the city in the midsummer heat. It was unbearable. The governor nodded in agreement. Something had to be done. 'Everything is promised,' Robson observed, 'nothing done.'[21]

Finally, Consul Brant requested of Ahmad Pasha that he intervene with the 'officers of the Kurds'—presumably the Kurdish *aghawat*—'to give up the women and girls the Kurds had carried off.' Increasingly, survivors reported instances of sexual violence against women in Damascus. For many, the very words were too offensive to repeat. 'Tongues would not describe, and pens would not write about the condition of the modest Christian women of Damascus,' one contemporary chronicler noted. 'The crowd did not limit their violence to murder but went further in the vile acts they committed against the virgins and respectable [i.e., married] women, something previously unheard of among the Druze and Shi`ite communities. Many girls and women were lost with no trace of where they went.'[22] Consul Brant demanded that the governor take immediate action to secure the safe return of all women who had suffered abduction during the riots. The governor nodded.

After Consul Brant and Mr Robson departed, Ahmad Pasha attended an emergency meeting of the Majlis of Damascus. One of the army officers posed a question to the assembled notables: 'If the Druze attack the Citadel, what do we do with the Christians, given we don't have the forces to defend them?' The first to respond was al-Sayyid Ahmad al-Hasibi, father of the diarist Muhammad al-Hasibi: 'This matter will discredit us [i.e., the notables of Damascus].

By God, I'm ready to drive all [the Druze] from Syria to hell [before allowing them to attack the Christians].' Another notable, 'Abdullah al-'Azm, stood to show his agreement with al-Hasibi's response, recognising that, as the notables of the city, they would ultimately be held to account for the acts of the mob they failed to control. However, the rest of the assembly remained seated in disagreement. 'They wanted to see those in the Citadel killed,' al-Hasibi recorded in his diary. 'Had a group of fifty Druzes showed up at that moment, they would have surrendered all those inside the Citadel [to be slaughtered].' Amir 'Abd al-Qadir, also in attendance, stormed out in protest against the passivity of the governor and the other notables, 'for they went on smoking their pipes and would do nothing.' As Ahmad Pasha remained seated, al-Hasibi believed the governor counted among those who wanted the Druzes to massacre the surviving Christians of Damascus.[23]

That day, Ahmad Pasha drafted his first report on the Damascus Events to his superiors in Istanbul. It is perhaps a measure of the paralysis of the man that it took four days for him to inform the Sublime Porte that Damascus was burning. The report is almost incoherent, a collage of random facts. The violence of Mount Lebanon had spread by contagion to Damascus. Crosses were drawn on shops in the Christian quarters, provoking a riot (no mention of the Muslim boys sent in chains to sweep the crosses). He was limited in responding to the crisis by the inadequate number of troops he had at his disposal. The soldiers could not reach the Christian quarters to expel the rioters. There was a fire in the Christian quarters. The situation risked deteriorating into a rebellion against the government and spreading to Beirut. He made oblique reference to the incident when Christians shot the men from al-Salihiyya on the third day, provoking renewed conflict. 'After that,' he recorded, conflicting with the accounts of al-Hasibi and Amir 'Abd al-Qadir, 'the officials convened a meeting of the Council of the leading notables of the city, where they discussed rapid responses for the resolution of this unseemly behaviour and the restoration of order.' He reported that he had recalled soldiers from other parts of the province and had alerted government officials in Homs, Hama, and Aleppo. The report created the misleading impression that Ahmad Pasha had the situation in hand. The minister reviewing his report noted optimistically that 'this incident will be pacified, and conditions improved in a short while.'[24]

The fourth day of violence drew to a close with the Christians concentrated in the Citadel, their safety assured only by 'Abd al-Qadir's Algerian soldiers. The destruction of the Christian quarters was more or less complete by the end of the day. There were no Christian houses left standing, and all religious structures—churches, convents, and monasteries—had been destroyed. All of the consulates except the British had been attacked. Fires still burned here and there, and 'Abd al-Qadir's men continued to circulate to pull ever fewer Christian survivors from the ruins.

The fifth day of the Events was a Friday, but no one went to the mosques for Friday prayers. Even Shaykh Muhammad Sa'id al-Ustuwani, the preacher of the Umayyad Mosque, was too afraid of the lawlessness and disorder in the city's streets to leave his home. As he noted in his diary, 'Your humble servant did not say Friday prayers out of fear, nor those of Wednesday or Thursday. The Umayyad Mosque and all the other mosques were closed as fear spread among us all.'[25] Obviously, Muslim notables like al-Ustuwani were not the crowd's target, but in the breakdown of law and order, disorder reigned supreme. Witnesses reported a lull in the violence on the fifth day. As more and more Christians took refuge in the Citadel, there were ever fewer left to attack in the streets of the city, and there were no more Christian shops, houses, or places of worship left to attack.

By the following day, Saturday, 14 July, the number of Christians in the Citadel was estimated to have reached between eleven and twelve thousand. There were touching scenes as family members separated in the violence were reunited, but many households remained dispersed, with wives in search of husbands and children desperately seeking their parents. All remained in a state of heightened anxiety, fearful that at any moment the mob would force the gates. The murderers circled the Citadel night and day baying for the Christians' blood. Food and water remained in short supply in the Citadel. The government promised each Christian a flat bread, a cucumber, and an apple each day, but everyone went hungry. Increasingly, the townspeople of Damascus began to suffer shortages as well, after six days of riot. The markets remained closed, and local farmers did not dare bring their produce to the turbulent city.

Governor Ahmad Pasha still had not left his office and had taken no measures to reestablish government control over Damascus. The dreadful mob took possession of the streets, no longer worried about the army intervening or the government holding them accountable for their crimes. The city was largely cut off from the outside world, sparing the Damascenes news of the growing reaction to the first accounts of the massacres in both Istanbul and the capitals of Europe.

The dead remained unburied where they lay in the Christian quarter, casting a horrible smell over the whole of the city. Townspeople took matters in their own hands, throwing scores of bodies into the wells of destroyed Christian houses and into the Barada River, to be carried downstream away from the city.

The sun rose on the seventh day of the crisis on Sunday, 15 July. The longer that law went unenforced, the breakdown in order grew ever more entrenched. Without effective government, Damascus had been reduced to a Hobbesian state of nature where life was literally nasty, short, and brutish. Aside from the small detachment of regular soldiers inside the Citadel, which preserved a modicum of discipline, the local army and police had joined the mob wreaking havoc and destruction throughout the city. Each town quarter appointed its own guards to protect its residents from the marauding crowd in the absence of police or soldiers. The disorder extended to the kavasses, who had played an essential role in protecting foreign diplomats and protégés. Suddenly, kavasses refused orders from their consuls. British consul Brant claimed he no longer counted on his guards to protect him. The Austrian consul's kavass was accused of delivering nine Christians to the mob for slaughter. Only Amir ʿAbd al-Qadir's Algerians could be relied on to preserve discipline and protect the surviving Christians from annihilation.

'Abd al-Qadir's men continued to find survivors and escorted them to the dubious safety of the Citadel. Conditions inside the Citadel continued to deteriorate as the inmates suffered exposure to the sun, dehydration, and hunger. The risk of sickness was omnipresent as sanitation collapsed because of an estimated twelve thousand refugees sharing limited toilet facilities. It was the uncertainty of their fate, and the way the crisis continued with no end in sight, that placed the most stress on the Christians. Their situation was very similar to that of the doomed Christians who took refuge in the citadels of Hasbayya, Rashayya, and Dayr al-Qamar.

Business remained at a standstill in Damascus. The shops, bazaars, and khans lay shuttered after a whole week of riot. Some bakeries were reported to have opened, and they no doubt found keen customers after a week without fresh bread.

In the governor's Saray, Ahmad Pasha seemed concerned only for his own safety. He no longer trusted his soldiers and feared that the lawless crowd might try to kill him. He probably knew that the Ottoman government in Istanbul had already named a new governor to replace him and had dispatched Foreign Minister Fuad Pasha as the sultan's special representative to investigate the crises in Mount Lebanon and Damascus. Ahmad Pasha would soon have to answer to the sultan for his catastrophic failures in Damascus.[26]

On Monday, 16 July, the new governor arrived to take up his post. Mu'ammar Pasha entered Damascus via the northern suburb of al-Salihiyya, where he stopped to pray at the grave of the revered Sufi mystic Ibn 'Arabi. From al-Salihiyya, the new governor rode into central Damascus. He ordered town criers to circulate through the city to assure all residents of their security. Townspeople were forbidden to carry weapons. Strangers—those not normally resident in Damascus—were ordered to return to their native towns and villages and leave Damascus. For Shaykh al-Ustuwani, the arrival of the new governor marked the end of eight days of violence. The Christians sheltering in the Citadel must still have felt in danger.

When he reached the government quarter of Marja, overshadowed by the Citadel along the banks of the Barada River, Mu'ammar Pasha found his official residence still occupied. Through eight days of riot, murder, and arson, Ahmad Pasha had never set foot outside his palace. The governor left his residence only when summoned to Beirut for questioning by the sultan's special envoy on 20 July. 'What we heard, which seems to be true, was that [Ahmad Pasha] went to the hospital, shielded by soldiers, showing fear of the people of the city, may God protect us from his wickedness,' Shaykh al-Ustuwani recorded in his diary.[27]

In the days after Mu'ammar Pasha's arrival, some semblance of normalcy returned to the devastated city of Damascus. Shops finally reopened. Households reprovisioned. Residents and shopkeepers began to sweep the detritus from their streets. Yet in the Citadel, thousands of Christian survivors waited in heightened anxiety for their ordeal to end. The anxiety was not confined to the Citadel. The Muslim townspeople of Damascus, as if waking from a nightmare, must have looked around and asked themselves, 'What have we done?' Behind the new governor, the Ottoman foreign minister was coming with thousands of disciplined Ottoman troops. There were rumours of intervention by the European powers. There was no hiding the crimes the Damascenes had committed against their Christian neighbours. If the reckoning were to be proportionate to the crime, dark days lay ahead for the Muslims of Damascus.

What just happened?

Society in the ancient and cosmopolitan city of Damascus, one of the birthplaces of Christianity and Islam alike, collapsed into communal violence that went to the brink of genocide. Dr Mishaqa said it quite succinctly: 'There was a general commitment to kill all of the Christians from all sects and denominations and classes without exception.' Smiley Robson confirmed Mishaqa's view, claiming that 'the design of the rioters was to exterminate the adult male population, take possession of the women and compel them to apostatize, bring up the children as Mahometans, and destroy the Christian quarter utterly and for ever.' The goal was to exterminate the Christian presence in Damascus once and for all.[28]

The term *genocide* had yet to be coined when Mount Lebanon and Damascus dissolved into sectarian mass murder, but these events were the kind of historical antecedents that international lawyer Raphael Lemkin had in mind when he gave a name to the crime against humanity that Nazi Germany had committed against the Jews of Europe in the Shoah, or Holocaust. The term gained the force of international law in 1948 when enshrined by the United Nations in the 'Convention on the Prevention and Punishment of the Crime of Genocide.' The convention defines genocide as 'acts committed with intent to destroy, in whole or in part, a national, ethnical, racial or religious group.' As the convention makes clear, there are many different means to eradicate a community. In the course of the Events, Damascene Christians suffered many of the practices of a genocidal moment.

Mass murder is the most direct form of genocide, and thousands of Christians were murdered during the Damascus Events. In a report submitted to the US government in September 1860, Dr Mishaqa compiled the most precise figures available from Ottoman and local sources. In all, Mishaqa estimated that 5,000 Christians were murdered in Damascus, half of them residents of the city and the rest refugees from neighbouring towns and villages. The figure of 2,500 Damascene Christians killed from a community of 15,000–18,000 would have represented about 15 percent of the city's Christian population.

Although there were certainly women and children who were killed in the massacre, the mob targeted Christian men. The only option that men had to save themselves was to convert. Forced conversion is another genocidal practice, for by assimilating to the Muslim majority, conversion contributed to the extermination of the Christian community. However, conversion was not guaranteed to save a man's life. As all contemporary eyewitnesses agreed, the mob was a heterogeneous group composed not just of Sunni Muslims but of Druzes, Shi`ites, Yazidis, Bedouin, and others who had no stake in Christians converting to Islam. There are numerous accounts of Christian men who professed their belief in the oneness of God and Muhammad as His Prophet only to be murdered by the crowd, presumably because they were attacked by men who weren't Sunni

Muslims and for whom conversion was immaterial. Others had their conversions accepted and were subjected on the spot to circumcision (Islam, like Judaism, requires men to be circumcised) under conditions that would have been humiliating at best and mutilating at worst. Dr Mishaqa reported that some four hundred Christian men converted to Islam in the course of the massacres. After the restoration of law and order, the Ottoman government encouraged forced converts to return to their original Christian faith, and most did. However, a few chose to remain Muslim as their best insurance against the risk of future attack.[29]

Women were for the most part spared from murder themselves. As Dr Mishaqa wrote, 'The Shari'a does not permit the killing of women on religious grounds.' However, adolescent girls and women of childbearing age were in many cases abducted and taken into Muslim households, where they were raped with the deliberate intention of making them pregnant. In his report, Mishaqa claimed that four hundred women had been abducted during the Events and that 'a group of girls had been raped and were pregnant.' Robson speculated that the number of women who suffered from sexual violence was greater than the sum of men who were killed, but he provided no figures to support his claim. Such sexual violence is another recognised genocidal practice. Rape devastates the community as well as the victim, violating notions of honour and shame in ways that often leave women ostracised and unable to return to their own community. For instance, it would be nearly impossible for a pregnant Christian woman to find a Christian man willing to marry her, leaving her with a choice between making life in the

Muslim household where she was raped or returning to her family to live out the rest of her life as a source of shame to them and herself. Moreover, the child of a woman of any faith made pregnant by a Muslim is, under Islamic law, born Muslim. Christian women did not even need to convert to Islam for their children to be claimed as Muslim. Forced impregnation thus turned women's wombs against themselves and their Christian community as part of a strategy of extermination.[30]

Throughout the massacres, Muslim clerics exhorted their followers to spare children—boys and girls before the age of puberty—from all violence. As Dr Mishaqa explained, 'Muslims claim on the authority of the Prophet that all children are born Muslim.' In other words, it was only when children in Christian and Jewish families came of age and adhered to their parents' religion that they 'split' from Islam to become Christian or Jewish. By abducting children of Christian families into their households, Damascene Muslims would ensure that the children never parted from Islam. Following the return of law and order, when the Ottoman authorities restored children to their families, the boys nearly always had been circumcised. Here again, a clearly genocidal logic prevailed, for in raising Christian children outside their own faith community, their abductors intended to hasten the extinction of their community.[31]

As though it were not enough to massacre the men and assimilate the women and children into the Muslim community, the violent mob set about the systematic destruction of Christian houses and workplaces within the city walls of Damascus. The arson was not random. The burning went on far longer than the limited wood in Damascene houses would normally have permitted. Arsonists must have circled through the Christian quarters to reset fires that, starved of combustible material, had gone out. They sought to obliterate every trace of the Christian presence in Damascus, leaving a scarred cityscape reminiscent of firebombed towns in the Second World War: not a roof, door, or window left in place. By Dr Mishaqa's count, some 1,500 houses were burned to the ground. Another 270 homes were destroyed by looters but not put to the torch, to protect neighbouring Muslim houses from fire. Damages to commercial properties included 200 shops robbed and burned in the Christian quarters, and all Christian shops in the central markets robbed but not burned. Fifty workshops—stables, bakeries, and looms—were also destroyed. In all, Mishaqa estimated the total property value stolen or destroyed at over 237 million piastres (£2.15 million, or $10.8 million, at 1860 exchange rates).

The Damascus massacre was a genocidal moment, but it was not a genocide. Outside the city walls, working-class Christians in the al-Maydan quarter were protected by their Muslim neighbours, and as a result the quarter witnessed no communal violence during the Events. Within the city walls, a small but influential group of Muslim notables of Damascus rescued as much as 85 percent of the Christian population from mob violence. Men like Mahmud Efendi Hamza and his brother Sharif As`ad, Shaykh Salim Efendi al-`Attar, `Abdullah Efendi al-`Imadi, `Uthman Jabri, Salim Agha al-Mahayni, Sa`id Agha al-Nuri, `Umar Agha al-`Abid, and Dr Mishaqa's own saviour, Muhammad al-Sawtari, took great risks in providing shelter to hundreds of desperate Christians. More than anyone else, though, it was Amir 'Abd al-Qadir al-Jaza'iri who saved the Christians of Damascus from extermination. His close relations with the Druze community and his network of informers alerted him to the imminent risk of violence. With funding from the French consul, he armed his eleven hundred Algerian veterans and, through them, had a loyal militia under his command. When the governor failed to take the necessary measures to intervene, and when the police and irregular soldiers crossed over to join forces with the rioters, 'Abd al-Qadir was the only person with an armed militia capable of quelling the mob, escorting Christians from their hiding places to safety, and providing armed guards for their places of refuge. Through the efforts of these courageous Muslim leaders, the Christian community of Damascus survived, and genocide was averted.[32]

The survival of the Christians of Damascus presented the Ottoman government with unprecedented challenges. It had to restore law and order in an anarchic city and begin the painstaking work of rebuilding what was destroyed and reintegrating the Christian community back into the urban fabric. Damascus had gone to the brink of genocide. The Ottomans now faced the daunting task of bringing Syria back from that terrible brink. The challenge was compounded by the fact that, after the unspeakable horrors of the Events, the Christians could never look on their Muslim neighbours in the same way again.[33] Rebuilding the city would require more than bricks and mortar. The victims of the Events needed to see those responsible for their suffering brought to justice. And the government would need to encourage a new social order binding the different communities of Damascus in a common future. It is no small thing to bring a city back from the brink of genocide.

The Ottomans needed to act quickly, both to revitalise one of the most important provincial capitals in their Arab lands and to prevent the European powers from using the violence to justify colonising Syria. The Ottomans entrusted this most delicate mission to one of their highest ranking and most experienced political figures of the day: the foreign minister, Fuad Pasha. In no small way, the future of Ottoman Damascus rested on that one man's shoulders.

6

Punish the Guilty and Restore Order

A gruesome sense of carnival descended on Damascus in the aftermath of the massacres. Smoke continued to rise from the ruins of the Christian quarters for a full ten days after the end of the violence. Only determined arsonists could still find combustible material in the ruins of the Christian quarter. Rubble filled the streets in Bab Tuma and Bab Sharqi, in some places six feet deep or more. The roofless, doorless houses stared blankly onto narrow lanes like empty sockets whose eyes had been gouged out. In the markets, gutted Christian shops alternated with shuttered Muslim stalls. Once-beautiful Damascus was disfigured by the violence that had devastated the city.

Beneath the rubble and floating in household wells lay hundreds of the dead. Stray dogs had moved into the ruins, where passersby saw them burrowing into the soil to feed on human remains. The dead took their revenge on the dogs. Months after the massacre, a foreign visitor reported masses of dead dogs heaped in the lanes of the Christian quarters: 'A horrible thing to think and to say! I saw in that unhappy quarter, the Harat al-Nassara [the Christian quarter], hundreds of dogs who died from having devoured too much human flesh.' There was no escape from the stench of death that hung heavily over the city in the summer of 1860. Damascus was no longer 'the Fragrant.'[1]

Breathing the foul air, the Christians crowding the open yards of the Damascus Citadel were constantly reminded of the horror that lay just beyond the castle's gates. As if to reinforce the point, violent men roamed around the Citadel baying for more blood. 'Let us finish the Christians, let us exterminate them,' they shouted, leaving the refugees inside the castle walls ever fearful for their lives. The murderous mob was enflamed by rumours of Christian violence against Muslims in neighbouring Syrian towns. 'There is no truth to these accounts,' Dr Mishaqa reported to his superiors in Beirut, 'though many of the people of this city believe them.' Without law and order, a return to violence seemed highly likely. Foreign diplomats expected a second massacre at any moment.[2]

Hopes that the new governor, Mu'ammar Pasha, might restore law and order were quickly disappointed. His investiture took place on Friday, 20 July. Following midday prayers in the Umayyad Mosque, an official read the sultan's decree naming Mu'ammar Pasha governor of Damascus. Muhammad Abu al-Sa'ud al-Hasibi described an atmosphere of disrespectful levity at the reading of the *firman*, the congregation distracted by 'laughter and games.' Following the reading of the decree, a guard launched a flare to signal to the gunners in the Citadel to fire the traditional salute in the new governor's honour. The flare misfired and struck a bystander in the eye. The superstitious took the mishap as a bad omen; the riotous took it as a sign of further disorder. Either way, it was a blow to the prestige of the new governor.[3]

In his first day in office, the governor called on the townspeople to lay down their arms and reopen their shops. He ordered all strangers out of the city. Yet without a credible military force, Mu'ammar Pasha had no means to impose his authority on the city. After a brief respite in violence, while the wary city took the measure of the man, the crowd returned to lawlessness and disorder. Mu'ammar Pasha found his residence surrounded by armed criminals who openly flaunted his commands. The new governor, like his predecessor, retreated behind the walls of his residence, fearful of the crowd.[4]

The crowd *was* fearsome. The violence had changed Damascenes. Murderers, rapists, arsonists, and thieves brazenly strolled the streets of the city in their hundreds. They recognised no authority because through the worst of their crimes, no one had succeeded in imposing any authority on them. Under normal circumstances, the notables of the city—members of the Majlis (ruling council), the leading Muslim religious scholars, the most influential merchants, and the traditional commanders of the paramilitary groups in Damascus— would have used their influence to put an end to the carnage before it got out of hand. Some of the notables had played a key role in rescuing Christians from violence, but others either were cowed into passivity or gave their tacit consent to the anti-Christian violence. Either way, in the aftermath of the massacres, public morality simply collapsed. As the young Muslim notable Muhammad Abu al-Sa'ud al-Hasibi recorded in his diary, 'There was open drunkenness and depravity and homosexuality and adultery without fear of anyone great or small.' Dr Mishaqa despaired of the breakdown in public order. 'In truth, the sun never rose on a place more beset with evil than this city of ours,' he lamented.[5]

This was the city that Fuad Pasha entered on 29 July 1860, entrusted by Sultan Abdülmecid with the mission of punishing the guilty and restoring order.

The sultan and his government recognised the gravity of the events in Mount Lebanon and Damascus, and the threat they posed to Ottoman rule in the Arab lands. The Sublime Porte knew that if they failed to take decisive action, the European powers would almost certainly intervene in defence of Syrian Christians themselves. Just six years earlier, a relatively trivial dispute between Christian denominations over privileges in the holy places of Palestine had led to the Crimean War. The sultan and his ministers knew that the wholesale massacre of Christians in Syria and Lebanon, left unaddressed, would almost certainly result in a foreign occupation and the dismemberment of the Arab provinces of the Ottoman Empire. The Porte needed to dispatch a statesman who could restore the sultan's control over Syria and keep the European powers at bay. They ultimately entrusted the mission to the Ottoman foreign minister and celebrated reformer Fuad Pasha.

Mehmed Fuad Pasha (1815–1869), commonly known simply as Fuad Pasha, was one of the most powerful Ottoman politicians of his day. As a young man, he secured admission to the Ottoman medical faculty, where he mastered French, the language of instruction. His language skills took him further than his medical training. In 1837, in a dramatic career shift, he abandoned medicine to join the translation bureau of the Ottoman foreign ministry, where he came to the attention of the influential grand vizier Mustafa Reshid Pasha, one of the framers of the Tanzimat reforms. Once under Reshid Pasha's wing, Fuad had a meteoric rise through the diplomatic corps that led to posts in London, Madrid, and St Petersburg. In 1852, at the relatively young age of thirty-seven, Fuad won his first appointment as foreign minister. By that stage, he was a well-known figure in the courts of Europe, experienced in the language and practices of European statecraft.

Along with his mentor, Mustafa Reshid Pasha (1800–1858, six times grand vizier), and his peer Mehmed Emin Ali Pasha (1815–1871, seven times foreign minister and five times grand vizier), Fuad was one of the most important men of the Tanzimat era. He wrote much of the 1856 Reform Decree, which first conferred legal equality on non-Muslim Ottoman subjects—a measure that contributed significantly to communal tensions in Damascus in the lead-up to the 1860 massacres. The Syrian crisis was the gravest challenge to the reform measures of the men of the Tanzimat. Fuad's appointment demonstrated the Porte's commitment to upholding the reforms.

The sultan announced Fuad Pasha's appointment as the special imperial commissioner plenipotentiary to Syria on 8 July 1860. His mission at first was confined to restoring order in Mount Lebanon but soon expanded to include Damascus in the aftermath of the massacre there. The firman of investiture placed a heavy burden on Fuad: 'You, my vizier full of intelligence, one of the glorious ministers and…great advisers of our empire, possess all our imperial trust.' The sultan praised his minister's discretion: 'In short, we trust your intelligence and sagacity with full powers, civil as well as military, to take the necessary measures' to restore order and punish the guilty.[6] The sultan essentially gave total authority to Fuad to impose such measures and inflict such punishments as he saw fit—down to the death penalty. If he succeeded, Fuad's efforts would be crowned in glory. But if he failed—and, given the complexity of the task ahead, failure seemed a likely outcome—Fuad would have no one but himself to blame.

Fuad Pasha sailed from Istanbul on 12 July and arrived in Beirut five days later. Deliberate and methodical, Fuad remained ten days in Beirut preparing for his dual mission in Mount Lebanon and Damascus. He met with European consuls to solicit their views and to reassure them of his determination to protect the Christians and punish their persecutors. He negotiated a truce between the Druzes and Maronites in Mount Lebanon. He dispatched agents to Damascus to collect intelligence and report back to him in advance of his entry into the city. Crucially, he waited until his military escort reached full strength before proceeding to Damascus. Fuad was determined to enter the rebellious city accompanied by a large and disciplined army to restore the townspeople's fear of their sultan and his government.

Fuad Pasha's strategy worked. The first thing that Damascenes noted when the minister plenipotentiary entered the city on 28 July was the size of his army escort. The four thousand regular troops were the largest armed force to enter Damascus since the Egyptian occupation in the 1830s. The grim-faced soldiers took up positions before Fuad entered the riotous city. He posted detachments to each of the neighbourhoods and placed a military cordon around the perimeter of the city. The Ottoman minister dispensed with ceremony. He entered the city in his travel clothes, not in official dress. He accepted the official welcome by the city's notables but refused to open his doors to the Muslim leaders of Damascus. He made an exception only for Amir 'Abd al-Qadir, in recognition of the Algerian's role in rescuing Damascene Christians. Fuad welcomed the Algerian amir with full honours. After 'Abd al-Qadir took his leave, the doors of the governor's palace slammed shut behind him. By this gesture, Fuad sent a clear message to the notable families of Damascus that he held them responsible for the breakdown in order. They had failed in their role as intermediaries between the state and society.[7]

Shunning the notables, Fuad went first to the Citadel to meet the Christian survivors of the massacres. He was overwhelmed by their accounts and their fears, confined to an open-air fortress in the midst of a hostile city. 'The crowd came to him, crying and entreating him to provide security and tranquillity as they had been promised,' Dr Mishaqa reported. Many wanted to leave Damascus altogether to take refuge with the Christian community in Beirut. The Christians could not remain in the Citadel indefinitely, were not safe outside the fortress's walls, and had no houses to return to. Beirut seemed the only reasonable solution. Fuad promised pack animals and provisions for those wishing to make the journey. Good to his word, Fuad provided 150 mules and, beginning on 2 August, sent the first caravan of Christian refugees from Damascus to Beirut under armed guard.[8]

Three days after entering the city, Fuad finally opened his doors to the Muslim elite of Damascus. Sixty notables were given orders, rather than invitations, to attend to the minister plenipotentiary in his offices—no regrets were accepted. In their first meeting, Fuad quite literally put the fear of God and His shadow on Earth, the sultan, into the Damascene elites. 'The city of Damascus was loved and esteemed before His Majesty the Sultan and all the Great Powers,' he claimed. 'However, as a result of the atrocious acts which took place here, it has now fallen under the wrath of God, His Prophet and the Sultan.' Looking directly at the notables, he continued: 'This has come about because you failed in three ways: You violated Islamic Sharia, you schemed against the laws of the Sultan, and you have caused the Sultan problems that are difficult to solve. It is now your responsibility to provide the names and details of those who have committed crimes.'[9]

The Ottoman minister then expanded on the bigger issues behind his mission. He was charged with preserving Syria under Ottoman control—literally, 'in the hands of the Sultan.' The actions of the people of Damascus and their notables, he warned, 'were contributing to placing the [Syrian] lands in the hands of the Europeans.' To avoid foreign intervention, Fuad needed to demonstrate that the Ottomans had themselves restored full law and order in Syria. If the notables did not work with Fuad, they risked finding themselves under European colonial rule.

To defuse the threat of European intervention, Fuad informed the assembly, he was ready to impose the full force of the law on anyone responsible for the horrors in Damascus, up to the highest level of the elites. Former governor Ahmad Pasha was at that moment returning under arrest to Damascus, he explained. Stripped of his rank and medals, and now referred to as Ahmad Agha, the former governor would soon be tried and, were he to be found guilty, would face 'exemplary punishment.' The words must have had a chilling effect on the gathering. The urban notables had no illusions about their own immunity if Fuad were willing to bring down a pasha. The only way to protect themselves from 'exemplary punishment' would be by cooperating with Fuad. It was clear that someone was going to pay for the Damascus massacres. The notables could either deliver their neighbours to the hangman or wear the noose themselves.[10]

The meetings in Fuad Pasha's office went on for several days. Under intense pressure, the notables cracked. They drafted a joint declaration pledging their full cooperation with Fuad's investigations and appended their seals to the document. They drew up preliminary lists of names of those suspected of taking part in the violence. And they agreed to Fuad's proposal to establish commissions in each of the eight administrative districts (*thumn*) of the city to continue the work of gathering information on those accused of taking part in the violence. By August 2, Fuad Pasha had succeeded in getting the notables to work for him. He ordered all the city gates shut, placing Damascus into lockdown, and sent his agents to work.

In addition to the preliminary lists provided by the Damascene notables, Fuad Pasha had already secured names from foreign diplomatic missions and Christian notables who survived the violence. British consul Brant provided Fuad with 'a list of the most notorious murderers and plunderers,' and Dr Mishaqa submitted a more modest list of the eight 'individuals who wounded me.' The French,

Greek, and other consuls submitted similar lists, which Fuad tallied against his own intelligence sources and began to make arrests.[11]

The first Damascenes arrested practically handed themselves in. The government put out a call for people to return property stolen from Christian households to a designated depot in their districts. It was assumed that those who returned property would be thanked for their honesty. Instead, they found themselves under arrest and escorted to a detention centre set up in the sixteenth-century Taki-yya Sulaymaniyya, a mosque complex overlooking the Barada River on the western outskirts of Damascus. Fuad claimed that his forces arrested 330 men on the first day alone. As word spread of the arrests, panic gripped the city. Commoners waited until nightfall before throwing all plunder from their windows to clear their homes of incriminating property. Clothing, bedding, and personal property rained down into the alleys and streams of Damascus, in many cases spoiling the property, which was recovered by officials the following morning. Treasures were mixed with common household goods. One of Dr Mishaqa's neighbours found Mishaqa's American consular seals in a nearby lane, and a group of Muslims delivered to the authorities a sack full of silver worth more than Pt. 40,000 that they claimed to have found in the street, all five vouching for the innocence of the others. The officials gathered thousands of horse loads of stolen items to be restored to their rightful owners.[12]

The pace of arrests accelerated in line with the work of the committees in each administrative district of the city. Shaykh Muhammad Sa`id al-Ustuwani, the preacher in the Umayyad Mosque, served unwillingly on the committee for al-`Amara along with scions of the most illustrious families in the city—the `Azms, Muradis, Barudis, and Mardam Beys. The committee met in the al-Kurdi Garden, where the officer presiding kept registers of the names of those accused of violence against the Christians. Al-Ustuwani listed the names of individuals from his quarter who were caught up in the arrests. Sa'id al-Sayyida was surprised by soldiers who entered his home from a neighbour's property to arrest him, whereas Ibrahim al-Sha''al, who sparked the riot to release the Muslim youths sent in chains to sweep the Christian quarters on the first day of the massacres, managed to elude his captors, possibly after being tipped off by a sympathetic notable. Each day, hundreds more were sent to the Takiyya under arrest—more than a thousand by the end of the first week.[13]

On Sunday, August 5, Muhammad Abu al-Sa'ud al-Hasibi received the knock on his door. A lieutenant accompanied by seven soldiers asked al-Hasibi to follow them to a meeting with Fuad Pasha in the Saray. Al-Hasibi should have had no reason for concern. As he noted in his diary, he had made only one trip into the city centre during the troubles, when he tried to rescue the son of his father's Christian clerk. Unable to reach the Christian quarters, he had returned home, where he sat out the remainder of the Events: 'By God Almighty I didn't go out or witness [violence] after that. I did not return to perform despicable acts. I didn't enter a Christian house, nor the Christian quarter, nor did I harm a Christian or a Muslim or anyone else [for which] God might hold me to account with my soul in his hand.' Yet as he faced the young officer and seven armed soldiers, he must have felt anxiety in the pit of his stomach. The very fact that he had been seen approaching the Christian quarters carrying a weapon on the first day of the violence could have been enough for someone to have denounced him.

Al-Hasibi was ushered directly into Fuad Pasha's office, where he found the Ottoman minister standing before a window while a servant buttoned his tunic. Al-Hasibi pressed his right hand to his lips and forehead in a respectful gesture of greeting to a man of high office. The interview lasted half an hour, but al-Hasibi did not record their exchange. He simply noted that at the end of the interview, Fuad instructed the lieutenant to take him to General Khalid Pasha, the commander of the armed forces, 'as our guest, and tell Khalid Pasha to put him in a suitable place.' Al-Hasibi repeated his respectful greeting and withdrew. Khalid Pasha kept him waiting for half an hour while he paced about his office in search of a 'suitable place' for the young notable. In the end, he ordered a captain to clear his room and turned to al-Hasibi. 'You sit here, guest,' he instructed ironically, as orderlies brought in a mattress. The shock of al-Hasibi's sudden incarceration sank in. 'I had to place my trust in God and commit myself to God, knowing God sees all,' he recalled.

Over the next days, al-Hasibi came to share his room with other notables arrested by the authorities. His diary reads like a who's who of the Damascene elite, now in state custody. There wasn't enough prison space in Damascus to accommodate the hundreds arrested daily, and the detainees were assigned to facilities according to their social rank. Merchants and commoners were held in the courtyard and cells of the Takiyya mosque complex, whereas notables were detained in officers' quarters in military barracks situated around the government quarter in Marja, to the west of the city walls. The highest-ranking detainees were assigned to a courtyard house called the Bayt al-Baltajiyya, near Marja. As the days passed, al-Hasibi grew increasingly depressed by his incarceration. 'Things got harder for me,' he wrote, 'and I began to have regrets, when regrets were not useful. All I wanted was to gain my release along with my friends. I knew I needed to show patience, if God would only give me patience.' Indeed, patience would be called for. Al-Hasibi was only at the beginning of his ordeal.[14]

The mass arrests heightened tensions in Muslim communities across Damascus. It was widely assumed that those arrested had been denounced by Christians, provoking Muslim calls for revenge. A butcher named Habib al-Lahham mixed arsenic into halwa, a sweet sesame paste, and offered the sweets to his customers in the Citadel and in the al-Salihiyya quarter. Two Christian women in the Citadel subsequently died from the poison, while those in al-Salihiyya fell ill but recovered. The poison was traced back to al-Lahham, who was arrested and confessed to the crime. On 8 August, the authorities hanged al-Lahham in a public square—the first public execution after the Damascus massacres. The hanging provoked outrage among many Damascenes. Dr Mishaqa reported Muslims saying, 'Fine, for every Muslim they kill we will kill another [Christian].' Sure enough, the day after Lahham's hanging, the body of a Christian man was found murdered in the ruins of the Christian quarter.[15]

Fuad Pasha could not allow such vigilante killings to spread. Further murders risked derailing his mission. He responded swiftly and decisively to strike terror into the hearts of the Damascenes. He convened an 'extraordinary tribunal' to try the men accused of violent crimes in the Damascus Events and began to hear their cases with more care for speed than due process. The cases were conducted in total secrecy, the sentences known only to Fuad and his officials on the court.[16]

Late at night on Sunday, 19 August, Muhammad Abu al-Saʿud al-Hasibi lay on his mattress, unable to sleep. Suddenly, the late-night calm was disturbed by the opening of the barrack gates. It was unusual for people to be moving about at that time of night. Al-Hasibi rose quietly, so as not to disturb his five sleeping cell mates, to ask the guard what was happening. Speaking softly, the guard replied that prisoners had just been brought to the building in chains. Al-Hasibi moved to the window to see what was happening in the courtyard below. He saw a group of fifty or more prisoners and heard the general Khalid Pasha giving orders to imperial troops to remove their chains. He could hear the officers speaking with the prisoners, advising them that 'those who want to perform their ablutions should hurry, and those who wished to designate executors should do so now, and those who want to perform a whole-body ablution should wash now.' The last suggestion was particularly ominous. Muslims perform ablutions on arms, feet, and face before all prayers, but they reserve the ritual washing of the whole body for death.

Looking down on the condemned men, al-Hasibi saw people he recognised. There was Mustafa Bey al-Hawasli, the Kurdish *agha* (military commander), who commanded a detachment of police in Dr Mishaqa's quarter at the time of the massacres. Here he was now, flanked by two of his nephews, at the mercy of the authorities. Months after his execution, the Islamic court of Damascus conducted probate on al-Hawasli's estate and found he was heavily in debt to Christian creditors. His debts far exceeded the net value of his property, leaving his estate nearly Pt. 50,000 in debt. Perhaps al-Hawasli hoped the massacres might eliminate his Christian creditors or that stolen Christian property might offset his debts. Whatever the reason for his conviction, al-Hawasli was about to take that secret with him to the gallows. Al-Hasibi could identify eight more men—perhaps not his closest associates or even people he particularly liked, but Damascenes of rank, all now being herded toward execution. 'May God have mercy on them,' he prayed, 'since many of them are innocent of any crime.'[17]

Shortly after sunrise, Dr Mishaqa rose to the sound of commotion on the street. Opening his door, he could see bodies hanging from makeshift gallows. Papers attached to the dead men confirmed their crime: convicted of murder and condemned to death. Mishaqa was shocked to see notables of the city hanging like common criminals. These were people he knew personally. He saw the lifeless body of Mustafa Bey al-Hawasli, his adversary in Suq Wadi Barada and the man who denied him shelter on the first day of the massacres. Whatever Mishaqa's views of the Kurdish agha, it must have been shocking to confront his body hanging from a post. Mishaqa had personally denounced two others to Fuad Pasha as men 'who wounded me with weapons' and now found them both hanging nearby. The condemned men, fifty-seven in all, were hanged in public places near intersections and coffeehouses, in some cases near the places of their crimes. The men faced the gallows in silence in the dark of night while Damascus slept. Their bodies were left hanging all day for Damascenes to witness.[18]

At 2:00 p.m. on Monday, 20 August, a phalanx of 800 soldiers assembled a group of 110 prisoners in the Takiyya complex to the west of the city. Some of those held with al-Hasibi in the military barracks had been taken to the Takiyya to join this group, raising everyone's concerns after the previous night's hangings. Al-Hasibi and his cell mates sent one of their servants 'to see where they are taking them.' All 110 were members of the police and irregular army units convicted of 'participating in the disturbances with weapon in hand.' The condemned assembled in the Takiyya, where soldiers tied them together and told them they were being transferred. Their journey ended abruptly in a field in al-Marja, where they watched as officers distributed a single bullet to each of the 800 soldiers and then ordered them to fire on the prisoners. The prisoners' servant went running back to the barracks to report what he had witnessed: 'They took them to al-Marja and lined them up and shot them with bullets.' It was carnage, with 800 men firing on the 110 prisoners at random, 'each prisoner shot with two bullets, three, four.' Inevitably, some of the condemned were initially wounded and tried to escape, only to be cut down by the soldiers' sabres. 'No one in the town was aware this was happening,' Shaykh al-Ustuwani recorded. 'The people struggled with this tribulation. You would see one man whose relative was hanged struggling to cut him down, while his friend [recovered the body of a relative] killed by firing squad on the soil of al-Marja.'[19]

By the day's end, Fuad Pasha's soldiers had executed 167 Damascene Muslims from all levels of society and every quarter of the city for their role in the Christian massacres. The scale and severity of the executions shocked Damascenes to the core—just as Fuad Pasha had hoped. In a report to Grand Vizier Ali Pasha in Istanbul, Fuad noted that 'among those hanged were some of the greatest notables of the city. No account was taken of their rank or dignity. The city has been struck with terror.' Here indeed was 'exemplary punishment.' For these harsh measures, Damascenes came to call Fuad Pasha 'Father of the Rope.'[20]

While striking terror into Damascenes, Fuad Pasha also sought to impress the European powers that the Ottomans were taking meaningful action to bring justice to the Christians of Syria. His door was open to all foreign consuls, and he used his conversations as a barometer reading of their governments' views. The consuls were impressed at first. Many had doubted that Fuad would dare to impose capital punishment on Damascene Muslims.

However, European views were changeable. Before long, the consuls revised their opinion and argued that the punishments fell well short of the magnitude of the crime, noting that only 57 men had been executed for the murder of 5,000 Christians (the 110 executed by firing squad were accused of armed robbery but not murder). One British official told Fuad that because it would have taken thousands to kill so many Christians, 'the great bulk' of those who had committed murder 'were yet free' and 'that it was to be hoped the others would not escape.' The British commissioner Lord Dufferin, in his first meeting with Fuad Pasha, applied a multiplier of 3 to the 5,000 Christian victims to declare that as many as 15,000 should be on trial and facing capital punishment. Clearly, the Europeans wanted to see more executions—many more executions.

The European diplomats also wanted to see more prominent people brought to account. At the top of their list were some of the leading theologians of Damascus, members of the Majlis, whom they accused of encouraging the violence against Christians, such as Shaykh 'Abdullah al-Halabi, the dean of the Damascene 'ulama, and 'Umar Efendi al-Ghazzi, the mufti of Damascus. And, of course, the former governor, Ahmad Pasha, who most of the consuls held fully responsible for the massacres.[21]

No doubt Fuad was frustrated that his severe punishments had made such a fleeting impression on the European consuls. Yet he too wished to see more notables held to account. Despite his many meetings with the leaders of the Muslim community, they categorically refused to break ranks and denounce fellow notables. On 7 August, Fuad dissolved the influential Majlis and placed many of its leading members under house arrest. When this measure failed to secure cooperation from key notables, Fuad raised the stakes. Immediately after the executions, while the city was still in a state of shock, Fuad ordered the arrest of Shaykh 'Abdullah al-Halabi and 'Umar Efendi al-Ghazzi, and had the two men imprisoned in the army barracks until they faced trial before the military tribunal. Among Damascenes, word of these arrests 'caused sorrow and pain to the hearts of the Muslims and enflamed their anger yet again.' But the arrests spread fear among the elites that if they continued to withhold their cooperation from Fuad's investigation, they might well face stern justice themselves.[22]

In line with arresting prominent Muslim theologians, Fuad sought to discredit their arguments justifying violence against Christians. European consuls frequently accused Abdullah al-Halabi and 'Umar al-Ghazzi of stirring the masses to hatred against the Christians. Leading Damascene religious scholars reportedly claimed that Christians were contractually bound to observe certain fiscal obligations, and restrictions on their behaviour, to claim protection under Islamic law. The Christians' failure to respect those obligations, even when they had been overturned by Tanzimat legislation, made the shedding of Christian blood permissible—or so the theologians reasoned. Fuad worked to dispel such arguments to impress the foreign powers, to prevent further violence against Christians, and to uphold the Tanzimat reforms.[23]

At the end of August, Fuad invited mosque preachers from across Damascus to a meeting in his office. Shaykh al-Ustuwani was among them. After expressing his respect for the work of the preachers, Fuad shared a copy of a sermon drafted by Mahmud Efendi Hamza (1820–1887), a Muslim theologian and member of the Majlis who was decorated by the sultan for his role in rescuing Damascene Christians during the Events. Fuad recommended Mahmud Hamza's sermon to his guests and suggested that 'they might preach from it or make similar points' in their own sermons the following Friday. The preachers had little choice. They took their copies of the text and preached the state-sanctioned sermon the following Friday. It read, in part:

> And now, ye men, fear God and know that injustice makes those who commit it hateful and disliked in this life and leads them to torments in the life to come.
>
> Is not he who sheds the blood of a Moslem, a Zimmi [*dhimmi*—i.e., a Christian or Jew] or a refugé [refugee, here referring to Christians from surrounding villages who sought refuge in Damascus] the most unjust man?
>
> Yea; is not he that violates a Moslem, Zimmi or refugé woman the most unjust man?
>
> Yea; is not he who robs the property of a Moslem, a Zimmi or a refugé the most unjust man?

Yea; is not he who destroys the house of a Moslem, Zimmi or refugé the most unjust man?...

How did the perpetrators of those acts then feel justified in committing them? How did they think it lawful for them to shed blood, insult women and rob property?... Indeed this evil work is no less than pulling down one foundation of religion...and whoever says that it is not right to chastise and punish those perpetrators he is one of these deceivers and offenders.

Wake ye up ye creatures of God from your sleep and slumber and submit to the decrees of God and obey your rulers. Those who despised the law of God and disobeyed it and offended the Zimmies shall be punished in this life and a severe punishment awaits them in the life to come.[24]

The text conveyed Fuad's message precisely. The Muslims of Damascus had violated God's law, and the Ottoman state was fully justified in punishing 'unjust men' who committed murder, rape, theft, or arson against Christians with the full weight of the law, leaving to God to impose justice in the afterlife.

Even if Damascenes accepted the message of the sermon, they still objected to Fuad's use of capital punishment, which many saw as a violation of their interpretation of Islamic law. In Islam, there are four schools of jurisprudence (in Arabic, *madhhab*), each drawing on the same sources (the Qur'an, the sayings of the Prophet

Muhammad, analogical reasoning, and the consensus of the community) but coming to different conclusions on certain points of law. The Hanafi madhhab was the official school of law in the Ottoman Empire, whereas the Damascenes subscribed to the Shafi`i school. The two schools have very different views on capital punishment. For Hanafis, murder is a capital offense regardless of the religion or social standing of the victim; in Dr Mishaqa's words, 'thus the learned [should face death] for [killing] the ignorant and the Muslim for the dhimmi.' The Shafi`i school, on the other hand, maintains that a Muslim should face capital punishment only for the murder of another Muslim. The murder of a non-Muslim was punishable only by the blood price, a fine set by the court as an alternative to capital punishment (the Muslim victim's family had a choice between demanding the death penalty and accepting the blood price instead), with Christian and Jewish victims incurring only half the blood price of a Muslim victim. 'Thus, should a Muslim kill a large number of Christians,' Mishaqa explained, 'no more should be exacted of him than the blood price. The Muslims of the city believe they have suffered an injustice since some of them were sentenced to death,' instead of being assessed a fine, in keeping with their Shafi`i interpretation of Sharia law.[25]

For Fuad, working on behalf of the Ottoman government, capital punishment was a legitimate instrument to punish the guilty and restore order. His challenge was to limit the numbers and prominence of those he put to death to avoid driving the Damascenes to revolt, while inflicting severe punishment on enough people in positions of authority to restore Ottoman control over the restive city and to satisfy the minimum European expectations of justice.

There were other means to inflict severe punishment than hangings and the firing squad. Starting on 22 August, 139 civilians accused of armed violence were clapped into wooden manacles and marched to Beirut, sentenced to life imprisonment with heavy labour. Another 145 Damascenes were sent into exile in Cyprus and Anatolia, convicted of having taken part in the violence *without* a weapon. Another 186 were condemned to fixed periods of hard labour and kept in Damascus to work on the roads. Yet more extensively, starting 27 August, hundreds of young men were drafted into the army. As Dr Mishaqa reported, the authorities 'locked the gates of the city and prevented the people from entering and leaving and began to arrest disgraced Muslims to conscript them into military service.' For years, Damascus had failed to provide its required share of conscripts for imperial service. Fuad set himself the goal of pressing two thousand Damascene men into the army. Many of those sent into exile or to prison with hard labour were diverted to military service to help make up this ambitious target. In this way, Fuad took troublemakers off the streets of Damascus and put them in uniform to serve their sultan.[26]

Of all those arrested for taking part in the Damascus massacre, the most controversial by far was the former governor, Ahmad Pasha. Dr Mishaqa and many of his colleagues in the consular corps believed that Ahmad Pasha played a direct role in provoking the massacres. Others, like British consul Brant, held Ahmad Pasha guilty of crimes of omission, of failing to use his authority and armed forces to intervene and put a stop to the violence before it got out of control. Views in the Muslim community of Damascus were also divided, with some like Shaykh al-Ustuwani condemning the former governor for his 'wickedness' and others, like his biographer al-Bitar, extolling his virtues in glowing terms as an enlightened governor and pious Muslim. It remained to be seen what view the Ottoman government would take of Ahmad Pasha and his failings.

Following his ignominious withdrawal from Damascus in late July, Ahmad Pasha was summoned to Beirut to meet with Fuad Pasha. After what by all accounts was a catastrophic interview, in which Ahmad threw himself at Fuad's feet in a desperate plea for clemency, Fuad asked the former governor to surrender his sword, placed him under arrest, and dispatched him to Istanbul for trial. Once back in the imperial capital, Ahmad faced predictable hostility from Grand Vizier Ali Pasha and his government. His failures had led to unprecedented destruction in a provincial capital and embroiled the empire in dangerous diplomacy with the European powers. The Sublime Porte stripped him of his honours and demoted him from the ministerial rank of 'pasha' to the simple honorific of 'agha.' Ali Pasha sent Ahmad Agha back to Damascus by return steamer to face trial, claiming that 'his conduct could only be adequately inquired into or dealt with' at the scene of his crimes. Ahmad Agha returned to Damascus in disgrace on 15 August. His trial opened that very day and lasted one week.[27]

The trial of a former governor required a higher level of court than the extraordinary tribunal that was then examining the notables and commoners of Damascus. Fuad created a special court-martial to hear Ahmad Agha's case. The new governor of Damascus, Mu'ammar Pasha, as well as the commander of the garrison, Halim

Pasha, presided over a distinguished group of ranking military officers and two civil servants to hear the case. Fuad served as prosecutor, leading the questioning of Ahmad Agha in what proved to be the
trial of the century for Ottoman Damascus.[28]

Given the tremendous sensitivity surrounding the case, the trial
was conducted in secret. Yet the rumour mill was hard at work. By
all accounts, Fuad Pasha's primary concern was to ascertain if the
massacre had been the result of a conspiracy or something more
spontaneous. Of all the foreign diplomats in Damascus, British consul James Brant was closest to Ahmad. In their conversations at the
time of the massacre, he found the former governor inconsistent on
the question of a broader conspiracy: 'I observed to Ahmet Pasha
that when the Mussulman boys were sent to sweep the streets of the
Christian quarter in chains, precautions should have been taken to
repress a possible outbreak; he replied that it would have been use-
less, as the plot was prepared, and, had not this pretext been found,
some other would have served the purpose.' Yet at other points in
their conversations, Ahmad insisted that no such plot existed. In
his trial, Ahmad 'utterly denied all knowledge of any such plot,' and
conspiracy was eliminated as a factor in the deliberations.[29]

In his defence, Ahmad Pasha claimed that his ability to intervene
in the growing tensions of July 1860 had been critically undermined
by the Ottoman government's redeployment of the Damascus garrison for service in the Balkans earlier in the year. This had been
Ahmad's recurring complaint with the government, that he had
been left with too few soldiers to ensure security in his province and
had been forced to recruit irregular forces to make up the shortfall—
irregulars who proved criminally insubordinate and played an

active role in the violence. The court-martial conducted an audit of the number of regular Nizami troops under Ahmad's command in Syria in July 1860 and concluded that he had more than 1,200 soldiers at his disposal—less than full strength, but more than enough to have intervened to stop the violence. After all, Amir 'Abd al-Qadir intervened effectively with his 1,100 Algerian veterans to protect as many as 85 percent of the Christians of the city.[30]

The court-martial completed its hearings by 23 August without coming to a verdict. There seemed little doubt of Ahmad Agha's guilt in the catastrophic breakdown in order that resulted in the destruction of the Christian quarters with a loss of some five thousand lives. But would Fuad Pasha actually condemn a former governor, one of the highest-ranking officials in the Ottoman administration, to death? The British consul-general, for one, doubted that he could: 'Such an event would shock every feeling of the Mahometan populace and soldiery to its very centre, and raise a storm of fanatical fury which it might be dangerous to evoke.' Lord Dufferin, appointed as Britain's representative on the European commission dispatched to 'advise' the Ottoman authorities following the massacres in Mount Lebanon and Damascus, took a very different view: anything short of a death sentence would grievously undermine Ottoman authority. In their first meeting in early September, Dufferin found that Fuad spoke of Ahmad 'with some slight degree of favour,' as if probing to see if the British might support clemency. When they met the next day, however, Fuad continued to test Dufferin's reactions, hinting that 'he had thoughts of ordering [Ahmad's] immediate execution.' Dufferin 'said nothing to discourage' Fuad, remarking that 'the greater the vigour he displayed [against Ahmad] the less occasion would the Commission find for usurping his authority.' It was a hardly veiled threat that might have tipped the scales of justice in Fuad Pasha's mind.[31]

On 7 September 1860, the court-martial issued its verdict: 'Given that the former *mushir* Ahmad Agha was in command of the army at the time of the distressing Damascus events, and that he recruited and dispatched [irregular] imperial soldiers deliberately to the Christian quarters in order to kill Christians, rob their money and property, and burn their houses, and that he gave the villains every assistance, do these reasons make it necessary for the death sentence to be imposed on the aforementioned man?' The twenty members of the court unanimously concurred that, on the basis of the evidence, it was necessary to condemn Ahmad Agha to death and appended their seals to the document. In addition to the former governor, the court-martial passed death sentences on three other high-ranking civil and military officers for their roles in the massacres in Damascus, Hasbayya, and Rashayya.[32]

The following day, soldiers led the condemned men to an enclosed yard in a barracks. Though closed to the public, the executions were witnessed by soldiers and officers. Fuad respected Ahmad Agha's wishes to hold his funeral and be buried in the mosque of Shaykh Muhyi al-Din ibn 'Arabi, the venerated Islamic mystic, in the al-Salihiyya quarter on the slopes of Mount Qasiyun. Contrary to expectations, contemporary reports suggest that Ahmad's execution did not make a big impression on the Damascenes, given that it took place 'in an enclosed yard, and, so far as regarded the inhabitants, in a manner entirely private.' Yet Fuad could now reassure European critics that Ottoman justice had reached the very highest levels of government and that he had not hesitated to impose the ultimate punishment on those found guilty.[33]

That Damascus was calm and European demands were satisfied was, for Fuad, an ideal outcome. Although there remained a great deal of work to be done, Damascus was stable for the moment. Immediately after the executions, Fuad set off for Beirut, where French troops had landed over two weeks earlier under the energetic command of General Charles de Beaufort d'Hautpoul (generally referred to simply as General Beaufort) and where the European commissioners were beginning to assemble to decide the fate of Mount Lebanon and Damascus. His sudden departure concerned the Christians, but the Muslims of Damascus were pleased to see Fuad go. 'May God compensate the Muslims for his wickedness,' Shaykh al-Ustuwani confided to his diary on the day of Fuad's departure. 'There is no power and no strength save in God.'

Over the course of the forty-three days he spent in Damascus, Fuad Pasha largely completed the task of punishing the guilty. One gets the impression from his conversations with European diplomats that Fuad had no stomach for capital punishment, and indeed there were very few executions after 8 September. He resisted European pressures to put leading theologians such as Shaykh Abdullah al-Halabi and 'Umar Efendi al-Ghazzi to death, arguing that he could not secure a single Muslim witness willing to give evidence against either man. Playing on European notions of the rule of law, Fuad argued to foreign officials that it would be unjust to execute a man without firm evidence. Yet these same notables proved obstructive to

Fuad's overall mission of restoring Ottoman control in Damascus, and he had his own reasons to wish them gone. However, the fate of the notables in the Majlis was for the moment deferred.

Fuad's work in Damascus was far from complete. His ultimate goal was to preserve Ottoman sovereignty in Syria against the threat of European intervention. Punishing the guilty was but one part of his task. The Europeans would also judge him, and the Ottoman government, by how well they dealt with the humanitarian crisis confronting the Christian survivors of the Events. Fuad had made little progress in addressing the plight of Christian survivors and the reconstruction of those parts of the city destroyed during the Events. The return of stolen property; compensation for losses; reconstruction of destroyed shops, homes, and places of worship; and interim measures to stem the flow of Christian refugees from Damascus to Beirut and provide accommodation for the homeless Christians in Damascus—these tasks and more remained to be done before Fuad could claim to have restored order as well as to have punished the guilty.

7

Beetles and Scorpions

As Fuad Pasha entered Beirut in September 1860, he was reminded at every turn of his unfinished business in Damascus. Thousands of Christian refugees from both Mount Lebanon and Damascus thronged the streets and public spaces across the city. A few men, but mostly the refugees were women and children— widows and orphans. They had escaped Damascus with their lives and the clothes on their backs. Destitute, they were dependent on the Ottoman government and foreign-aid agencies for everything. Punishing the guilty was only the beginning. The essential task of rebuilding houses and restoring lives still lay ahead. In case Fuad got distracted, the refugees were there to remind him.

The Damascus refugees were in Beirut because Fuad Pasha had sent them there. He visited the Citadel in late July, shortly after arriving in Damascus, and found an estimated eleven thousand Christians sheltering within its walls. They wanted to leave the Citadel as soon as possible but did not feel safe in Damascus. They were terrified of the mob that bayed nightly for their blood. They had no homes to return to, for nearly all had been burned to the ground. Because they were already homeless, it was better to be in a city that was safe for Christians. They wanted to go to Beirut, with its large Christian population, extensive European presence, and the rumoured arrival of a French army to protect the Christians from further harm.

Following his meeting in the Citadel, Fuad Pasha offered mules and provisions at the government's expense to carry Christian refugees from Damascus to Beirut. The first caravan set off on 2 August, arriving in Beirut two days later with some three thousand survivors, all 'in a very sad plight.' In the course of August and September 1860, thousands more followed as the refugees began to evacuate the Citadel.[1]

Once in Beirut, however, the Damascene Christians faced serious hardships. They found the city, which had a prewar population of between forty and fifty thousand, already flooded by refugees from the war in Mount Lebanon. The local government in Beirut was overwhelmed trying to provide food and accommodation for more than ten thousand destitute Lebanese Christians. As thousands more Christians from Damascus began to make their way to Beirut, local churches and international-aid agencies did their best to provide from their insufficient resources. Beirut simply did not have the capacity to cope with an emergency of this magnitude. While continuing to support the caravans to Beirut, Fuad also sought ways to accommodate homeless Christians in Damascus itself. The solution he adopted was radical and did little to calm Muslim hostility.[2]

On 16 August the government in Damascus ordered Muslim residents of the al-Qanawat quarter to evacuate their houses to provide accommodation for homeless Christians. Rich and poor, notables and commoners, the measure applied to everyone without exception. The al-Hasibi family were long-standing notables of al-Qanawat, and news of their evacuation reached even their son Muhammad Abu al-Sa'ud in his prison cell. The police gave residents just twenty-four hours to vacate their properties and 'inflicted all sorts of wickedness upon the people, not giving anyone extra time,' al-Hasibi lamented in his diary. 'God forbid, there were respectable families who had lived in Qanawat for two hundred years and had never left their homes.' In the rush to clear their houses, residents were forced to deposit their personal belongings in the streets, where thieves had a field day. 'That day in Qanawat was like the day the Christian Quarter was plundered,' al-Hasibi claimed with some hyperbole (after all, no one was murdering the residents of al-Qanawat or setting fire to their houses). He viewed the forced evacuations as one more collective punishment inflicted on respectable Damascenes innocent of any violence against the Christian community—a view shared by the preacher of the Umayyad Mosque. 'The greatest distress, shame and fear fell over Damascus,' Shaykh Muhammad Sa'id al-Ustuwani observed, as the evacuation measures were extended to Muslim homes in the districts of al-Qaymariyya, Bab Tuma, and al-Jura. 'I saw homeless [Muslims] with no idea where to go carrying their clothes to the Umayyad Mosque and other places.'[3]

As soon as the Muslim proprietors had vacated their homes, Ottoman officials made them available to Christians from the Citadel. Some two hundred families left the castle for al-Qanawat at the end of

August. They were the bold ones. Most Christians chose to remain in the relative security of the Citadel, fearing the reaction of the Muslim community evicted from their own homes. The authorities provided armed guards to reassure the nervous Christians of their security in the Muslim quarters. It was a tense situation, with resentful Muslims cursing Christians in the street by day and stoning their houses by night. However, over time, ever more Christians accepted to move from the Citadel into vacated Muslim houses. By the end of August, Fuad discontinued government assistance to refugees fleeing Damascus for Beirut. By mid-September, the last of the Christian refugees vacated the Citadel after nearly seventy days of confinement.[4]

That still left eight thousand Damascene Christians in Beirut, nearly half the estimated twenty thousand refugees thronging the city. Unlike earlier waves of migrants, who brought trade and prosperity to the rapidly growing port town, these people were destitute. And they were angry. Once their gratitude for survival had passed, resentment for all they had suffered took its place. They vented their anger against the Ottoman authorities, who could barely keep up with refugee demands for food and accommodation. And they targeted the caravans of Muslim convicts and conscripts making their way from Damascus to Beirut, taunting the manacled men as they marched under armed guard toward the garrison:

'Where are the axes? Where are the swords?'

'Tough luck that they caught you, you'll end up in a noose!'

'Tomorrow we're heading back to Damascus. We'll drop by your place and take your house.'[5]

By September, the authorities in Damascus were actively calling on refugees in Beirut to return. Fuad Pasha sent flyers to be posted in churches and public places in Beirut advising Christian refugees that 'Damascus is at present under the protection of His Imperial Majesty [the sultan] and in the enjoyment of tranquillity and security. It is incumbent upon you to return to it; you will find there all that you require as regards lodging and subsistence.' Misery in Beirut drove some to return. Others needed convincing that it was safe to go back. The fact that Fuad himself had left Damascus and gone to Beirut left many Christians questioning the wisdom of returning to Damascus. But the Ottoman minister had good grounds for turning his attention to the situation in Beirut.[6]

Fuad Pasha's decision to leave Damascus for Beirut was driven by international politics. The Events were front-page news in Europe and the United States. Correspondents in Ottoman lands telegraphed horrific accounts of the violence in Mount Lebanon and Damascus to atrocity-hungry editors in Paris and London. The London *Daily News* published one of the early accounts on 15 July as 'the work of plunder, burning and murder' was still ongoing. The newspaper gave eyewitness evidence of fanatical mobs baying to 'kill all the dogs of Christians, not to spare one, to burn their houses, plunder their property, dishonour their wives, tear in pieces their children, and rid the holy city of all save the true followers of the true prophet.'[7]

These graphic accounts enflamed public opinion, trickling down to popular culture. A contemporary ballad, 'The Sorrowful Lamentation on the 40,000 Christians Massacreed in Damascus,' reproduces the sensational details of the newspaper accounts set to popular music:

Good Christians pay attention to what I now unfold,
The subject now I mention will make your blood run cold,
It's of the Syria massacre where thousands suffered sore,
By the uncivilized Mahometans upon the Turkish shore.

For forty thousand Christians it grieves me to explain,
Were slaughtered without mercy by a Christian taunting train,
They speared and shot them through the heart to please their
*   base desire,*
Their property they plundered and their dwellings set on fire.

It would grieve your heart with pity to see how they were used,
The men at first were put to death, the women then ill used,
Each village street was covered all over with a crimson flood,
We hope their souls are happy as they suffered for their God.[8]

With the press and the music hall taking up the cause of Syrian Christians, Western governments were swift to respond. The French daily *Constitutionnel*, a mouthpiece of Napoleon III's government, asserted that France was 'prepared to see the government of Syria pass into firmer hands' than those of the Ottoman government that had proven so powerless to protect its Christian minorities. Napoleon III's foreign minister, Edouard Antoine Thouvenel, proposed the dispatch of a European intervention force to protect Syrian Christians and pressure the Ottomans to resolve the crisis to the West's satisfaction. The British government viewed French overtures through the lens of imperial rivalries and interpreted Thouvenel's call less as a humanitarian intervention than a first step, 'and it is a very long step, towards ending the rule of the Sultan on the borders of the Mediterranean,' a prospect that British commentators found 'scarcely less alarming to us than it is to the Turks.' British commentators discerned a French strategy to dominate the African and Asian shores of the Mediterranean and, through the Suez Canal project, to control Britain's access to India. Britain was thus committed to preserving Ottoman sovereignty in Syria to deny French ambitions.[9]

Though unwilling to contribute ground forces to the French-led humanitarian expedition, Britain fully supported the convening of an international commission to oversee Ottoman measures to resolve the crisis in Syria and Lebanon, and to restructure the dysfunctional system of governance in Mount Lebanon. As the European commissioners began to assemble in Beirut, and the French army reached the shores of Lebanon, Fuad took his leave of Damascus, the better to contain European initiatives that directly threatened Ottoman sovereignty in Syria.

The French intervention force of six thousand soldiers, dispatched by Emperor Napoleon III to protect Syrian Christians from further violence, reached the Lebanese coast in mid-August, and its soldiers were encamped in the pine forests to the south of Beirut. From Fuad's perspective, they were a ticking time bomb. He worried that the large European army would reawaken communal tensions across Syria and that the smallest incident might spark renewed violence. Fuad's correspondence with the commander of the French force, Marquis General Charles Marie Napoléon de Beaufort d'Hautpoul

(1804–1890), only reinforced Fuad's concerns about the clear and present danger posed by this army.

Beaufort was a fighting general determined to secure battle glory for himself and his soldiers. When addressing his troops, Beaufort invoked the dubious precedents of the French Crusader Godefroy de Bouillon (1058–1100) and Napoleon's campaigns in Egypt and Syria (1798–1801), promising his soldiers that they too would make history in the Levant. But to do so, they would have to engage an enemy in battle, swords drawn. The enemy in this case were those who killed the Christians: the Druzes in the first instance, but Syrian Muslims were a viable alternative. Ideally, Beaufort would have liked to resettle Christian survivors in their home villages in Mount Lebanon and kill any Druzes who got in his way. This was Fuad's nightmare. If the French engaged the Druzes in Mount Lebanon, Fuad believed the conflict would draw in the Druzes of the Hawran and their Bedouin allies 'so that, opposed to greatly superior numbers, the French honour might possibly become involved, when it would be quite impossible to say where the warfare or intervention might end.' Such a scenario would almost certainly lead to the dispatch of more European soldiers and the lengthening of the military expedition, putting Ottoman rule over Syria in jeopardy.[10]

When General Beaufort reached Beirut, he was a man in a hurry. The terms of reference imposed by the European powers placed a time limit of six months on his mission. They also required Beaufort to work in concert with the Ottoman authorities. Upon arrival in the port of Beirut on 20 August, Beaufort drafted a letter to Fuad Pasha: 'A French expeditionary corps, which the Emperor [Napoleon III] placed under my command, has been sent to Syria...with

the principal goal of aiding Ottoman troops in the mission of energetic repression which they must pursue under Your Excellency's
high command. I need not tell Your Excellency how desirable it is for
that repression to be as prompt as it is energetic.' Prompt, energetic
repression: Fuad had grounds for concern.

As a precaution against Beaufort's zeal, Fuad requested the
French general to deploy his troops in Christian territory around the
Beirut-Damascus Road, where they would be least at risk of engaging
the Druzes in hostilities. Beaufort, denied the opportunity to lead
his men in battle, was outraged. As Beaufort later recounted, 'When
the paper containing the proposition was handed to [me, I] tore it
in two in the face of the gentleman who brought it.' Beaufort's reaction redoubled Fuad's resolve to move to Beirut as soon as possible to
keep the French under control, to ensure that there was no reason to
dispatch more foreign troops, and to see that their mission ended on
schedule six months later. Anything else risked total catastrophe for
the Ottoman Empire. Yet to contain Beaufort, Fuad had to turn his
attention from Damascus to Mount Lebanon, and in his absence the
city proved highly volatile.[11]

Throughout the tense summer months of 1860, Dr Mikhayil Mishaqa remained in Damascus. The injuries he sustained on the first day
of the massacres left him bedridden and convalescent for thirty days
in the home of his friend Muhammad al-Sawtari. He never contemplated joining the Christian caravans to Beirut—he simply wasn't
strong enough to make the journey. Five weeks after the attack,
Mishaqa still could not use his right hand. His son Nasif served

literally as his right-hand man, drafting Mishaqa's correspondence and conducting consular business on his father's behalf. Nasif also kept Mishaqa fully up to date on the news of the town and regularly reported to Consul Johnson in Beirut.[12]

As he recovered from his near-death experience, Dr Mishaqa began to count his losses as well as his blessings. It was remarkable that he and all his family survived the horrors of July 1860. Their house had been stripped down to the brickwork, but, as it was situated between Muslim homes, it was left standing—one of a small number of Christian houses spared from arson attack. However, the Mishaqas lost everything else. In his free time, Mishaqa sat with his family to draw up an inventory of their personal losses, which he sent to Consul Johnson in Beirut in the hope of compensation. It makes for a poignantly intimate list, the material profile of an upper-middle-class Christian family in nineteenth-century Damascus.

The list suggests that Mrs. Mishaqa was a richly dressed and well-accoutred woman. She claimed to have lost gold and jewellery worth Pt. 115,800 (more than £1,000) and clothes worth Pt. 50,900 (£462). Dr Mishaqa, by comparison, had a modest wardrobe valued at just Pt. 13,760. Their children also claimed to have lost extensive clothing and property: their sons Nasif (twenty-two years old, Pt. 32,723), Salim (sixteen years old, Pt. 8,000), Ibrahim (nine years old, Pt. 3,000), and Iskandar (about two years old, Pt. 1,500), as well as their seven-year-old daughter, Salma (Pt. 6,000), whose wardrobe clearly exceeded those of some of her brothers.

The list also confirmed Dr Mishaqa's cultural depth and professional breadth. He valued his private library at Pt. 50,000, his personal pharmacy and medical instruments at Pt. 60,000, and his musical instruments at Pt. 1,400. He also suffered extensive financial losses when his house was plundered: Pt. 125,000 in cash and the records for Pt. 156,000 in loans. In addition to personal property, there were the standard household items: silverware, pots, pans, and plates, Syrian furniture, European-style tables and chairs, clocks, pocket watches and chains—the list goes on for pages. The total of the Mishaqa family's claims came to more than Pt. 1 million in all (nearly £9,700)—an enormous sum. Of course, Dr Mishaqa might have padded the figures a bit, knowing that the authorities were likely to repay only a part of all claims. But to give some sense of the magnitude of the family's losses, in October 1860 Mishaqa was offered (and declined) a job as a doctor in a new Anglo-American hospital for a monthly salary of Pt. 1,250 (£11). At that rate of pay, it would have taken Mishaqa 71 years to earn back what he claimed to have lost in the Damascus Events.[13]

Dr Mishaqa's list of stolen property confirms his image as a devoted father, a scholar, a doctor, and a gentleman. Yet one line in his inventory shatters that image entirely: a list of miscellaneous 'purchased goods' comprised of 'merchandise, fabrics, wooden goods, a female slave, a mare, a mule, several horses and different tools.' The word *jariya* ('female slave') looks so incongruous among the livestock and household goods that you might be forgiven for thinking you have misread the handwritten Arabic. But no. To confirm the point, Mishaqa added a note in his cover letter to Consul Johnson:

We found the female slave who fled from our home [during the Events] and asked for her to be returned.

She was taken to the government who has refused to deliver her to us. She has been placed in the house of the *Naqib* (the leader of the descendants of the Prophet Muhammad), the government claiming that the Sultan has emancipated the slaves—even though no such thing has ever occurred in Damascus, and no one has heard of such a measure. So I have included her price in the list of stolen goods.[14]

Dr Mishaqa was in fact correct in claiming the Ottomans had not banned slavery in Damascus. It wasn't until February 1871 that the government notified Damascene traders that they were no longer allowed to sell slaves, 'and the places where slaves were sold were closed.' Even then, pilgrims returning from Mecca continued to smuggle slaves to Damascus in small numbers: two in 1871 and 'male and female slaves valued at Pt. 3,000' in 1872. In 1860 these restrictions had yet to take hold.[15]

Whatever his personal views on slavery, Consul Johnson did not respond to Dr Mishaqa's callous reduction of a young woman to an item of merchandise. The issue of slavery was very divisive in the United States in 1860 and was a major contributing factor to the outbreak of the Civil War in April 1861. This revelation would have appalled Mishaqa's admirers among the American Protestant missionaries. The Boston-based American Board of Commissioners for Foreign Missions was staunchly abolitionist. On the other hand, the American ambassador in Istanbul, James Williams, was an outspoken advocate for slavery and later resigned his diplomatic mission to adhere to the Confederate cause. In terms of this issue, Mishaqa revealed himself opposed to his adoptive church but fully aligned with his ambassador.

More immediately, Dr Mishaqa was destitute and needed financial assistance to begin rebuilding his life. He did not draw a salary for his work as vice-consul. The job brought other benefits like tax exemptions and discounts on tariffs. Under present circumstances, those benefits were of no value to the cash-strapped Mishaqa household. Mishaqa hoped to leverage his consular position to pressure the Ottoman authorities to indemnify him for his losses. In the first instance, Mishaqa wrote to Consul Johnson in Beirut asking him to intervene with the Ottoman government on his behalf. 'I no longer have a thing to live on,' Mishaqa pleaded. Given that the attack on his house was in fact an attack on an American diplomatic mission, aided and abetted by Ottoman soldiers, and that the local government had taken no measures to provide security, Mishaqa believed Johnson should have an easy time making the case. But Consul Johnson refused to take up Mishaqa's claims, explaining that he believed the Ottoman government would want to complete their own procedures before making compensation for damages and theft. His response provoked a rare outburst of anger from Mishaqa: 'I submit to Your Excellency that the Government does not want to give anything to anyone, not now and not later, not to us and not to others. If they give anything, it will be against their wishes.'[16]

Truth be told, the Ottoman treasury had no funds to compensate Damascenes for their losses in 1860. According to Ottoman figures, the annual revenues for the whole of the province of Damascus in 1860 totalled Pt. 22.6 million (£205,000). The best they could do was to offer individual Christians a per diem of 1.25 piastres—a penny a day—to provide enough money for their daily bread. Even those payments, which cost the Ottoman treasury between Pt. 500,000 and 600,000 per month, were running forty days in arrears. Fuad Pasha would need to find a mechanism to raise the necessary funds to finance the reconstruction of Damascus. Until they had money, the Ottoman authorities relied on bureaucratic hurdles to delay action on Christian claims for compensation.[17]

To be fair, the Ottomans were doing more for Dr Mishaqa than they were for most Damascene Christians. As one of the few Christian homes left standing, the Mishaqa house had been among the first designated for restoration at government expense in August 1860. After thirty days sheltered in the home of Muhammad al-Sawtari, the Mishaqas moved into a vacant Muslim house in their old neighbourhood. From their temporary accommodation, the Mishaqas could keep an eye on the renovation works on their own home. Yet the move was not without its dangers. British diplomats reported that Mishaqa faced open hostility from Muslim men who 'cursed the [US] Consul and his religion, assuring him that he need not think Fuad Pasha would be always at Damascus to protect him.' Mishaqa made no reference to these threats in his own reports, but they clearly contributed to his growing sense of anger at the situation in which he and the Christians of Damascus found themselves in the months after the Events.[18]

Anger was the dominant mood in Damascus as summer turned to autumn. The Muslim majority could ill disguise their fury at the series of punitive measures that Fuad Pasha and his administration had imposed on them in the aftermath of the Events. Mass arrests, public executions, exiles and imprisonment, an unprecedented conscription of men for the army, the forced evacuation of whole urban quarters—Muslims feared their own government as a threat to their lives and property. Moreover, the economic life of the city had been devastated, with shops in the markets frequently closed either out of precaution or in protest. Worse yet, Fuad Pasha would not allow the returning pilgrimage caravan from Mecca into the city, denying Damascus one of its most important religious and economic events of the year. All of this to satisfy a now-despised Christian minority and their European patrons. Who would protect the Muslims from such calamities if even the Ottoman state refused to do its duty to protect Islam and its law?

The Christians of Damascus were also angry. They had suffered unspeakable violence; lost friends and family, their homes and businesses; and been forced to shelter in the Citadel for weeks, fearing that at any moment the mob might break through the gates to massacre them all, just as had happened in Hasbayya, Rashayya, and Dayr al-Qamar. They had to live on a penny a day, in evacuated Muslim houses without a stick of furniture or bedding and endure daily insults and nightly threats from resentful Muslims in the city. For all the government's talk about rebuilding their houses and returning their stolen property, bodies lay unburied in the ruins of the Christian quarters, and few Damascene Christians were any closer to resuming their shattered lives. They had suffered, were suffering still, and wanted to ensure that the Muslims suffered too.

In September 1860, the government ordered the evacuation of Muslim houses in Qanawat al-Barrani, the latest in the series of house clearings to accommodate Christian refugees. Shaykh 'Abd al-Rizaq al-Qadiri, a respected Muslim cleric, piled his personal property on the street outside his house. He was accosted by a group of Christian men who accused him of holding property stolen from Christians. When he tried to defend himself from the charge, they pointed to a carpet and an overcoat they claimed had been stolen from their homes, and dragged the venerable shaykh to the Saray, where he was arrested and imprisoned pending investigation. The Christians had found a new way to use their limited power to make Muslims suffer.

As Shaykh Muhammad Sa'id al-Ustuwani recorded,

> Over the past five days, the Christians have been circulating, men and women alike, and accusing Muslims of crimes. They might grab a man and say to him 'That's my coat' or accuse him of theft or arson. A Christian woman might seize a Muslim woman and say 'That is my dress, show me what you have, what's under your coat?' Whatever she was wearing, the Christian would say 'That's mine!' They pursued such charges [with the authorities] who decided in the Christians' favour. Anxiety and distress spread among the Muslims.[19]

Dr Mishaqa vented his own frustrations at Ottoman justice by denouncing fellow Damascenes he accused of taking part in the plunder of his house. He accused his neighbour Muhammad al-Mukhallilati, an artisan with a shop in the clog-makers market, on the testimony of Mishaqa's servant, who had just returned from

Beirut. More dramatically, Mishaqa accused Husayn al-Qaltaqji and his son of assaulting his wife and of stealing her jewellery, a horse, a mule, and the female slave who featured in Mishaqa's list of stolen property. Crucially for the viability of his claim, Mishaqa named a Muslim notable as an eyewitness to al-Qaltaqji's crime. The slave was pregnant, Mishaqa claimed Qaltaqji had made her pregnant, and Mishaqa refused to have her back, demanding her full price—Pt. 5,500 (£50)—instead: 'I also request judicial punishment against Qaltaqji and his son for armed attack against the consulate and robbing the women of this household, and theft of the female slave, and that in accordance with the law to serve as a deterrent to others.' The police subsequently arrested the men and opened investigations into Mishaqa's charges.[20]

Dr Mishaqa provides very few details about the slave woman. In his documents, he never mentions her name, age, or origins. We don't know where Mishaqa bought her, but slaves were still traded and taxed in mid-nineteenth-century Damascus. For instance, Shaykh al-Ustuwani wrote how officials detained pilgrims returning from the Hajj in 1860 'searching for coffee and slaves to tax.' Although she was certainly not Muslim herself (even in the Tanzimat age, a Christian would not want to, or be allowed to, buy a Muslim), she was made pregnant by a Muslim, so her child would be born a free Muslim. As Mishaqa wrote, 'Given her pregnancy, which has been imposed on her [the closest Mishaqa comes to confirming she was raped], we are not able to accept her.' It would have been impossible to raise a Muslim child in a Christian household in mid-nineteenth-century Damascus. Even allowing for the difficulties posed by her bearing a Muslim child, there is a real sense of repudiation in Mishaqa's correspondence. He subsequently declined the government's offer of Pt. 3,000 compensation for the female slave, demanding her full purchase price of Pt. 5,500. He never mentioned her again, and we have no idea what became of either the enslaved woman or her child.[21]

Returning to the Christian allegations against Muslims in Damascus, the string of accusations heightened Muslim hostility toward the Christians of Damascus. 'Some of them say "We were wrong to leave some of the Christians [alive], for had we killed them all there would not be any left to complain [to the authorities],"' Dr Mishaqa reported. 'Others say "We killed the beetles and left the scorpions,"' or in other words, those murdered in the July Events were harmless, whereas the survivors had the capacity to 'sting' Muslims. Predictably, on 4 October 1860, anonymous figures chalked crosses on the doors of houses inhabited by Christians as if marking them for attack. Panic swept through the Christian community of Damascus, provoking renewed flight to Beirut. Fuad Pasha had not been gone one month, and already the fragile equilibrium he had struck between Muslims and Christians in Damascus had come undone.[22]

Fuad Pasha had spent the month in Lebanon containing General Beaufort's martial enthusiasm. After meeting with the French commander in Beirut, the two agreed on a plan of action. Fuad would sail to the southern Lebanese port of Sidon to join an Ottoman campaign force of five thousand soldiers. Ottoman forces would march through the Druze southern district of Mount Lebanon to reestablish Ottoman control and to arrest all local leaders implicated in attacks on Lebanese Christians. Beaufort and his French forces would then escort Christian refugees back to the mixed town of Dayr al-Qamar, proceeding inland from the coast to reinforce the Ottomans in their pacification campaign. The French would thus be in position to strike should Druze leaders resist arrest or engage in hostile action against Ottoman troops. It wasn't the action that Beaufort yearned for, but it was action enough to secure the French general's cooperation. As Fuad confided to British commissioner Lord Dufferin, the plan gave Beaufort 'the opportunity of employing his troops without allowing him to assume an independent line of action.' In this way Fuad hoped that the campaign would be confined to 'a military promenade.'[23]

Fuad set off from Beirut to Sidon on 23 September to begin his march through Druze territory. Word of the Ottoman army's approach preceded him, leaving Druze leaders ample time to flee to the Hawran to evade capture. Only compliant Druze villagers remained to receive Fuad and his forces. No shots were fired in anger, and by the time that French forces reached Dayr al-Qamar, the town was perfectly calm for the resettlement of Christian survivors. Fuad congratulated Beaufort on a successful campaign. For his part, the French general complained to all and sundry about how Fuad had let all the Druze brigands escape punishment. Fuad had to prevent Beaufort from leading his men into the Hawran in hot pursuit and ordered him instead to accompany Ottoman forces to the town of Zahleh in order to continue confidence-building measures and the restoration of Christian refugees to their hometowns. Fuad persuaded Beaufort to put his soldiers to work helping Christians in both Dayr al-Qamar and Zahleh to clear the rubble and rebuild. Here was the genius of Fuad, in getting the French soldiers to lay down their rifles to pick up shovels and hammers instead. With the French soldiers occupied and their commander neutralised, Fuad returned to the Druze stronghold of Mukhtara, where he had made his headquarters. It was while he was in Mukhtara that Fuad learned of the deteriorating situation in Damascus. With Mount Lebanon stabilised, Fuad set off immediately for the Syrian capital, which he reached on the morning of 10 October.[24]

The cannons in the Citadel fired a salute to mark Fuad's unexpected return to Damascus. He met with his officials to take stock of the situation. Tensions were on the rise between Muslims and Christians, causing panic and renewed Christian flight to Beirut. Fuad was determined to stem the flow of refugees, fearing that the new wave would encourage the European powers to intervene in Damascus.

The representatives of the five European powers—Austria, France, Great Britain, Prussia, and Russia—had recently arrived in Beirut and convened the first session of the Syrian Commission on 5 October. As agreed among the European powers, the commission was tasked with 'repression, reparation and reorganization': to investigate the causes of the violence in Syria and Lebanon and to ensure that those responsible were brought to justice, to determine the extent of Christian losses and to ensure that they were compensated, and to review the administrative arrangements in Mount Lebanon to prevent any future recurrence of violence. Fuad was determined to keep the administrative inquiry restricted to Mount Lebanon, with its large and diverse Christian population and its particular institutions of governance. He did not want the Europeans to interfere in Damascus, which was an Ottoman provincial capital with an overwhelming Muslim majority. However, the flow of refugees from Damascus alerted the commissioners to the troubles in the city, and in their second session, on 9 October, the French commissioner, Léon-Philippe Béclard, called for the commission to transfer its meetings from Beirut to Damascus to respond to the breakdown in order there. By their presence in Damascus, Béclard reasoned, the commissioners would not only reassure the Christians but would 'determine the punishment of those truly guilty who have yet to be dealt with.' From Fuad's perspective, this was dangerous mission creep.[25]

Fuad Pasha moved quickly to neutralise the situation. The day of his arrival, Fuad dispatched a message to the European commissioners reporting that he found Damascus 'in a state of tranquillity as satisfactory as when I left it.' His Christian sources confirmed that the crosses found on doors had 'most likely' been drawn by a handful of their fellow Christians eager to go to Beirut themselves and hoping to provoke their family and friends to move with them. Yes, the Christian community had panicked, and some had fled the city. But now that Fuad was back, he would restore their confidence and reassure them of their safety in Damascus. The commissioners, he implied, really needed to focus their attention on the problems facing Mount Lebanon. Fuad had everything in hand in Damascus.[26]

But did he? Whoever was responsible for drawing the crosses, they had contributed to a growing Christian panic, and the flood of new refugees to Beirut did not stop with Fuad's return. By British count (and the British were working *with* the Ottoman authorities to discourage flight), some 1,200 Christians left Damascus for Beirut between 4 and 26 October. Fuad needed to reverse the migrant flow and convince Damascenes that it was safe, and their needs would best be met, in their hometown. He also used a bit of coercion. Fuad sent notices to Christian churches in Beirut calling on all Damascene refugees to return to their native city. He also warned that Damascenes would no longer be eligible for state assistance in Beirut but would receive support only in Damascus.[27]

While reassuring Damascene Christians, Fuad still had to address the growing antagonism in the city's Muslim community. His task was made more difficult by European demands for the leading notables of Damascus to be brought to justice. Once the shock of the first hangings and the execution of Governor Ahmad Pasha had subsided, European diplomats took stock of the situation and decided that Ottoman justice still had not gone far enough. The consuls and commissioners singled out the leading members of the religious establishment (the 'ulama) and notables from the influential provincial council (the Majlis) for exemplary punishment. They focused in particular on Shaykh 'Abdullah al-Halabi, the dean of Islamic scholars in Damascus, as 'the chief instigator in the murder of the Christians.' Other notables targeted by European diplomats included the Shafi'i mufti, 'Umar Efendi al-Ghazzi, and former members of the Majlis like Ahmad al-Hasibi, the father of the diarist. Fuad had no sympathies for these men, whom he saw as opponents to his Tanzimat reform measures. However, they were held in such reverence by Damascene Muslims that Fuad needed to proceed with care to avoid provoking outrage that might set off a fresh round of violence.[28]

Shortly after his return to Damascus, Fuad ordered Shaykh 'Abdullah al-Halabi and the other leading 'ulama and notables detained—230 men in all. Most of these men had been in and out of government detention or under house arrest since Fuad first arrived in Damascus in July 1860. The leading notables were taken to the Bayt al-Baltajiyya, where Muhammad Abu al-Sa'ud al-Hasibi was still being held without charge. He recorded the names of each of the notables as they entered the detention facility, leading to a brief but touching reunion with his father: 'I felt the greatest joy when I saw my father enter, and when he saw me, his eyes filled with tears.' The authorities did not allow al-Hasibi father and son to share a room, although they did put the two men in adjoining rooms.[29]

Muhammad Sa'id al-Ustuwani was a former student of 'Abdullah al-Halabi. He held his teacher in deepest reverence and consistently referred to him as 'the Shaykh.' Al-Ustuwani closely followed news of the shaykh's many sessions before the extraordinary tribunal, waiting outside the courthouse in the hope of catching a glimpse of his mentor. According to al-Ustuwani, witnesses consistently testified to the shaykh's innocence of all charges. In al-Halabi's final appearance before the court on 14 October, the prosecutor focused on his appeal to the men of al-Salihiyya to help extinguish the fires in Damascus on the third day of the violence. Many Europeans, drawing on the accusations of Damascene Christians, claimed that the shaykh in fact had called on the men of al-Salihiyya to join in the attacks on the Christian quarters rather than to douse fires. Yet 'all confirmed the innocence of the Shaykh on that day.'

The detained notables began to grow impatient with their incarceration and repeated questioning by the extraordinary tribunal.

After one session in mid-October, the tribunal dismissed Shafi'i mufti 'Umar Efendi al-Ghazzi and ordered him back to detention. 'After sixty days of questioning I am sent back to the Bayt al-Baltajiyya?' al-Ghazzi asked, incredulous. 'What am I guilty of? What is it that I did in this city?' The members of the tribunal were unable to answer the mufti. They weren't sure themselves. Witnesses simply refused to testify against the Muslim notables, and through repeated interrogations the tribunal had yet to get any of the accused to contradict their original statements.[30]

In the end, it proved impossible to convict the leading notables and 'ulama of capital crimes. Without clear and damning evidence, Fuad would not pass a death sentence. But he could not release the notables without exacerbating Christian fears, provoking further flight to Beirut, and running the risk of European interference. Instead, Fuad pursued a compromise solution, by finding the notables guilty of 'not having used their influence over the people to stop the uprising against the Christians.' For this lesser crime, Fuad explained, 'I have condemned some to life imprisonment or for fixed periods in a citadel, and others for a period of exile.' Shaykh Abdullah al-Halabi was condemned to life imprisonment, al-Hasibi's father to fifteen years, and the Shafi'i mufti 'Umar Efendi al-Ghazzi to ten years. The sentences were harsh, but families could hold out hope for a reprieve or amnesty. The condemned were dispatched to Beirut on 20 October for transport into exile in Famagusta on the island of Cyprus. The sentences gave rise to a popular saying in Damascus for anyone in a difficult situation: 'Brother, they cast me in this Famagusta and left.'[31]

Once Fuad passed judgement on the city notables, he began to wind down the work of the extraordinary tribunal in Damascus.

Many of those who had been denounced by Christians and held under arrest were released back into the community without charge. Some Christians complained that the government had grown lax and was not serious about bringing the guilty to justice, but the emptying of prisons eased tensions in the Muslim community. It was a difficult balancing act, for Christians continued to abandon the city. Another thousand reached Beirut on 31 October, and by 3 November there were no more than two thousand Christian adults left in Damascus. 'If the stream of emigration continues unchecked,' British commissioner Dufferin observed, 'none but the scanty dregs of the Christian population will remain.' Fuad and the Ottoman officials in Damascus would need to push the refugees from Beirut and pull them back to Damascus, but that would take time.[32]

After two intensive weeks in Damascus, Fuad Pasha returned to Beirut. Although Christians continued to flee Damascus, there were ample soldiers in place to ensure security. The Muslim community was subdued. The exile of so many 'ulama and notables had struck fear without provoking outrage. The situation in Damascus was thus stable. The most immediate threat to Fuad Pasha's mission now lay in Beirut, where the five commissioners from the European powers continued their deliberations as the Syrian Commission. The commissioners had shown growing interest in expanding their labours into Damascus, and Fuad needed to focus their attentions on Mount Lebanon instead.

Fuad Pasha chaired his first meeting of the Syrian Commission on 26 October 1860, and he took the opportunity to update the five European commissioners on his recent work in Damascus. He upheld the conviction and exile of eleven leading notables as a shield against further European accusations of laxity toward the Muslim elite in Damascus. Looking over the faces of the commissioners, Fuad could see they weren't entirely persuaded. Those savage Europeans believed that the situation called for more hangings. They had such different stakes in the Syrian crisis. The foreign diplomats seemed driven by short-term goals of satisfying domestic public opinion by imposing exemplary punishment on those who massacred Syrian Christians. Some might even have looked to use the crisis in Syria to extend their own imperial interests in the Levant—the British, who advocated the preservation of the Ottoman Empire, suspected France and Russia of such ulterior motives. Fuad had his eyes on the long term: restoring law and order and advancing Ottoman reforms in a crucial Arab province. He needed to strike a modus vivendi between Muslims and minorities. And he needed to preserve Ottoman sovereignty over Syria. Given the differences in their perspectives and priorities, Fuad knew that the European commissioners were no less a threat in Syria than General Beaufort and the French army.

Consider, for instance, the British commissioner, Lord Dufferin (1826–1902). Britain had a long-standing commitment to the preservation of the territorial integrity of the Ottoman Empire. Britain pursued this policy across the nineteenth century to prevent conflicts between the European imperial powers over geostrategic territory that the Ottomans were too weak to defend, and to serve as a buffer between Russia and continental Europe. One would expect Dufferin's policies in Syria to have been sober and moderate. Yet his proposal, in light of the renewed outpouring of Damascene Christians to Beirut in October 1860, was nothing short of ethnic—or in this case, sectarian—cleansing. Declaring the Damascus massacres 'a criminal attempt by Islamism on Christianity,' Dufferin believed that Islam as a whole, not just individual Muslims, should face punishment: 'Europe, as it has the power, so has it the right, to inflict on Islam some signal and permanent mark of its displeasure.' By way of punishment, Dufferin proposed a population transfer between Damascus and Jerusalem:

> Might not, then, the double object of securing an asylum for the [Damascus] refugees, and of exacting from their persecutors an appropriate retribution be accomplished, by our requiring that this should be made the occasion for the restoration to Christendom of the city of Jerusalem; and that the fugitives from Damascus should be established in the quarter which [Jerusalem's] Moslem population shall be invited to vacate. In the streets of its holiest city, Islam has poured out Christian blood like water. Of so great a crime the forfeiture of Jerusalem would be no inappropriate memorial.[33]

Admittedly, Dufferin made this proposal to British ambassador Bulwer in Istanbul, not to Fuad himself. Still, it gives insight into the thoughts of the man: European supremacy, civilisational conflict, Crusader restoration, collective punishments imposed on Jerusalemites completely innocent of crimes against Damascenes—there were many grounds to object to Dufferin's proposal. With allies like Dufferin, Fuad had to manage the European commissioners with great care.

The French commissioner, M. Léon-Philippe Béclard (1820–1864), was a more obvious danger for Fuad, given Napoleon III's active imperial interests in the Levant. Already in early October, Béclard had proposed moving the meetings of the Syrian Commission from Beirut to Damascus—a suggestion that the Ottomans were quick to reject. In November 1860, Béclard suggested that Damascus be treated like a 'city taken by assault' and that a draconian tax be applied on all its Muslim residents to compensate Damascene Christians for their losses. Anticipating resistance from Muslim notables, Béclard proposed seizing 'a certain number of hostages, chosen from among the richest and most influential of the inhabitants,' and making them responsible for raising the money, with a strict deadline. If they missed the deadline, the rich hostages' own property would be expropriated by the state. Given their hostage status, Béclard held out the possibility of inflicting further punishments on uncooperative notables. Whatever the merits of the proposal, it had no grounding in the rule of law. Such provocative and counterproductive proposals raised by European commissioners like Dufferin and Béclard were clearly conceived with European public opinion in mind rather than the long-term stability of Ottoman Syria. They redoubled Fuad Pasha's resolve to keep a close watch on the Syrian Commission and to keep it as far as possible from Damascus.[34]

The Syrian Commission was entrusted with three tasks: repression, reparation, and reorganisation. Fuad insisted to his European colleagues that he had addressed the question of repression in Damascus through the work of the extraordinary tribunal there. He thus focussed their attention on the pursuit of justice in Mount Lebanon and on the activities of extraordinary tribunals convened in Beirut and in the Druze town of Mukhtara. The protocols of their meetings confirm Fuad's success in that regard. However, he acknowledged that the work of reparation was still in its initial phases in Damascus. Masses of stolen property had been recovered in Damascus, and committees in the city quarters had overseen the return of property to its rightful owners, to the best of their ability. This still left the major question of funding the reconstruction of damaged properties in Damascus. All agreed that the Damascene Muslims should contribute a major part of the cash for reconstruction and that a tax should be imposed to fund indemnities to Damascene Christians. Fuad referred the matter to the Sublime Porte for decision on the size and modes of implementing the punitive reconstruction tax.

While the authorities in Damascus waited for Istanbul's response on indemnities, Christian refugees continued to flood from Damascus to Beirut. The commissioners renewed their quest to move their deliberations to Damascus, to assess the problems there for themselves and to reassure Damascene Christians and stem the tide of migrants. To make the point, French commissioner Béclard read a petition signed by the spiritual heads of the five main Christian denominations expressing their willingness to return to Damascus on condition of a security guarantee from the Syrian Commission. The suggestion provoked a strong reaction from Fuad Pasha, who insisted that the commission had no authority to issue such a guarantee and that the Christians should put their trust in their government: 'To give the Christians the confidence they lacked, if further measures were needed, [Fuad Pasha] would take them, and towards that end he would always welcome the advice of his colleagues [the

European commissioners]. In transgressing this limit, however, the Committee would overstep onto the rights of his Government.' To defuse the heated exchange, the matter was deferred to a later meeting for decision.[35]

Fuad continued to resist every attempt by the commission to visit Damascus. In a long and stormy session at the end of November, the French commissioner raised the matter once again. Fuad argued forcefully that the timing was wrong, given that the Porte was due to announce its plans for an extraordinary levy on Muslims to indemnify the Christians in Damascus. A visit by Europeans at that moment would compromise the integrity of the measure by making it appear that the Porte was acting under European pressure rather than on its own initiative. He would have to advise the Porte to postpone the announcement of the extraordinary levy on Muslims indefinitely. That argument made no impression on the commissioners, who put the matter to a vote and roundly overruled Fuad Pasha. The commissioners went home to pack their bags, and Fuad prepared for a hard week of damage control.

Damascus was in no state to receive a high-level European delegation at the start of December 1860. The economic life of the city had ground to a halt, and the markets were dead. The Muslim majority was more antagonistic toward Europeans than ever, and tensions between the Muslim and Christian communities in Damascus remained at a fever pitch. The Christians huddled in fear and cold, with no money for food, wood, or charcoal to feed themselves or heat their borrowed accommodations. Only a minority remained in Damascus—the majority of Christian survivors had already demonstrated their lack of confidence by taking refuge in Beirut. There was nothing Fuad could do about any of these problems before the Europeans reached the city. The one thing he could do, and should have done long before, was hire workmen to begin clearing the rubble and the human remains that still choked the streets of the Christian quarters. The day before the commissioners arrived, Fuad ordered one thousand workers and three hundred mules to be deployed to clear the rubble. They worked straight through the commissioners' visit, hauling out rocks and soil and disinterring the remains of Christians killed in the massacre nearly five months earlier. The bones were taken to the Christian cemetery for burial.[36]

The commissioners set out from Beirut on 29 November and reached Damascus on 1 December. As they made their way through the city markets, they were openly insulted by the Ottoman soldiers on duty, but the local government received them 'with honours suitable to their status.' They visited the homes of Christian families in Damascus to see firsthand how they were faring. For the most part, 'Their supply of bedding, blankets and cooking utensils were inadequate.' The commissioners met with Christian religious and communal leaders to hear their concerns and to learn what measures needed to be taken to stop the continual flow of Damascene refugees to Beirut. A delegation of clergy from six denominations set out their recommendations: punishment of murderers and 'of those who violated our harems'; compensation of losses; rebuilding of churches and convents, of houses and workplaces 'according to their original form'; and the provision of security against future threats. Finally, the commissioners walked through the ruins of the Christian quarters to see for themselves the extent of the devastation, while the workers continued to clear the rubble and bones from the streets.[37]

The commissioners made a point of calling on Muslim notables who had distinguished themselves by sheltering Christians from the mob during the massacre. The most illustrious of all was, of course, the Algerian amir 'Abd al-Qadir. In the intervening months, the amir had been honoured by several governments for his gallant actions. The Ottoman sultan awarded him the Mecidiyye, first class; the French bestowed the Grand Cross of the Legion of Honour upon him; and US president Lincoln sent a brace of fine pistols in a display case. (Queen Victoria conveyed her admiration through Her Majesty's consul without sending a more substantial token of her esteem.) Yet the more he was honoured by foreigners, the more estranged 'Abd al-Qadir became from the local government and Damascene notables. They came to see him as a foreign agent while he condemned their criminal passivity during the massacres in July, 'for they went on smoking their pipes and would do nothing.' In his conversations with European officials, 'Abd al-Qadir divided the Muslims of Damascus into twenty-four parts: 'Of these, twenty were actively inciting to a massacre; of the remaining four parts, three and a half wished such an event, but did not excite, and the remaining half portion alone were really opposed to such a proceeding.' In 'Abd al-Qadir's view, Fuad Pasha should have executed ten times the number of Muslims to reimpose respect for the Ottoman government in Damascus.[38]

Such views endeared 'Abd al-Qadir neither to the Muslim notables of Damascus, who had welcomed him to their ranks when he first moved to the city in 1855, nor to Fuad Pasha, in his mission to restore Ottoman authority in Damascus. Among European proposals for the future reorganisation of Syria was a plan to create an Arab kingdom in Syria with 'Abd al-Qadir on its throne. The plan had few supporters—it was seen as a transparent bid to extend French influence over Syria—but the fact it was proposed at all marked the amir as a threat to Fuad's mission.[39]

One of the measures the European commissioners had called for to improve security was general disarmament in Mount Lebanon and Syria. Fuad hesitated to apply the measure with any vigour because it would have provoked widespread Syrian resistance. Many Damascenes hid their weapons in the women's quarters of their homes, where Ottoman soldiers could not search without provoking outrage. However, Fuad took advantage of the commissioners' calls for disarmament to act against 'Abd al-Qadir's Algerians. He still had a force of more than 1,100 armed men who were answerable only to the amir. In November the government began to forcefully disarm 'Abd al-Qadir's retainers. When the commissioners asked Fuad Pasha to explain this, he reminded the European diplomats of their repeated demands for disarmament and noted that, although he had offered to leave 'Abd al-Qadir 'a body-guard of 200 armed men... it was out of the question to make an exception in favour of the whole 1,500.' Whatever the gains for Fuad and his administration, the sudden and forceful disarmament of Algerians raised Christian fears anew. The Algerians had proven to be the only reliable defenders of the Christians in Damascus. 'If they complete this process,' Dr Mishaqa observed, 'then the remaining Christians in Damascus will leave and I might be among them.' But the commissioners did nothing while in Damascus to stop the process.[40]

The commissioners did not convene a formal meeting while in Damascus. They waited until their return to Beirut to resume their work. And when they did, they placed their focus squarely on Mount Lebanon. Perhaps their visit impressed on the commissioners the enormity of the work that remained to be done in Damascus. They certainly showed less interest in intervening in Damascus and more willingness to leave the Ottoman authorities to take responsibility for the city's reconstruction. After resisting the commission's demands to visit Damascus for months, Fuad could not have hoped for a better outcome.

By the end of 1860, Fuad Pasha had seen off the two greatest European threats to Ottoman rule over Syria and Lebanon in the aftermath of the massacres. His measures to contain the military ambitions of General Beaufort held until the end of his mission. The French army never engaged in a single combat operation for the duration of its stay. The French general toured Mount Lebanon and the Lebanese coastline in search of an opportunity for battlefield glory. Each of the campaigns that Beaufort proposed—in the Hawran, the Laja', and the Bekaa—was deftly deflected by the Ottoman minister. The worst violence associated with the French army was revenge killings by Maronite villagers against Druze civilians while under the protection of Beaufort's troops. Although the murders were atrocious, they did not lead to any fresh disturbances. Fuad secured all the benefits from the French army's presence—reassuring the Christian population in Mount Lebanon and assisting in rebuilding their homes and villages—without allowing the army to disrupt his plans.

The one battle that Fuad lost to Beaufort related to the extension of the French mission in the Levant. As the six-month term of Beaufort's commission drew to a close, the French general sought by all means to extend his stay. The Ottomans and the British tried to veto the request, but Napoleon III insisted that his forces should remain in Lebanon to protect the Syrian Commission until the commissioners had completed their work. The French negotiated a formal extension of Beaufort's term from mid-February to 5 June 1861. Fuad accepted the defeat with good grace but ensured that there was no reason for the French to stay beyond June.

To the north of Beirut, the Nahr al-Kalb (Dog River) carves a path through dramatic cliffs to empty into Jounieh Bay. Here, since antiquity, armies that believed they had conquered Lebanon have commemorated their campaigns with monumental inscriptions. The Egyptian pharaoh Ramses II, the Babylonian king Nebuchadnezzar II, the Romans, the Byzantines, and the Mamluks have all left their mark on the cliff face overlooking the medieval bridge spanning the river. As a last gesture before leaving Lebanon, Beaufort commissioned a monumental stele to honour his emperor, himself, his commanders, and his units:

1860–1861

Napoleon III

Empereur des Français

Armée Française

General de Beaufort d'Hautpoul

Commandant-en-Chef

Colonel Osmont

Chef d'État Major General

General Ducrot

Commandant d'Infanterie

A list of the nine military units deployed in Lebanon completes the inscription. With no heroic slogans or any glorious battles to record, the inscription simply suggests, 'We were here,' lest history forget. In June the six thousand French troops boarded ship for the journey home. After a round of touching farewell parties, General Beaufort set sail on 10 June, the last member of the expeditionary force to leave Lebanon.

After returning from Damascus in December 1860, the Syrian Commission focused the remainder of its meetings on restructuring the governance of Mount Lebanon. The Ottomans and the Europeans agreed that the division of Mount Lebanon into Maronite and Druze administrative districts, introduced after an earlier round of sectarian conflict in 1842, had proven a catastrophic failure. However, they all had different ideas on how best to restructure the region's administration. The commissioners debated a wide range of proposals in the spring of 1861 before coming to an agreement on a new unified structure under a single Ottoman Christian governor. The plan satisfied European demands that the Christians of Mount Lebanon should be governed by a Christian, and the Ottomans were satisfied that the new structure drew Lebanon closer to Istanbul's direct rule. In May the commissioners withdrew to Istanbul for an ambassadorial-level conference to conclude the agreement, and on 9 June the Ottomans and the European powers ratified the agreement establishing the new governing structure of Mount Lebanon. The new system of government, known as the 'Mutasarrifiyya,' or 'governorate,' ushered in a period of unprecedented peace and stability in Mount Lebanon that was to endure until the outbreak of the First World War, in 1914.[41]

Although Fuad Pasha had staved off the many threats posed by the European powers in the aftermath of the massacres, Damascus remained in a state of crisis. Tensions persisted between Muslims and Christians. The flow of Christian refugees from Damascus to Beirut continued unabated. The city's economy was in deep recession, with both trade and manufacturing yet to recover from the impact of the Events. The serious work of reconstruction had still only just started by the end of 1860, hindered by a lack of funds to pay for the rebuilding of Christian homes, workplaces, and churches. Fuad Pasha and his Ottoman soldiers proved able to provide security in Damascus, but the new obstacle to restoration in the city was money. It would be impossible to persuade Christians to return to the city if their losses were not to be indemnified. To advance the reconstruction of Damascus and the reconciliation of its communities, the government would have to find the means to pay.

8

Rebuilding Damascus with Money Grown on Trees

O n the first anniversary of the Events, in July 1861, Fuad Pasha urged the governor of Damascus to organise a dinner party where the Christian and Muslim elites of the city could mix and mingle socially. The events of the past year had deepened the cleavages in Damascene society, and Fuad was determined to see life brought back to some semblance of normality—although everyone knew that relations between Muslims and Christians remained far from normal in the strained city.

A Muslim notable named Abu Ahmad al-Salka hosted the dinner party in his home, lit by one thousand lamps, with a band playing Arabic music for the occasion. The lights sparkled off the medals and insignia of the bishops and consuls who rubbed shoulders with Muslim notables and government officials. Dr Mikhayil Mishaqa, the US vice-consul in Damascus, was among the two hundred men invited. He would have enjoyed the opportunity to be out in society once again, after a slow recovery from his injuries and the general turmoil that had overtaken his city. The guest list had been carefully curated. None of the Muslims present had been implicated in the violence. The governor joined the party after guests sat down to dinner, only to be called away to the new telegraph office by urgent messages. The telegraph office had opened just three weeks earlier, and this instant form of modern communications had attracted widespread interest. All the same, it was a bit self-important of the governor to withdraw to deal with his telegrams. Or perhaps the gathering wasn't entirely to his liking.[1]

Dr Mishaqa's host could afford to throw such a lavish dinner. Through his connections to Christian survivors of the massacre, Abu Ahmad al-Salka had recently received an exemption from the extraordinary tax imposed on the Muslims of Damascus to help pay for the reconstruction of the Christian quarters. Only those Muslims known to have intervened to protect Christians were spared from this punitive tax. Hence, the lights shone brightly in the Salka household, and the band played on into the night.[2]

The mood was much darker in the other houses of Damascus. Just a month earlier, the majority of Damascene Muslims had been presented with a stiff bill for the Christian indemnity fund that was all the more unwelcome coming after the economic shocks of the past year. The mood among the Christians of Damascus was just as sombre. Their homes still lay in ruins, and the indemnities they were being offered in most cases promised to pay as little as half the total of their losses. It felt as though everyone's life was on hold and at risk on the first anniversary of the Damascus Events.

Money was the problem. The devastation wrought on the Christian quarters and on the economy of Damascus would cost a fortune to repair, and the Ottoman treasury was depleted. The expenses of modernising the army and the catastrophic Crimean War forced the Sublime Porte to take out its first public loan on European markets in 1854. Borrowing as a means of dealing with cash shortages proved a slippery slope. Further loans followed in 1855, 1858, 1859, and 1860, on ever worse terms, reflecting declining confidence in the Ottoman economy, taking the empire down the path to eventual bankruptcy in 1875. Neither Fuad Pasha nor the Ottoman governor in Damascus could count on Istanbul for help. The reconstruction of Damascus would have to be financed primarily from local sources.[3]

Given the state of the Damascene economy in 1861, it would take some creative accounting to generate reconstruction funds from practically nothing. Ottoman officials looked for any assets that they could use instead of cash to indemnify Christians for at least part of their losses and to start reconstruction. They played for time, drawing out the repayment schedule, and they found creative means to devalue Christian claims to enable the provincial treasury to stretch its limited cash resources as far as possible. This left the whole agenda of reconstruction fraught with uncertainties and anxiety as the local government struggled with the seemingly contradictory challenges of rebuilding and restoring normalcy with little or no financial resources in post-massacre Damascus. Yet the government had no choice. Without reconstruction funding, Damascus would never recover, and its estranged communities would never reconcile. Someone would have to pay. The question was who.

The European representatives on the Syrian Commission returned to Beirut from their one visit to Damascus in December 1860 impressed by the magnitude of the challenge of rebuilding the Christian quarters. For the remainder of their mission, they focused on Mount Lebanon, leaving Damascus to the Ottomans to solve—with the one exception of the indemnity tax that the European powers believed was essential to finance reconstruction. The Europeans were determined to impose a punitive fine on the Muslims of Damascus to serve as further retribution for the Christian massacres. After extensive discussion, the Syrian Commission recommended that the Ottomans create a fund of Pt. 150 million to compensate all Christian losses and rebuild their homes, workplaces, and churches. The Sublime Porte accepted the commission's recommendations in March 1861 but halved the size of the fund to Pt. 75 million 'because of budgetary constraints.' To avoid further European intervention, Fuad waited until the Syrian Commission had completed its work and departed for Istanbul in May 1861, and for General Beaufort and the French army to withdraw from Beirut in early June, before returning to the delicate task of taxing the Muslims to indemnify the Christians of Damascus.[4]

Even allowing for a certain amount of official foot-dragging to see the Europeans out of Syria, it took time to establish a viable system to process Christian claims. Since Fuad Pasha's arrival in Damascus, the Ottoman authorities had encouraged Christian survivors to itemise their losses, divided in two categories: houses and other urban real estate burned by arsonists (*mahruqat* in Arabic), and stolen property (*maslubat*). Starting in August 1860, thousands of such claims were filed by the Christian subjects of the Ottoman Empire, by foreign protégés, and by the different Christian churches in Damascus. Although we have no record of the grand total of all Christian claims, Dr Mishaqa estimated the value of stolen property and real estate losses at nearly Pt. 240 million—far more than the Ottomans had the means to honour. The Ottoman authorities set to work almost immediately to try to build up an indemnity fund. They needed some sense of available resources before they could begin promising indemnity payments to Christian survivors.[5]

The Ottoman authorities engaged in creative accounting to build up the indemnity fund for Christian claims. One obvious strategy was to tax the rich. In the autumn of 1860, as the Ottomans conscripted young Damascenes into military service, the government preyed upon the elite's horror of sending their sons into the army. In September 1860, the government issued some three hundred exemption certificates and sent letters to prominent families with the options of either sending their privileged offspring to fight in the sultan's wars or paying Pt. 20,000 to secure a certificate of exemption. The government might have raised as much as Pt. 6 million had the issue sold out, but in the event it appeared that fewer rich families had the funds to buy out their son's military service than the government had hoped. The British consul reported that only eighty men paid the exemption fee, and Shaykh Sa'id al-Ustuwani could name only eleven families he knew who had actually paid the levy. Rumours circulated about officials selling exemption certificates for far less to line their own pockets, but the Damascenes always suspected their government of corruption. In December the government dropped its price to Pt. 10,000, but still there were few takers. As a result, proceeds from the exemption certificates made but a minor contribution to the reparations fund.[6]

Reasoning that reconstruction required building materials, the authorities found one effective strategy to help underwrite reparations. In December 1860, Fuad Pasha ordered Damascus and villages within a five-hour march of the city to provide 150,000 trees for reconstruction. Nine forestry officials were dispatched to count the trees and assign a quota to orchard owners. Once the tree census was complete, the Reconstruction Council ordered specific quantities of trees from each town quarter and village, ranging from one-half of all trees to the total deforestation of a given site. The impact on the Damascus environment was severe—the denuded gardens being just the latest assault on the once-beautiful city—but here at least the government found money literally growing on trees.[7]

While the government pursued these piecemeal strategies, Fuad Pasha and his advisors struggled with the logistics of the reparation tax to be imposed on the Muslim population of Damascus. No doubt Fuad would have preferred to avoid taxing the Muslims altogether. Following the mass arrests, executions, exiles, and house requisitions, tensions ran high. But Fuad had no choice. The European powers demanded the imposition as a matter of justice: the Muslims of Damascus massacred the Christians and destroyed their homes, so the Muslims would have to pay. Nor did Fuad have an alternative. The imperial treasury was in the red and could make little or no contribution to the indemnity fund. The city would have to pay for its own reconstruction. More specifically, the Muslims and Jews of Damascus, and the other towns and villages of the province, would have to provide the funding for the reconstruction of the devastated Christian quarters. As Christian claims for indemnities flooded his office, Fuad had a good sense of how much reconstruction would cost. What he and his officials didn't know was how much they might reasonably expect to raise from the non-Christian subjects of the province.

Whatever the tax that Fuad might impose, the measure would be deeply unpopular. He needed to ascertain that the sums raised, and paid out to the Christians, were justified. Although no one said it explicitly, the Ottomans had neither the means nor the intention to reimburse the Christians for *all* their losses. Their goal was to provide what the Christians needed to rebuild their homes and enough money to allow them to resume their working lives. Reparation to that extent was in everyone's interests: to allow the Christians to vacate their temporary accommodations in the Muslim quarters and to revive the city's flagging economy. Fuad's challenge was to find a mechanism to verify Christian claims and to implicate the Muslims and Jews of Damascus—the people who would pay the construction bill—in determining the magnitude of reparations.

In April 1861, Fuad created a special commission composed of key government officials—the governor, the police commissioner, the military commander, the treasurer, and the mufti—along with a distinguished group of Muslim notables. Intriguingly, the police commissioner swore each member to secrecy on pain of exile. Over the next few days, more notables were drawn into the commission's deliberations and were forced to take the same oath of secrecy.

'Yet the rumour spread in confidence,' Shaykh Sa'id al-Ustuwani recorded, 'that they were assessing the values of Christian houses and stolen property.'[8]

The formation of the secret committee was clearly the talk of the town. Dr Mishaqa reported on the creation of the committee in early May, adding that two Jewish members had also been appointed to serve. He also noted with interest the vow of secrecy and repeated the rumour that the committee was tasked with evaluating Christian claims. It was unusual to cloak a government committee in such an air of secrecy, and it is striking how poorly the secret was kept. Everyone, it seemed, knew that a group of Muslim and Jewish community leaders was advising Fuad on the final reconstruction bill and that the Christians had no say in the matter. As such, the committee served Fuad's purposes of implicating the Muslim and Jewish elites in the tax that their own communities would have to pay.[9]

Shortly after news of the creation of this secret board circulated among the Damascene elite, the government announced the outlines of the reparations tax to be imposed on the Muslims and Jews of the city and province of Damascus. The grand total came to 90,000 purses (a *kis*, or purse, was an Ottoman unit of accounting worth Pt. 500), or Pt. 45 million, divided between the city of Damascus (25,000 purses) and the four counties surrounding Damascus (35,000 purses), with the remaining 30,000 purses to come from the more distant towns of Homs and Hama and the remaining counties of the province. The tax would be imposed on all residents of the province except the Christians and those Muslims known to have intervened to protect Christians during the massacres. The sum was a far cry from what Dr Mishaqa estimated the total losses to represent (Pt. 245 million), what the European commissioners had recommended (Pt. 150 million), or even what the Sublime Porte had accepted (Pt. 75 million). But it was still a vast sum. By way of comparison, the total revenues for the province of Damascus in the year before the Events did not exceed Pt. 22.6 million—just half the amount of the proposed indemnity tax. The proposed levy raised predictable anxieties among the target communities as an unwelcome addition to the heavy tax obligations already imposed by the cash-strapped Ottoman state after a catastrophic economic year.[10]

Shortly after the plans for the reparations tax were made public, Dr Mishaqa reported further rumours about the workings of Fuad Pasha's 'secret' committee: 'I have recently learned that those individuals appointed by Fuad Pasha to undertake an appraisal of the losses of each Christian's real estate and stolen property worked as ordered and decided that the total sum was about ninety thousand purses.' It was no coincidence that the secret committee's assessment of the indemnity bill converged with the government's proposed indemnity tax. And by attributing the indemnity bill to a secret body of Muslims and Jews, the government distanced both itself and the Christian community from any responsibility for the scale of the bill.[11]

At the end of May 1861, the government sent requests for indemnity-tax payments to each quarter of Damascus and each county of the province. At the head of each list, the government named those Muslims exempted from payment in recognition of their services to protect Christians during the Events. All other Muslim and Jewish subjects were required to pay a contribution toward the indemnity tax in line with the value of their houses, gardens, and other properties. The tax bill divided the total levy into two parts: a general tax on all non-Christians and a particular punitive tax on those who were 'more seriously implicated in pillage or massacre.' To sweeten the pill, Fuad announced a general amnesty for all Muslims of Damascus not already charged and convicted for crimes in the Damascus massacre. The Christians of Damascus could no longer denounce their Muslim neighbours and have them arrested or tried for crimes alleged to have been committed in July 1860. The government also began to release men they had held in prison without charge. The young diarist Muhammad Abu al-Sa'ud al-Hasibi secured his release through this amnesty on 21 July 1861 after nearly a year in detention.[12]

From the moment the government issued the bill for indemnities, all those who were liable for the tax sought to join the list of those exempted. Amir 'Abd al-Qadir and his 1,100 Algerian veterans were of course all exempted, given their central role in rescuing Christians. Suddenly, hundreds of Damascene Muslims approached the amir to request a letter confirming that they were in fact North Africans, and he helped those whom he could. 'This went on until the number of those calling themselves Maghribis [North Africans] reached 5,000 men, protégés of the Amir,' al-Hasibi recalled, 'at which point the [Ottoman] government became annoyed and Fuad Pasha issued an order that only true Maghribis would be exempted from paying the tax.'[13]

Dr Mishaqa was appalled to find that the men who saved his life had not been granted exemptions from the tax. The kavass of the American vice-consulate, Haj 'Ali 'Ilwan, had sheltered Mishaqa with his own body against the violent crowd and had escorted him to safety, and Muhammad al-Sawtari had taken in the wounded Mishaqa and provided him and his family safe haven at the height of the violence and for a month, at great personal risk. Mishaqa called on his superior, Consul Johnson in Beirut, to lobby the Ottoman authorities to have these men exempted. Other consuls were making similar claims on behalf of Muslims they knew who had helped save Christians, but the Ottomans resisted as best they could. Mishaqa's petition for Muhammad al-Sawtari was rejected, and he was assessed an indemnity tax of Pt. 2,000, more than one month's salary for a middle-class Damascene.[14]

Another bold initiative sought an exemption for *all* the Muslims of the al-Maydan quarter in recognition of their success in protecting all the Christian households and churches in their neighbourhood from harm. The Christians of al-Maydan petitioned the Ottoman government in gratitude to their Muslim neighbours for their deliverance. Dr Mishaqa objected strenuously to the effort, arguing that while the Maydanis protected Christians in their own quarter, he believed that they inflicted more violence and damage in the Christian quarters of the old city than the men of any other quarter of Damascus. Moreover, he feared that if the Muslims of al-Maydan secured this concession, Muslims in other neighbourhoods would force the Christians of their quarter to draft similar petitions. However, the al-Maydan initiative failed to secure enough Christian signatures and collapsed, leaving the Muslims of al-Maydan to pay their share of the indemnity tax.[15]

The British authorities, in their role as patrons of the Jewish community in Ottoman domains, pressured the government to exempt the Damascene Jews from the tax altogether. The European powers continued to view the tax as a punishment on the Muslims of Damascus and objected to the Jews, who had played no role in the 1860 massacre, being subject to the punitive tax. For the Ottoman authorities, the tax was less about punishment than raising the necessary funds for reconstruction, and they sought to involve all taxable non-Christian males. They did not want to set the precedent of exempting an entire community. However, through British lobbying and careful negotiations, the Jewish community of Damascus was able to strike an agreement with the Ottoman government to pay a much-reduced contribution of Pt. 150,000 instead.[16]

Despite such efforts to secure exemptions, most Damascenes remained subject to the indemnity tax—and objected strenuously. As Dr Mishaqa observed, 'It was harmful to impose the indemnity tax on the innocent as a way of lightening the burden on the guilty. The innocent are aggrieved that, not having taken part in the plunder, they are fined along with those that did.' Damascenes could not help but believe the guilty, with their ill-gotten gains, were in a better position to pay than those innocent of any robbery. The perceived injustice of the extraordinary levy drove many Syrian Muslims to the brink of revolt. In August 1861 the Ottoman authorities got wind of an uprising among the Muslims of Damascus and intervened with extra security forces before the insurgents could act.[17]

Resentment extended beyond Damascus to the other counties of the province. Druze villagers in the Hawran and farmers in the southern region of 'Ajlun (today in northern Jordan) saw no reason why they should pay extra taxes because of massacres in Damascus. They threatened to rise in armed revolt if the government tried to impose the tax. The authorities in Damascus acted quickly to stamp out the resistance, fearing it might spread to other regions like the bigger market towns of Homs and Hama. The governor dispatched the army to the South of the province, warning the Druzes and 'Ajlunis that they would be forced to pay the army's expenses in addition to the tax, and that they would be financially liable for each soldier wounded or killed in performing their duties. The show of force deterred armed rebellion, but many villagers fled their homes and farms to evade a tax that they lacked the means to pay.[18]

Large-scale revolt was averted across the province of Damascus. However, evasion exceeded compliance, and the government never collected the full indemnity tax. By September 1864, when the government closed the books on the indemnity fund, it reported raising only Pt. 22,567,400—half the total that it had pledged to raise (Pt. 45 million). It was not enough, not nearly enough, to honour the full extent of Christian claims. The question remained if it was enough at least to cover the reconstruction of the Christian quarters and prime the Damascene economy back into activity.[19]

Of course, the Ottoman authorities did not accept Christian claims at face value. The government had detailed records for urban real estate and could determine the value of practically every building within the Damascus city limits. What worried Christian claimants was that the Ottomans were using the market value of houses as the basis for their reparations. Real estate in Damascus depreciated rapidly, and old houses sold for a fraction of their construction costs. Dr Mishaqa estimated that the purchase price of an established Damascene house was one-quarter of its construction cost. Were real estate indemnities to be made based on market value, he warned, the Christians would never be able to rebuild their homes to their previous standard.[20]

Claims for lost property were more complicated. Christian survivors could only approximate the extent and value of their household goods from memory. Dr Mishaqa reflected on the difficulties of documenting losses for 'one who left his home with his family, naked beneath the blows of gunshot and various weapons, whose every possession has been robbed from him down to his instruments and papers,' concluding 'that any legal evidence aside from his obvious misfortune and the testimony of those with knowledge of the state of his house is impossible.' Given the lack of hard evidence, the Ottoman authorities openly suspected the Christians of inflating their claims—and their cash losses in particular. In an age before banks, there was no way of confirming just how much money a claimant might have kept in their home. The challenge for the authorities was to create equitable processes for auditing Christian claims. The local government organised committees with Christian and Muslim members in each of the eight divisions of Damascus to review the claims of Ottoman Christians.[21]

Starting in late June 1861, the local government in Damascus began to award indemnities to Christian survivors of the massacre. The audit committees in each quarter operated in a black box, leaving the people of Damascus to speculate on how the committees decided each claimant's payout. According to Dr Mishaqa, 'A few did not suffer significant reduction in their claims, a few were greatly increased' (Mishaqa suspected 'treachery' here), but the majority of claims were grossly decreased. 'Perhaps the total allocated to one of the claimants in return for reparations [for their houses] and restitution of stolen property would not suffice to rebuild half his house.'[22]

The auditors were forced to be more open in deciding the claims of Syrian protégés of foreign powers. Fuad convened mixed panels of Western and Ottoman authorities to review the losses of each foreign country's citizens and protégés in the autumn of 1861, in line with the capitulatory privileges of Western powers. Each session of the mixed panels was minuted and the records shared with the foreign consulates. The American vice-consulate in Damascus supported claims for two of its Syrian Christian protégés, Yusif 'Arbini and Habib Khalid. Their experiences shed light on how the Ottoman government scrutinised Christian claims.

Yusuf 'Arbini was an Arabic-language teacher at the Greek Orthodox school in Damascus who became an American protégé through his work with the Protestant missionaries. The mixed panel, composed of three American and three Ottoman members, invited him to Beirut in October 1861 to review his claim of Pt. 85,257 for his house, library, and personal possessions. The panel summoned four witnesses to testify to the veracity of 'Arbini's claims. All four men, interviewed individually, confirmed they had visited 'Arbini's house frequently. Their descriptions provide a blunt snapshot of a middle-class Damascene Christian household:

> His house had seven rooms with mediocre furnishings consisting of divans, carpets, tables, chairs, a coffee service, and kitchen implements. He had a good library of some 300 manuscripts and books in Arabic on scientific, historic, religious, and medical subjects worth

between 20 and 30,000 piastres. He also owned some surgical instruments. The claimant was well dressed, as were the rest of his family. His wife wore jewellery typical of the middle class, including two floral sprays in diamonds, a pair of gold bracelets, a pair of gold earrings, and gold coins that she wore on her headdress. A woman of her class typically would own jewels and clothing worth between 15 and 18,000 piastres.

Property witnesses' testimony notwithstanding, the Ottoman auditors openly accused 'Arbini of inflating his claims. He responded by providing character references from a patriarch and some bishops and notables to vouch that he was a man of his word. After three sessions of the mixed panel, convened between October and November 1861, the authorities awarded 'Arbini Pt. 12,000 for the reconstruction of his house and a total indemnity of Pt. 50,000 for his library and personal property, or about 72 percent of his original claim.[23]

The Ottoman delegates on the review panel were far more sceptical of the claims of a second American protégé, Habib Khalid, for Pt. 71,000. In addition to his work in the US vice-consulate, Khalid claimed to practice medicine and law on the side. He gave his annual earnings from these sources as varying between Pt. 18,000 and 30,000, which the panel found to be too wide a salary range to be credible. 'The Ottoman delegates believe he has exaggerated his property claims which exceed what he might credibly have owned given his social standing,' the commission minutes record. They also accused him of claiming more furnishings than his modest three-room house could hold. They rejected outright his claims for Pt. 35,000 in cash savings lost when his home was plundered. Nothing that his property witnesses or character witnesses said swayed the Ottoman authorities. They slashed his claim in half and offered him an indemnity of Pt. 35,000.[24]

Dr Mishaqa, as already noted, submitted property claims totalling Pt. 1,000,408—an astronomical sum. Whether through his personal connections, his position as a foreign diplomat, or the scale of his claim, Mishaqa's indemnity was referred to Fuad Pasha for resolution. Mishaqa provided as much documentation as possible, but because of ill health—he never totally recovered from his injuries and was not strong enough to travel to Beirut to testify—he was unable to attend in person, designating two Christian notables and the mufti of Damascus to speak on his behalf. If Mishaqa hoped he might get special treatment from Fuad Pasha, he was to be sorely disappointed. The Ottoman minister reviewed the evidence for Mishaqa's Pt. 1 million claim and awarded him almost exactly half—Pt. 500,000.[25]

It is clear from these three examples that the Ottoman authorities were exacting in reviewing Christian claims. Bearing in mind that the protégés of foreign powers had the advantage of diplomats to help argue their cases, it is likely that most Ottoman Christian subjects who did not enjoy protégé status would have been in an even weaker negotiating position with the government's claims adjustors. Given that the government raised only half the projected indemnity funds, we can assume that the authorities paid around half of Christians' claims. The awards disappointed the Christian claimants, and many despaired of the injustice of the system. But they needed the money; faced with the choice of taking what was offered or pursuing an appeal, most chose to accept what the government offered.

The government, for its part, did all it could to drag out the repayment process. Buying time was a way to economise. In late June 1861 the government notified claimants of their indemnity settlement in a formal document known as a *mazbata*. The mazbata set out the terms of repayment for both real estate and personal property losses. Those with claims of Pt. 10,000 or less received their indemnity in full in one cash payment. Those with claims in excess of Pt. 10,000 would receive a separate government bond, or *sergi*, for house reconstruction and personal property claims. Sergis were to be redeemed in four instalments, the first falling due forty-five days after the sergi's date of issue and subsequent payments every four months thereafter. For house reconstruction, claimants needed to demonstrate that they had started work to receive their second instalment. This was to prevent those Damascenes who had left with no intention of returning from claiming reconstruction assistance to spend in their new place of residence. Second instalments were paid in timber from the 150,000 trees the government had culled. The third and fourth payments, in cash, were conditional on demonstrated progress toward completing house reconstruction. Indemnities for lost property were disbursed by the same schedule: a first payment forty-five days after the issuance date on the sergi, with three subsequent cash payments every four months. Once they had received the mazbata detailing the repayment of their claims, Damascene Christians often waited weeks for their sergis to be issued, starting the forty-five-day countdown toward their first payments. In this way, payment could be drawn out over fifteen months or more. The government knew

(Top) The gates of the Citadel of Hasbayya. (Bottom) Rashayya.

(Top) Zahleh. (Bottom) Dayr al-Qamar.

(Top) The courtyard of the British consulate in Damascus where thousands of Christians took refuge during the massacre. (Bottom) Another view of the Takiyya al-Sulaymaniyya, used as a detention centre for hundreds of Muslim men arrested after the massacre.

(Top) The Street Called Straight, facing Bab Sharqi (the Eastern Gate),
Damascus, 30 April 1862 in near total ruin. One rebuilt house can be
seen clearly and another glimpsed to the right of the palm tree. (Bottom)
Ruins of the Greek church in the Christian quarters, 30 April 1862. The
logs in the foreground were for reconstruction.

(Top) The new administrative quarter of Marja. This is where the road from Beirut to Damascus entered the city. (Bottom) Marja Square, looking south, showing the central jail, the governor's palace or Saray (with curved roofline), and government buildings, 1895.

(Top) The Suq al-Arwam. (Bottom) A pottery shop in Damascus, 1859. In 1863 the governor ordered benches such as this one to be destroyed to widen the streets and allow through wheeled traffic.

(Top) The Citadel of Damascus. (Bottom) The Suq Midhat Pasha provided a barrel-vaulted arcade stretching hundreds of meters along the Street Called Straight.

(Top) Students at the Maktab ʿAnbar in their school uniforms. These would have been Salah al-Tall's contemporaries. (Bottom) A street in the new Damascus after reconstruction.

it did not have enough money in the treasury to make all payments and hoped to manage its commitments by extending the payment schedule over a longer time frame.[26]

By the autumn of 1861, the government began to pay the first tranche of indemnities. The reparations encouraged the last of the refugees to leave Beirut to return and rebuild. Masons and carpenters went to work in the ruins of the Christian quarters. At long last, reconstruction had begun.

We have photographic evidence capturing the moment when Christians began reconstruction of their homes. In February 1862, Albert Edward, Prince of Wales, eldest son of Queen Victoria, embarked on a grand tour through the eastern Mediterranean. His route took him overland from Palestine to Syria. He visited Hasbayya and Rashayya, where he paid his respects at the sites of the Christian massacres. His caravan reached Damascus on 28 April. The following day, the Reverend Smiley Robson, himself a survivor of the massacres, escorted the prince through the ruins of the Christian quarters. 'We saw specially the ruins of the Greek Church and the house of a rich Christian, which once were beautiful, and are now a heap of ruins. We also went up an old minaret and had a good view of the desolate houses where once 25,000 Christians lived prosperously,' the prince recorded in his diary.[27]

Overwhelmed by the scale of the destruction, the Prince of Wales did not see what his official photographer, Francis Bedford, captured in his memorable images of Damascus: the very first stage of the reconstruction of the Christian quarters. In one photograph of the Street Called Straight, looking east toward Bab Sharqi, Bedford captured one house on the left with a second-storey room nearing completion. Leaning against the new structure are dozens of logs—part of the owner's indemnity payment in timber. Farther in the distance, near a palm tree, another second-storey room is under construction. Even Bedford's bleak photograph of the remains of the Greek church captures dozens of fresh tree trunks in the foreground, awaiting builders. The images are striking for the devastation and capture the magnitude of the reconstruction project ahead. But they also document that crucial moment when the Christians of Damascus began to rebuild their homes.

At the end of November 1861, news reached Damascus that the sultan had promoted his minister plenipotentiary and special commissioner to Syria, Fuad Pasha, to the office of grand vizier. Fuad must have been thrilled. He had already served four times as foreign minister, but this was his first appointment to the empire's top job. Fuad left Syria the next day to take up his post. His sudden departure raised Christian anxieties yet again, for no Ottoman official had done more to protect Christians and to constrain the Muslims of Damascus. But the end of his mission should have come as no surprise. Fuad was one of the most influential Ottoman statesmen and champions of the Tanzimat reforms. Inevitably, his services would be required back in the imperial capital (already in August 1861, while still working in Syria, he was reappointed foreign minister). He had dedicated sixteen months to resolving the massacres in Mount Lebanon and Damascus, and never put a foot wrong. He had overseen the trials and punishment of those convicted of taking part in the massacres. He had contained the European initiatives that threatened Ottoman sovereignty in Syria and Lebanon. He had encouraged Christian survivors to return to Damascus. And he had laid the foundations for rebuilding the Christian quarters through the indemnity tax and reconstruction fund. Having resolved the most difficult issues of the Syria crisis, Fuad left the task of implementing reconstruction to the governors of Damascus. That said, the path ahead for his successors, and for the Christians of Damascus, would not be straightforward.[28]

No sooner did reconstruction commence than the Christians were served eviction notices. They had been living in Muslim-owned houses around the city for over a year and a half, and the local government decided it was time to move them on. The Christian presence in Muslim quarters had been a regular source of tension, and the government seemed to balance every concession to the Christians with some benefit to the Muslims. However, the Christians were given no advance warning, and few if any had yet to make their homes habitable. By government order, dated 7 March 1862, all those who accepted their first repayment award would no longer be eligible for government-subsidised housing. They were required to evacuate the Muslim houses the government had provided and to find alternate accommodation, 'which they will rent at their own expense.' Dr Mishaqa was livid: 'Since the Christian who has just received one quarter of the value of his burned property is unable to rebuild his house in a day, and that the one quarter he has so far been paid is insufficient to rebuild his house, how can he be expected to pay rent for where he lives while using his [indemnity] to restore his house?' The Christians did what all Damascenes did when faced with unreasonable government orders: they petitioned and appealed to gain time. But the Christians were henceforth under pressure to rebuild and move on.[29]

The provincial government was having cash-flow difficulties of its own. It had enough liquidity for first payments on the Christians' sergis at the end of 1861. The second tranche for reconstruction was made in timber, but the treasurer was aware that cash reserves were running critically low. In March 1862, the government began to devalue the local currency in Damascus used for reparations by 10 percent to try to make its money go a bit further—or, as Dr Mishaqa put it, 'in order to lighten the burden on the Muslims, and to place a part of the burden on the Christians for that which they are paid in reparations.' No one, he predicted, would be paid their full indemnity.[30]

By August 1862, the indemnity fund was depleted. The government had insufficient cash to continue servicing all sergis. Dr Mishaqa called on Antun al-Shami, one of the Christian notables who served on the indemnity fund's board, who confirmed 'that the government had no money, and that the government had no wish to make payments if it could avoid it.' To its credit, the government prioritised the poor, and had from the start. For example, the government ordered the very first houses rebuilt in April 1861 be for the poorest Damascenes, built entirely at the government's expense. They continued to prioritise the poor in making indemnity payments. The treasurer of the indemnity fund, Qabuli Efendi, pledged to redeem all claims of less than Pt. 10,000 as a first priority. Once the smallest claims had been settled, the government would make payments of Pt. 20,000 or less and assist with the reconstruction of churches. Larger claims would follow. This was bad news for Mishaqa. His reparation bond, signed by Fuad Pasha no less, was for Pt. 500,000, and while he did receive his two first instalments of Pt. 166,000, the chances of securing his third and final payment looked slight.[31]

In spite of the shortfalls and delay, reconstruction continued apace. Christians facing eviction from their temporary accommodation poured whatever resources they had into rebuilding their houses, and between the indemnities paid for homes and stolen property, there appeared to be just enough money to keep the builders going. Donkeys and mules carried loads of stone, plaster, and wood through the lanes of the Christian quarters, which were coming to life again after two years of abandonment.

Reconstruction, however, did not bring peace to the troubled city. Relations between Muslims and Christians remained tense. The Muslims resented the heavy taxation imposed by the government, and the Christians condemned the discounts and delays on their indemnities that made reconstruction such a struggle. It probably worked to the government's advantage that the Christians complained loudly about the inadequacy of their indemnities—no one could accuse the government of impoverishing the Muslims to enrich the Christians. But sectarian crime was on the rise, and Dr Mishaqa's reports began to read like a police blotter. In February 1862 he reported an attack on an American missionary and his wife, an assault on a Christian merchant walking home after sunset, and an armed assault by a Muslim from the al-Shaghur quarter on two Christians in Bab Tuma. In March he reported how the police broke up a stone-throwing brawl between Muslims and Christians, and made a number of arrests. In March 1863 a group of armed Muslims attacked two Armenians as they returned home from a coffeehouse one evening during the Muslim fast of Ramadan, killing one and wounding the other. Christians reported hearing Muslims threatening to 'repeat the past in the Ramadan feast,' which reawakened Christian fears of massacre. This led many of the builders in the Christian quarter to down tools and seek refuge in safer towns like Zahleh and Beirut until Ramadan was over and the Eid had been celebrated. Although this was not a genocidal moment, communal tensions continued to run high, unabated by reconstruction.[32]

The government continued to face difficulties in paying indemnities. The treasury delayed the fourth and final tranche of payments to all but the smallest claimants into 1863 when, in March, it imposed a 19 percent discount on all sergi holders, promising to pay the balance 'when the treasury has the funding.' Few in the Damascene Christian community had any illusions of seeing the balance from their government bonds. Dr Mishaqa repeated his standard mantra in reporting these developments: 'There is no hope that the government here will pay anything to anyone.' Even with the discount, the government had difficulty completing payment to sergi holders and in January 1864 resorted to the last indignity of bankrupt governments: offering payment in freshly printed paper money. In a coin-based economy like Damascus, it was impossible to persuade people to trade in paper money. They were used to coinage of all varieties, and in the markets of Damascus traders moved easily between English pounds, French livres, Russian roubles, Austrian thalers, and Ottoman coinage from Istanbul, Baghdad, and Cairo. But you would not find many traders who would accept payment in paper banknotes printed in Istanbul, and those who did discounted the face value by 33 percent. They could hardly be blamed; even the government would not accept its own paper money for tax payments. With such devalued currency, the indemnity fund limped to the end of its mission and made final payments to those who would receive them.[33]

Dr Mishaqa declined final payment in paper money. He continued to petition for the Pt. 166,000 still owed him on his bond signed by Fuad Pasha to be paid in coin. He wondered why he faced such resistance from the governors of Damascus, but they probably thought he was wealthy enough to rebuild his life without them having to make that final payment. Their priority had never been about big principles like justice and restoring the Christians to the quality of life they had known before the Events. Their primary objectives had always been rebuilding the city, reintegrating the Christians, and revitalising the economy. In 1865 the British consulate agreed to add Mishaqa's claims to those of other British protégés (Mishaqa still enjoyed protégé status with both Great Britain and the United States), and he placed his sergi in British hands for satisfaction. But by that time, the Ottoman government had already succeeded in its primary objective: the reconstruction of the Christian quarters of Damascus.

In his annual trade report for 1864, Dr Mishaqa reported 'the completion of the rebuilding of the burned Christian quarters' and provided clear statistics to support the claim. Before the Events, he noted, there were 15,206 houses in Damascus. At the end of 1864, there were 14,921—a shortfall of only 285 units. Given Mishaqa's prior estimates of 1,500 Christian homes destroyed in the Events, and allowing for the numbers killed in the massacre and those who relocated to Beirut or other cities, this probably represents the total reconstruction of the houses of Christian survivors returned to Damascus. The number of shops in the city had actually increased since 1860, rising from 7,782 units to 7,796—an increase of 14 units. For the economic life of the city, the restoration of the markets must have been a very encouraging sign to all. The industrial life of the city had also recovered, although it had not reached pre-1860 levels. As Mishaqa recorded, 'The looms for weaving silk and cotton cloth in Damascus are fewer than in the past because of the Events but they have been restored and this year there are now about three thousand looms. In 1859 there were about 3,500 looms.' Given the centrality of weaving in the economy of Damascus, it was a very encouraging trend. Four years after the massacre, the Christian quarters were rebuilt, the surviving Christians reintegrated, and the economy recovering. Yet no one would say, after all the traumas of the previous four years and the cleavages that had emerged in society, that Damascus was back to normal.[34]

The reconstruction of the Christian quarters had been completed on the cheap. The houses were very rudimentary, and their residents struggled to make ends meet. Initially, this left the reconstructed areas impoverished and vulnerable to the forms of criminality common to disadvantaged neighbourhoods in any big city. Taverns cropped up near places where people gathered in Bab Tuma and Bab Sharqi, by the police station, next to bathhouses, even near mosques, all 'contrary to municipal regulations.' Respectable residents frequently complained of drunken and disorderly men committing assault and robbery. Prostitutes worked the streets of Bab Tuma, scandalising 'honourable folk' (*ahl al-'ird*) and further undermining law and order. Criminals and prostitutes made common cause to protect each other from arrest. The police and the headmen (*mukhtars*) of the quarters were accused of complicity, accepting bribes from the very people they should have been restraining, further encouraging criminals through the semblance of impunity. These developments left some Damascenes to despair that 'security has been lost in Damascus.'[35]

In his reports to Consul Johnson in Beirut, Dr Mishaqa captured the fragility of Damascene society during reconstruction: 'If the government can ensure real security to reassure the populace...and pay indemnities to the Christians so they have the funds, and restore security and confidence in trade, then the situation in Damascus will improve year on year. If it fails, then Damascus will decline each year from what it was before.' In his view, the future of the city hung in the balance.[36]

Furthermore, reconstruction had done little to ease tensions between the communities. Hostilities continued to rise to the surface, often in response to events far from Damascus, for which local Christians bore no responsibility. Between 1866 and 1869, the Greek Orthodox Christians of Crete revolted against their Ottoman governor in a major insurrection that troubled the peace in Damascus for more than two years. Dr Mishaqa was alarmed by notices posted in the Muslim quarters of Damascus 'informing the Muslims of what happened in the Greek uprising in Crete, and how their brethren there were slaughtered and plundered, and how many of their faith were martyred, and other inflammatory statements, asking for assistance from their Muslim brethren.' Predictably, the notices provoked outrage among Damascene Muslims and widespread fear among Christians. By the time of the final suppression of the revolt by the Ottoman authorities in January 1869, Muslim antagonism had reached such extremes that Christians feared a return to the horrors of 1860. Mishaqa remembered 'the dreadful event which befell the Christians of Syria in 1860' and warned that 'if the states of Europe don't take the decision to send soldiers, there will not remain a trace of the Christians in Eastern lands. The only ones who will be left will be those who abandon the Christian religion and become Muslims.' After nearly a decade, Christians and Muslims had yet to turn the page on the Damascus Events, leaving the spectre of massacre hovering over the city and its residents.[37]

Still, the governors of Damascus struggled to restore a sense of normalcy to their city. In June 1869 the Muslim notables of Damascus organised a dinner party in honour of the governor, Mehmed Rashid Pasha, who had just returned from a successful campaign against Bedouin tribes in Transjordan. It was a brilliant occasion, the venue lit with ten thousand candles. As in 1861, when Abu Ahmad al-Salka hosted a dinner for the then-governor, the party included notables from the Muslim, Christian, and Jewish communities. But this time there were Muslims attending who had been convicted of crimes in the Events. In 1865 the government had issued a general amnesty and allowed all Damascenes to return home from exile. Former members of the Majlis such as the revered Shaykh Abdullah al-Halabi and Ahmad al-Hasibi, father of the diarist, returned home in 1866 to public celebration. Both Shaykh Abdullah and Ahmad al-Hasibi had been invited to the dinner in 1869 (Hasibi declined), but the presence of former exiles must have made the seating plan difficult because dinner was served at tables with the guests seated 'by rank' in the European fashion. Protocol provides little guidance for such a complex situation, and the hosts clearly got it wrong—at least in the eyes of the Muslims present. 'There were many Christians seated in the hall,' Muhammad Abu al-Sa'ud al-Hasibi recorded in his diary, 'including the patriarchs and the consuls and one rabbi of the Jews. But the 'ulama of the best religion [i.e., Islam] were missing, since the Governor gave too much precedence to the Christians and the consuls. It was a shame for the Muslims.' He concluded with a pious invocation: 'There is no power and no strength save in God Almighty.'[38]

Nearly a decade after the massacre, and five years after reconstruction, the society of Damascus had yet to recover from its scars. Townspeople saw one community's gain to be necessarily at the expense of the others. It would take prosperity for the people of Damascus to grow more tolerant in transcending their sectarian divisions. Yet the revenues of the province were so limited that prosperity seemed beyond reach.

Fortunately, the city had a friend in power. As grand vizier, Fuad Pasha had not forgotten Damascus. And the latest reforms he was applying in the Ottoman Empire stood to bring tremendous benefit to the city of Damascus as the capital of a reorganised and enlarged province of Syria. As part of a new phase of Ottoman reform, Damascus would benefit from a massive injection in tax revenues that would transform the city, completing the process of reconstruction and reconciliation that would finally permit the Muslim and Christian communities to put the horrors of the past behind them.

9

Damascus Restored

L ooking out of the windows of his resplendent offices in down-town Istanbul, the grand vizier never lost sight of Damascus. Fuad Pasha's mission to the Syrian capital had left a mark on him. In his valedictory message to the people of Damascus and Mount Lebanon in 1861, Fuad declared, 'I now consider myself to be a Syrian at heart.'[1]

In 1864, four years after the Events, Damascene Christians still lived in fear of further massacres. All Fuad's good work in restoring Ottoman control and preventing European intervention in the city would be lost if the Muslims of Damascus rose against the Christian community again. Fuad was determined to use his powers as grand vizier to preserve the reconstruction of Damascus and to advance the reconciliation of its divided society. To do so would require good governance and a major injection of funding. Fuad had ideas about how to achieve both.

Fuad reached out to one of the most brilliant reformers of the Tanzimat era to draft a root-and-branch overhaul of Ottoman provincial administration. Ahmet Shefik Midhat Pasha (1822–1883) was governor of the province of Nish (in modern Serbia) and had spent most of his career in the troubled Balkans. He would subsequently also rise to grand vizier and was one of the drafters of the Ottoman Constitution of 1876. In Nish, Midhat confronted issues of maladministration and sectarian tensions similar to those that Fuad had witnessed in Damascus. Dysfunctional provincial government gave rise to separatist nationalist movements in the Balkans and sectarian conflicts in the Arab provinces that attracted European intervention and threatened Ottoman sovereignty. Both men saw provincial reform as essential for the survival of the Ottoman Empire as a whole.

Fuad and Midhat drew on their experiences in Syria and the Balkans to craft a new template for provincial government that could be applied not just to trouble spots like Syria and Serbia but stood to improve governance across the empire as a whole. The result was the 1864 Provincial Reform Law, a landmark of the Tanzimat, lauded in the British press at the time as 'a masterpiece of legislation' that 'if properly carried out,' would be 'adequate in every sense to ensure prosperity, and protect the lives and property of all nationalities and creeds in the Empire.'[2]

The Provincial Reform Law tackled many of the administrative problems that contributed to the breakdown in order in the Damascus Events. Never again would one administrator hold both the governorship and the command of the armed forces, as Ahmad Pasha had done. The new law created a division of powers, with checks and balances between the civil, military, and judicial officials, and established a clear hierarchy, with the governor (*wali*) at the pinnacle of authority. Each province was divided into regions, each with its own regional governor (*mutasarrif*). Each region was in turn subdivided into five or six districts, each headed by a district governor (*kaymakam*) who answered to his regional governor. Finally, each district was divided into clusters of villages headed by village headmen (*mukhtar*) answerable to the kaymakam of their district. This structure gave a direct chain of command and lines of communication from the lowest to the highest level of provincial government. Ottoman subjects took a step closer to citizenship, gaining the right to vote and even to stand for public office in administrative councils and the courts at every level of administration. Moreover, the law required both Muslims and non-Muslims to be represented in all elected bodies. Together, Fuad and Midhat crafted a provincial order fit for the modern age. The Ottoman government promulgated the Provincial Reform Law on 8 November 1864.[3]

Before applying the new law across the empire, Fuad chose to trial-run the legislation in the Balkans. The Balkans were a minefield of nationalist agitation and great-power intervention, as much in need of good governance as anywhere in the Ottoman domains. Fuad dispatched Midhat Pasha as governor of a newly formed superprovince on the Danube, the Tuna Vilayeti, created from the merger of three former provinces (Nish, Vidin, and Silistria) that straddled territory in modern Bulgaria and Serbia. The consolidation of three provinces generated a massive increase in tax revenues for the governor to apply where he saw fit. Midhat Pasha used the new powers and enhanced revenues generated by the Provincial Reform Law to embark on expansive public-spending projects. According to a contemporary British account, in his three years as governor of the Danube province, Midhat 'constructed more than 2,000 miles of road, built 1,400 or 1,500 bridges, with schools, hospitals, and other public institutions. He scrupulously applied the laws relating to the government of vilayets, introducing Christians [into administrative posts], and rigidly enforcing justice in all the newly-established courts.'[4]

Encouraged by developments on the Danube, Fuad turned next to Syria. As in the case of the Danube Province, Fuad chose to consolidate three existing provinces into a super-province. In April 1865 the Ottomans announced the creation of a new province of Syria (Suriye Vilayeti) that comprised the former provinces of Damascus, Sidon, and Jerusalem. Fuad appointed Mehmed Rushdi Pasha, the governor of Damascus, to head the new province. The announcement provoked widespread celebration across the Syrian lands in anticipation of investments and improvement in living standards. It also set off a fierce competition between Beirut and Damascus over which city would be declared the capital of this new creation, with all the honours and revenues the title bestowed.[5]

The Beirutis were the first to make a bid. A group of 219 Christian and Muslim notables of the city drafted a petition to the governor of Syria, Rushdi Pasha, inviting him to make Beirut the capital of his new province—or in their words, 'the soil for your footprints.' By designating Beirut as his capital, the bishops, patriarchs, imams, and leading merchants of the city argued, Rushdi Pasha would 'strengthen the basis of Beirut's success, would improve conditions for its residents, would enhance its progress and growth and the development of its trade, to the benefit of the imperial treasury [through customs duties].' Failure to promote Beirut, they warned, 'would lead to devastation and a reduction in trade and imports—something Your Excellency would never permit as it goes against sound principles and imperial aims previously expressed.' The notables of Beirut believed they had made a rock-solid case.[6]

The notables of Damascus begged to differ. They reacted with ill-feigned outrage at the parvenu boomtown Beirut flexing its commercial muscle in a bid to usurp Damascus's natural claim to preeminence. The Muslim notables of the city—Shaykh Muhammad Sa'id al-Ustuwani among them—drafted their own petitions to Rushdi Pasha, expressing their joy at the announcement of his appointment to head the new province of Syria. Reminding Rushdi of Damascus's history as the first capital of the Islamic caliphate in the seventh century of the current era, the Muslim petitioners flagged Damascus's singular role in the Muslim pilgrimage to Mecca, 'one of the highest priorities of the Sublime State.' They stressed the importance of Damascus as a shield at the edge of the desert protecting the agriculture of Syria from Bedouin nomads. The Muslim notables dismissed Beiruti claims that the commerce of their city was at risk, arguing that 'the growth in the city's trade is not dependent on it being Your Excellency's capital' and that its geographic location alone ensured Beirut's continued prosperity.[7]

The Christians of Damascus sent a separate petition, reaching out to Grand Vizier Fuad Pasha himself. After his handling of the immediate aftermath of the 1860 Events, Damascene Christians had more faith in Fuad than perhaps any other Ottoman official. They appealed to the grand vizier as if faced with an existential threat: 'We are slaves of the Sublime State from the Greek Orthodox and other churches, people of the city of Damascus, living in comfort and security, hoping for gradual progress towards felicity and the completion of the rebuilding of our quarters that had been reduced to ruins in the past Event.' They reiterated the same points raised by the Muslim notables about the priority of the Muslim pilgrimage and Damascus's strategic role in containing the threat posed by the Bedouin against settled communities. But they focussed on the Damascus Events as something from which they were still recovering and a reason to reinforce Damascus's fragile redevelopment: 'Were the safety and security so recently restored after the painful Events in Damascus to be put in doubt, this would drive your Christian subjects to emigrate and leave our houses and ruins.'[8]

The intense competition between Beirut and Damascus to secure recognition as the capital of the new province of Syria was all about money. Beirut was a prosperous port city that had witnessed explosive growth in the first half of the nineteenth century, rising from obscurity to become the third-largest port in the eastern Mediterranean (after Izmir and Alexandria). Since the 1840s, Beirut had served as the capital of the now former province of Sidon, and the burghers of Beirut were determined to prevent any change that might put their city's phenomenal growth in jeopardy.[9]

Damascus, on the other hand, was a city in decline. It was fragile before 1860, and the Events dealt Damascus a near-fatal blow and brought its economy to a halt while the state squeezed every last piastre from its subjects to finance reconstruction. The treasury in Damascus was chronically depleted. According to British reports, the revenues for the province of Damascus in 1860 were no more than Pt. 22.6 million. The new province of Syria combined revenues from Damascus, Beirut, and Jerusalem, representing a four- or five-fold increase in provincial revenues, with land revenues in excess of Pt. 100 million, 'in addition to the money from customs, from tobacco and salt.' Both Beirut and Damascus fought hard for the prize of controlling this vast new budget.[10]

In the end, Fuad Pasha confirmed Damascus as the seat of the new province of Syria. There is no evidence that he ever seriously considered Beirut's bid. As a consolation prize, he established the provincial commercial court in Beirut, given the city's preeminence in the Mediterranean trade. Fuad's primary concern was the regeneration of Damascus, and through the creation of the new province of Syria the tax revenues of Beirut, Jerusalem, and Damascus would now flow into the treasury of Damascus. This newfound wealth gave the governors of Damascus unprecedented resources for the development of their city, and over the next quarter century they embarked on a transformative spending spree. Like Midhat Pasha in the Danube, the governors of Syria would make massive new investments that would revitalise society and the economy by improving communications, expanding government offices, commissioning modern new markets for the city centre, and creating modern comprehensive schools to give young Syrians the education they needed to access the opportunities of a renascent Damascus.

The designation of Damascus as capital of the new Syria immediately raised confidence in the city. Wealthy Christian notables, who had hesitated to rebuild lavish homes in the face of recurrent sectarian tensions, flocked back and built some of the finest mansions the city had yet witnessed. Mitri al-Shalhub, an influential Christian notable, completed work on his house in 1866. 'It is very extensive,' the Damascene chronicler Nu'man Qasatli wrote, 'clad in fine stone with many white marble pillars, embellished alcoves, rooms, and salons,' and a courtyard planted 'in the most beautiful flowers.' Qasatli reported that the house cost Pt. 3 million, an astronomical sum at the time. Yet Antun Efendi al-Shami, another Christian notable, spent even more on his stately home—nearly Pt. 3.5 million—completed that same year. 'When the Russian crown prince visited Damascus in 1869,' Qasatli recalled, 'he said that it was the finest home he had seen in his travels in the Eastern Mediterranean.' Jewish notables also began to splash out on lavish houses. Between 1865 and 1872, Shum'aya Efendi, the Islambuli family, and the Lizbuna family all built prominent houses in the Jewish quarter that cost in the range of Pt. 3.5 million. Crucially, the building boom engaged the Muslim notables as well, with members of the prominent Quwwatli and Barudi families building modern palaces for unspecified fortunes in the later 1860s. This flourishing of fine houses in the Muslim, Christian, and Jewish quarters was the strongest signal yet that, since being named capital of Syria, Damascus was returning to its former glory.[11]

The creation of the province of Syria also marked a new stage in Muslim-Christian relations in Damascus, beginning with the petition campaign to secure Damascus's claim to be provincial capital. Through their separate petitions, the Christians and Muslims scored a joint victory for their city. It was the first instance since the 1860 Events of the different communities working toward a common goal, and they shared in the success of their effort. These developments did not put communal tensions to an end, but they did demonstrate a common stake in the future of their city. This common stake emerged clearly in the recommendations of the elected council that advised the governor on provincial development—the Muslim and Christian notables of Syria taking the lead in the economic development of their city and province.

Early in 1867, representatives from the eight regions of the new province of Syria—Acre, Beirut, Damascus, Hama, Hawran, Jerusalem, Transjordan, and Tripoli—assembled in Damascus for the first meeting of the General Council (*Meclis-i Umumi*). This was an elected body, created in conformity with the 1864 Provincial Reform Law, to advise the governor on development strategies for the province. The thirty-two councilmen, two Muslims and two Christians from each region, entered the meeting room, the Muslim delegates taking their seats on the right side of the chamber, the Christians on the left. In the course of the year, the council met twenty-eight times, sixteen of the sessions in Damascus and twelve in Beirut to ensure that the spending spree was shared equitably across the province. Divided by religion, the councillors were united in their ambitions for the economic regeneration of their province—the Muslims and Christians of Syria meeting together to set the development agenda for their province.

The General Council was tasked with oversight of 'the construction, maintenance, and security of imperial roads' in the province and with the 'construction, repair and maintenance of municipal buildings.' Council members also deliberated measures to enhance trade and agriculture, and 'to study questions relative to the levying of taxes.' Each councillor brought suggestions from his constituents for discussion with the governor, who chaired the council. Items reached the agenda only with the governor's consent. Each proposal was then raised before the full council for discussion. Those proposals that were adopted by the council were recorded and dispatched to Istanbul for the central government's approval.[12]

In the course of 1867, the council approved some eighteen major projects for Syria. These included the expansion of the road and communication network and markets; rural security and the sedentarisation of the nomadic Bedouin tribes that traditionally preyed on farmers and merchant caravans alike; the expansion of government buildings and offices, creating lucrative new jobs; and the opening of state schools across the province to provide young Syrians with the skills to apply for those prized government posts. There were proposals for new factories and for measures to promote trade in Syrian clothes and fabrics in Istanbul and the other major cities of the Ottoman Empire, where fine Syrian textiles enjoyed a competitive edge over cheaper foreign imports. The council's ambitions were so bold that many contemporaries doubted if any of the proposals would see the light of day. The governor himself showed no such doubts, giving every proposal his considered attention. When the council held its final session at the end of 1867, the governor presented each councillor, Christian and Muslim alike, with a certificate recording his gratitude for their services to Syria.[13]

The road network in Syria was a hindrance to both government and commercial activity. Before 1860, there was no paved road suitable for wheeled traffic between any of the cities of Syria. People travelled by horse or mule, and goods were carried on the backs of donkeys and camels. Travel times over hilly tracks took days and were fraught with dangers. Well before the General Council met in 1867, Ottoman officials looked to modernise Syria's road network to speed the transport of goods and persons.

The first modern carriage road in Syria linked Beirut to Damascus. Built as a commercial venture by a French company with a concession from the Ottoman government, work on the road began in 1858. The violence in Mount Lebanon in the summer of 1860 shook investor confidence in the project, forcing the company to suspend construction and to refinance before works could resume. The road was inaugurated on 31 December 1862, and the first string of mule-drawn carts carrying Mediterranean merchandise made a triumphal entry into Damascus the following day—New Year's Day, 1863. The new road revolutionised communications, cutting travel time between the two cities from three days to just twelve hours. The director of the company, Count Edmond de Perthuis, predicted that the Beirut-to-Damascus road 'would powerfully develop the commerce and industry of the land.'[14]

Dr Mishaqa confirmed de Perthuis's predictions. 'The carriage road to Beirut has brought benefit to the people of Damascus by facilitating the transport of commodities and by making faster travel for riders,' he noted in his commercial report for 1864. Charles Warner, an American traveller to Syria in the 1870s, described the heavy traffic 'of white-topped wagons,—like the Western "prairie schooner"—drawn each by three mules tandem. Thirty and forty of these freight vehicles travel in company, and we were continually meeting or passing them; their number is an indication of the large trade that Damascus has with Beyrout and the Mediterranean.' Warner and his party travelled in a three-horse passenger stagecoach that stopped at regular intervals at stations managed by the carriage-road company: 'At every station we change one horse, so that we always have a fresh animal.' Each horse had its own number, duly recorded along with the precise time of arrival and departure. 'All is life and promptness at the stations,' he noted approvingly; 'changes are quickly made.'[15]

The Beirut-Damascus Road demonstrated how improvements to communications enhanced prosperity. The General Council sought to replicate this first carriage road's impact on the rest of Syria, with Damascus at the centre of a burgeoning road network stretching northward to Homs and Hama, southward to Transjordan and Palestine, and west to the Bekaa Valley. In the late Ottoman Empire, maps were still drawn with distance measured in hours, on the assumption that one could ride or march five kilometres per hour. Given how they reduced travel times, the advent of carriage roads quite literally made the Syrian world smaller.

However much carriage roads might accelerate travel speeds— under good conditions, a horse-drawn carriage moved at about ten miles per hour—the telegraph could communicate at a velocity approaching the speed of light. Along with investment in road infrastructure, the Ottoman government was enthusiastic in bringing telegraphy to Syria. Never again would a city burn for three days before news reached the government centre. Instant communications also helped trade, enabling merchants to respond efficiently to changing market conditions. Already, a first telegraph line had been extended between Beirut and Damascus in 1861, with onward connections to Istanbul. The General Council now called for a major extension of telegraphy to all the major market towns in the province.

By the late 1860s, a telegraph grid began to take shape. One line followed the coast, linking port cities from Latakia to Tripoli, Beirut, Sidon, Acre, Jaffa, and Gaza. A second north-south line connected the inland cities of Syria, from Aleppo to Hama, Homs, Damascus, and the Hawran. A number of east-west lines linked the market towns between the coast and the inland cities. In 1868 the network comprised fourteen stations. By 1885, the system had grown to some forty-two stations linking towns and villages across Syria stretching as far south as al-Salt in Transjordan (near modern Amman). Syria was bound together by instant communications, transforming security, government, and trade.[16]

The advent of carriage roads and telegraph communications had a transformative effect on the markets of Damascus. The arrival of horse-drawn carriages exposed one feature of Damascene urban planning that, dating back to antiquity, was ill-suited to modern times. Streets built to accommodate animal caravans were too narrow for wheeled traffic. To make matters worse, shop fronts had stone benches that served as counter space to display wares or seats for shop owners and customers to socialise, further narrowing the already constricted passages. Starting in 1863, Governor Mehmed Rushdi Pasha initiated a scheme to remove the benches and pave the commercial streets to enable trade carts to access the town centre. Whatever the shopkeepers thought about losing their benches, it was the first major public-works project in the markets of the old city since the Events, and the investment was welcome. Works to widen the streets in the commercial centre continued through 1871.[17]

Along with the widening of the streets in the central markets of Damascus came a new level of investment in the commercial centre of the old city. In 1875 a leading Muslim notable endowed a new market linking the government centre in Marja with the traditional commercial centre of the city. `Ali Pasha al-Murahli was an administrator of the endowments for the holy cities of Mecca and Medina. His family had been in Damascus since the sixteenth century. The new market, or *suq*, bore his name. Suq `Ali Pasha represented a bold new form of urban design that combined eighty-six shops built around a central courtyard with two cafés, a reading room, and a fountain. The upper storeys provided office space and accommodation for visiting merchants and a hotel for general visitors. In the evenings, rooms were given over for public performances. The Suq `Ali Pasha was like a modern mall, combining hospitality, offices, shops, and leisure space for all Damascenes—Muslims, Christians, and Jews alike.[18]

In 1878 the former governor of the Danube Province, who coauthored the Provincial Reform Law with Fuad Pasha, was appointed as governor of Syria. Shortly after taking up his post, Midhat Pasha launched the second major commercial development in Damascus—Suq Midhat Pasha. Stretching over 470 meters, the market proved one of the biggest urban-development schemes that Damascus had yet witnessed. Taking the ancient Street Called Straight as his focus, Midhat Pasha ordered the razing of buildings along the southern side of the road to provide a wide, paved, and yet straighter street for the largest and most modern market in Damascus. The shops in

Suq Midhat Pasha were spacious and well lit, with rooms on the second floor to provide offices and accommodation. The Street Called Straight became a paved road wide enough to accommodate two-way carriage traffic. The new suq might have disappointed foreign tourists looking for the Thousand-and-One-Night's experience of exotic markets stocked with Oriental wares, but the Damascenes appreciated the modern amenities it provided.

No sooner was Suq Midhat Pasha completed than the city council of Damascus went to work on its most ambitious project for the regeneration of the commercial centre of the city: the famous Suq Hamidiyya. Named after the reigning Ottoman sultan, Abdülhamid II (r. 1876–1909), Damascus's grandest new market followed the southern perimeter of the Citadel for 450 metres, leading to the Umayyad Mosque. Thanks to the redevelopment of the disused moat of the Citadel and strategic demolitions, the paved road spread up to ten metres—an unprecedented width for the ancient city of Damascus. Works for this vast market complex were undertaken in stages, providing two-storey structures with spacious shops at ground level sheltered by a barrel roof in wood, very much on the model of nineteenth-century shopping arcades in Europe. Construction was completed between 1886 and 1889.[19]

These new markets—Suq Ali Pasha, Suq Midhat Pasha, and Suq Hamidiyya—led to the modernisation of the commercial centre of Damascus and became the focus of civic pride. As one Damascene noted in 1898, on the occasion of the visit of German Emperor Wilhelm II, 'The suqs of Damascus are famous for their spaciousness and beauty so that even some European dignitaries said that they did not have any architecture to rival some of the suqs in Damascus.'[20]

Within central Damascus, the government district in Marja Square experienced rapid development in the years after 1866. In that year, the city council paved over a stretch of the Barada River to create a vast open square where the Beirut-to-Damascus highway entered the city centre. Here the horse-drawn passenger coaches departed for Beirut. With the expansion of government offices after the creation of the province of Syria in 1866, the Marja district entered a period of rapid transformation.

Among the first of the new government buildings in Marja were the central courthouse, the prison, and police headquarters, built around 1880. These three institutions reaffirmed the government's central role in preserving law and order. In 1883 the local government erected a new post and telegraph office tucked between the central courthouse and the new commercial complex, the Suq 'Ali Pasha. Two luxury hotels also graced Marja Square: the Hotel Dimitri Karah and the Hotel Victoria, where visitors arriving from Beirut might alight in comfort. Several cafés provided leisure space for visitors, civil servants on their breaks, and townspeople who flocked to the government buildings to conduct their official business. A new theatre, the 'Flower of Damascus' (in Arabic, *Masrah Zahrat Dimashq*), provided a venue for increasingly popular dramatic performances. We have reports of the management interrupting a performance in 1911 when 1,100 people overwhelmed the theatre's 800-seat capacity. The development of the Marja quarter only accelerated in later decades, with a city hall, a land-registry office, and a new saray built between 1894 and 1910 in an unprecedented burst of urbanisation.[21]

This rapid development had a significant impact on social relations in Damascus. At one level, the major building projects provided work for masons and artisans, enhancing the welfare of the working people of Damascus. Within the new government buildings, jobs were created for educated Damascenes in government service. Government jobs were well paid, and civil servants enjoyed high standing in Damascene society. Moreover, the jobs were distributed among the different communities of the city, Muslims, Christians, and Jews alike, in conformity with the terms of the Provincial Reform Law of 1864. This meant that each morning, Damascenes of all faiths would converge on the government offices in Marja Square as they went to work in the courts, or the post office, or the governor's Saray. They would take their breaks in the same cafés and probably crowded the same performances of popular plays. The barriers between the Muslims and Christians of Damascus, raised by the horrors of 1860 and the pressures of reconstruction, began to fall in places like Marja Square.

Access to government jobs was restricted to Damascenes with higher education. The work of modern bureaucrats required fluent reading and writing skills, advanced mathematics, some history and geography, and the command of several languages—Arabic to communicate with the people of Syria, Turkish for exchanges with the Ottoman government in Istanbul, and French to deal with the growing European presence. These prerequisites privileged Christians over Muslims in the competition for government jobs. Catholic and

Protestant missionaries opened modern schools in Syria, forcing local churches to raise their standard or risk losing members of their flock to rival churches. Irish Presbyterians founded the Evangelical School in Damascus with 6 teachers training 120 boys, the Catholic Patriarchal School boasted a faculty of 10 teachers with 250 boys, the Greek Orthodox School hired 7 teachers to teach 290 boys in Arabic, and the Greek Catholic Azariyya School had a faculty of 8 for 160 boys. In the 1870s the different Christian communities of Damascus operated a total of 9 boys' schools with a total of more than 1,100 pupils, and 7 girls' schools with 1,070 students, all receiving the kind of education that opened doors to jobs in the expanding Ottoman bureaucracy.[22]

Educational opportunities for the Muslim children of Damascus lagged far behind those for the Christians in the 1870s. The traditional Damascene boys' schools, run by religious clerics, taught children to read and memorise the Qur'an. There was no separation of pupils by age or ability in these Qur'an schools: all students sat through the same lessons in the same classroom. According to official government figures, there were 74 boys' elementary schools teaching 1,250 pupils the basics of reading and writing, and 28 girls' schools for 300 students. The only higher education was provided by 5 lower-secondary schools, known in Turkish as *rüshdiye* schools. The rüshdiye schools were a failing product of the Tanzimat education reforms that were later merged with the primary school system. Still, until the late 1880s, the rüshdiye schools were the best the state had to offer its Muslim pupils, with a three-year curriculum covering Turkish, Arabic, and Persian language training, the different divisions of mathematics, and a range of humanities disciplines like Islamic history and world geography. In the early 1870s, there were only 250 Muslim boys registered in the rüshdiye schools of Damascus.[23]

The Ottoman authorities in Damascus recognised they faced a serious problem with the education system. Although the Christians represented no more than 15 percent of the total population in Damascus, Christian schools were turning out a much higher number of well-trained graduates than did the Muslim religious authorities and the Ottoman state system combined. As a modern Turkish historian observed, 'Thanks to their educational superiority over the Muslims, non-Muslim [Damascenes were] able to hold important positions in the local administration,' threatening the government's efforts to restore communal harmony in post-conflict Damascus.[24]

In 1869 the Ottoman government introduced a new Regulation of Public Education to launch a complete overhaul of the education system. The law called for the expansion of state primary (three years) and rüshdiye (three years) schools across all the provinces of the empire, with plans for the subsequent development of high schools. The law sought to limit the teaching staff in state schools to graduates of teacher-training colleges, although in practice the shortage of trained teachers forced many schools to hire members of the Islamic religious establishment instead, few of whom could teach the more secular subjects of the new state curriculum.[25]

Immediately after the 1869 reform, the authorities in Damascus opened a new professional training school known as the *Madrasat Sanayi*`, or the 'trades school.' For the first time in Damascus, a state school recruited a mixed student body of thirty-eight Muslims and twelve Christian students. The Ottoman authorities raised funds locally with public contributions and revenues from the government press to launch the trades school, providing room and board for the students. Students were given primary education in reading and writing Arabic and French alongside vocational training in sewing, tailoring, and other trades. Many Damascenes had high hopes that the school could prove of 'great benefit to the people.' It was not to be. The school ran out of funds in its first year, and the student body became increasingly 'disorderly.' All but one of the Christian students abandoned their studies, presumably to return to church- and missionary-run schools. Reduced to just thirty-six students by its second year, the trades school was abandoned and its buildings repurposed to serve as a rüshdiye school. Yet the experiment reveals the provincial government's strategy to use education as a means both to train the young for careers and to encourage the integration of Christians and Muslims in post-reconstruction Damascus.[26]

After the failure of the trades school experiment, the Ottoman authorities turned their energies to enhancing the state primary and rüshdiye school system. By 1880, the government had opened primary schools in each of the eight districts of Damascus (with two in al-Salihiyya), training more than one thousand boys and nearly four hundred girls. Each school typically had two teachers dividing the lessons of a three-year curriculum. Two rüshdiye schools provided a higher level of training for successful graduates of the primary system. The Çakmakiyya Rüshdiye School developed a four-year curriculum for more than a hundred students taught by six teachers who provided a diverse curriculum in foreign languages, advanced mathematics, and professional skills like bookkeeping and calligraphy. A second, smaller institution, the Malik al-Zahir Civil Rüshdiye

School, preserved the older three-year curriculum, with three teachers training thirty students.[27]

Deep into the 1880s, the Ottoman state school system still lagged behind schools operated by Western missionaries and local Christian churches. In 1887 the governor of Syria, Rashid Nashid Pasha, petitioned the central government to expand funding for education across his province. His report was nothing short of a call to arms:

> American and English missionaries, Jesuit and Lazarist priests (who obtain the practical protection and financial support of the French state), and many Italian and Russian individuals—by establishing very large and exalted schools in nearly every subdistrict in Syria in the service of the political aims of the states with which they are affiliated—are educating Muslim and Christian children gratis and seducing and convincing the children of those who do not send their children to their schools by any means available and are corrupting the subjects' upbringing. In spite of this, so far no schools have been built by the [Ottoman] state as is necessary to be beneficial and to compete with them.[28]

In response, the Ottoman government opened its first civil high school in Damascus: the celebrated Maktab 'Anbar.

After a long planning period, the Ottoman government began opening high schools (in Turkish *idadî*, literally 'preparatory') in the 1880s. The Damascus high school, established in 1887, was one of the first. At last, the government created a school that largely surpassed all the Christian and missionary establishments. Housed in a sumptuous mansion in the heart of the old city, the school enjoyed a level of prestige and exclusivity on a par with the finest British public or American prep schools. As one graduate wrote in later years, Damascenes looked on a Maktab 'Anbar diploma 'the way people of the present generation respect the holder of a doctorate.'[29]

The school took its name from the mansion in which it was based. Yusuf Efendi 'Anbar was a prosperous Jewish merchant who began work on his house in 1867, in the building boom that followed the designation of Damascus as the capital of the province of Syria. The 'Anbar house surpassed all others in size, luxury, and expense. As already noted, the costs of some of the most extravagant mansions built after 1865 exceeded Pt. 3.5 million. Yusuf Efendi 'Anbar spent more than Pt. 5.3 million to create what a contemporary deemed 'the second largest and one of the most splendid houses in Damascus.' The scale of the mansion eventually surpassed 'Anbar's means. When he declared bankruptcy, the Ottoman government took possession of the still-unfinished house. It was here that the Ottomans chose to establish their most prestigious institution of higher education, the Damascus idadî school known as the Maktab 'Anbar.[30]

Salih al-Tall (b. 1872), a country boy from the village of Irbid (70 miles/115 kilometres south of Damascus, now in northern Jordan), was one of the first students admitted to Maktab 'Anbar. Having excelled in his village primary school, Salih secured a nomination to the high school shortly after Maktab 'Anbar opened. Salih at first demurred and stayed in Irbid to work and make a bit of money. One of his classmates took up the offer and returned from Damascus during school holidays with stories of 'the beauty of the school, the elegance of its uniforms, the sumptuous food,' until Salih could no longer resist. He rode to Damascus before the start of the next academic year (probably the autumn of 1888 or 1889) to attend the admissions interview at Maktab 'Anbar.[31]

In Damascus, Salih al-Tall found that the school was the talk of the town. He overheard a conversation between civil servants and townspeople extolling the qualities of Maktab 'Anbar—the beauty of the campus, the rigour of the teachers, and the quality of the uniforms and food. He met a public prosecutor who encouraged Salih to do his best in the interview and secure his place, claiming to have three sons already registered in the school, which was then in its second or third year of operations. Encouraged, Salih made his way to the school and crossed the threshold into the lush courtyard, shaded by tall trees. The other students waiting to be interviewed took one look at the village boy, in bright red boots and peasant's overcoat wearing his long hair in braids under a Bedouin headdress, and burst out laughing.

Salih had just enough time to compose himself before he heard his name called for interview. He entered a lavish room with rich furnishings and mirrors on the wall to find himself facing a stern group of men. One spoke to him in Turkish, asking him to take a piece of chalk. Salih's Turkish failed him, and he stared blankly at the man, who barked in broken Arabic: 'Here—this white stuff.' He then went to a blackboard and began to perform dictation in Turkish and Arabic and math problems. Writing in his memoirs a half century after this interview, Salih could still remember the questions the interview board set him. When they were done, they dismissed Salih and called in the next candidate. Hours later, he learned that his interview had been successful and that he had secured a full scholarship to join the elite ranks of the state high school students, who gained the title 'Efendi' as a mark of distinction. From now on, Salih al-Tall would be known as Salih Efendi. However, to carry the title, a student needed to look the part. The deputy principal took Salih Efendi aside and told him to cut his braids as they would not fit under the *tarbush*, or fez, of the school uniform.

Salih Efendi marvelled at the luxury of it all. The school issued him both summer- and winter-weight uniforms with European-style shoes, socks, shirts, and underwear. He found that the food lived up to everyone's praise and was far better than village fare back home. He took to dorm life instantly, luxuriating in his surroundings in the palatial 'Anbar mansion. An enthusiastic student, he was stimulated by the full range of lessons the school offered. And he made close friends with 'the brightest students of praiseworthy morals.' He wasn't an entirely virtuous student, though. Older than many of his classmates—Salih Efendi was in his late teens when he entered the school—he was already a smoker. Like many rebellious high school students before and since, Salih Efendi and his fellow smokers took to the lavatories to hide their vice. More than once Salih Efendi was forced to flush his tobacco down the toilet and rinse his mouth to evade detection. Yet he was intolerant of other vices and denounced one of his teachers for drinking alcohol and kissing a young schoolboy in his office. The combination of paedophilia and alcohol abuse was taken very seriously, leading to two commissions of enquiry and the ultimate dismissal of the offending teacher. The incident seemed to reinforce Salih Efendi's confidence in the school and the system, as 'the party that had strayed was shamed and humiliated.'

After five years of study, Salih Efendi sat his final examinations for his high school diploma. They were given mock exams in the middle of their last year, to prepare them for the rigours of finals. Final exams, held in July 1896, were given orally with three or four days between subjects. External examiners from both the civil and military services were drafted in, alongside the school's teachers. The rigour of the process and the reliance on outside examiners served to elevate the prestige of the high school diploma. Salih Efendi distinguished himself with high pass marks in all thirteen of his subjects. He graduated with honours, ranked seventh in his class of thirty-one.

Salih al-Tall's school memoirs reflected the prestige and drama of attending Maktab 'Anbar. At long last the Ottomans had created a school that surpassed the finest missionary and church schools in the land. Not only did the high school curriculum provide practical skills, but the school was also a tremendous door opener for its graduates to secure respectable government jobs. In the decade following his graduation, Salih Efendi secured posts as a schoolmaster in primary and rüshdiye schools in Ma'an, Irbid, and 'Ajlun; served as chief administrator of one of the counties in the 'Ajlun district; administered the local census office in Irbid; and rose to deputy inspector of police in the central Syrian city of Hama. In later years, Maktab 'Anbar graduates were recruited to higher-level institutions in the imperial capital, Istanbul, such as the prestigious Mülkiye Mektebi, or Civil Service Academy.[32]

Maktab 'Anbar grew in stature and numbers over the 1890s and early 1900s, with a dozen teachers training a student body that expanded from 250 to 550 pupils over its first two decades. The provincial yearbooks provide no details on the origins or faiths of the students. Although neither of the surviving memoirs of Ottoman-era alumni makes any reference to Christian students, it would have been in keeping with the laws and practices of the Tanzimat reforms for the school to admit Christians, Muslims, and Jews. Yet it is clear from contemporary accounts that, in its culture and community, Maktab 'Anbar was a school for the city's Muslim majority, counterbalancing the dominant role that Christian-run schools had played in Damascus until the late 1880s. In the interest of communal harmony, it was at times necessary to privilege the Muslim community.[33]

The burghers of Beirut had never reconciled themselves to their city's subordinate status in the province of Syria. For years after their original petitions of 1865, when the Muslim and Christian notables tried to persuade the government to declare Beirut the capital of Syria, the leaders of the port city continued their campaign to have Beirut either established as the capital of Syria or designated as the capital city of a new province of its own. In March 1888, Sultan Abdülhamid II finally conceded to their demands and divided Syria, creating a new coastal province with Beirut as its capital.

Although the decision held grave consequences for Damascus, the city responded to the news without comment or emotion. The most immediate impact would be on the revenues of Damascus, which fell by about one half.[34] Yet Damascus was no longer as fragile as it had been in 1865. The years of investment and development had transformed the city. The roughly rebuilt houses of the Christian quarters had been restored to their former glory. The markets of Damascus were more beautiful and modern than ever, with broad paved lanes for carts to deliver and collect their wares. The trade of Damascus adapted to changing times, with more goods arriving from Beirut via the secure carriage road, displacing the overland trade routes with Baghdad and the Hijaz of yore. The looms of Damascus continued to turn out high-quality silk and cotton fabrics that enjoyed a privileged market across Ottoman domains. The government quarter grew substantially, providing jobs and workplaces for Damascenes of all faiths. Thousands of children attended modern schools which provided the kind of diverse education that opened doors to well-paid jobs in both government and trade. In short, after a twenty-three-year spending spree, Damascus was strong enough to stand on its own without having to rely on the revenues of Beirut to survive—and thrive.

Crucially, the spending spree had reduced tensions among the different communities of Damascus. The new opportunities provided by the Ottoman government drew Christians and Muslims into ever more regular contact. They worked toward the same goals when petitioning the Ottoman government to make Damascus the capital of Syria. They sat together in government committees and in the courts. They shared in the opportunities that came with the building boom, the modernisation of markets, the opening of new schools. Tensions still bubbled to the surface in times of political crisis, as in the Balkan crises of the 1870s. But the fear of massacre, omnipresent in the first few years after the 1860 events, was gone.

Nor would it ever return. It took a quarter of a century to consign the horrors of 1860 to the past. By 1888, Damascenes had their eyes firmly on the present and the future, and had every reason to hope that their children would enjoy a better future. It was perhaps this hope, more than anything, that allowed the Damascenes to turn the page on the Damascus Events and move on.

Conclusion

Dr Mishaqa Retires to Write His Memoirs

In March 1870, Dr Mikhayil Mishaqa suffered a stroke. He was within days of his seventieth birthday, and his health had been deteriorating over recent years. He never fully recovered from the injuries he sustained in the 1860 Events, and as a physician he was able to put a name to every malady ('no less than seven,' by his own count) that he suffered in the decade following that horror. He was frequently bedridden with gout but always recovered. However, the stroke did lasting damage, leaving him partially paralysed on the right side of his body. Too ill to perform his duties as vice-consul, Mishaqa wrote to his superior in Beirut, J. Augustus Johnson, to tender his resignation after eleven years of faithful service to the United States of America.[1]

In his letter of resignation, Dr Mishaqa nominated his eldest son, Nasif, to serve as his successor. Nasif was thirty-two and had worked for years in the British consulate as both a dragoman and a clerk.

A worldly man, Nasif was fluent in English, French, and Turkish as well as in his native Arabic. He knew the ways of the diplomatic service and the workings of the Ottoman administration in Damascus. Consul Johnson accepted the suggestion and by July had secured all the necessary paperwork from Istanbul to confirm Nasif Mishaqa as America's second vice-consul in Damascus.

The change might well have come as a relief to Consul Johnson. Dr Mishaqa was a brilliant man, but he wasn't a natural diplomat. Since he was first appointed in 1859, Mishaqa had clashed with practically every Ottoman governor appointed to Damascus. He was intensely principled and argued his case relentlessly. Little wonder the governors of Damascus tried their best to avoid the man. Nasif, on the other hand, demonstrated better social skills than his illustrious father. He would represent American interests in Damascus ably for more than forty years, until the outbreak of the First World War, in 1914.[2]

For the first time in his life, Dr Mishaqa found himself without gainful employment. Like many prominent men plunged into sudden retirement, Mishaqa decided to write his memoirs. Or something bigger than just *his* memoirs. On the urgings of friends and family, he decided to commit his vast store of knowledge on the modern history of Syria to paper, weaving his family's history and his personal eyewitness accounts into that story. It was an ambitious undertaking that consumed the next three years of his life. The book was completed on 22 October 1873, and Mishaqa titled it after those who inspired it: *The Response to the Suggestion of the Loved Ones*. Circulated in handwritten copies during his lifetime, *The Response* was instantly recognised as a masterpiece. His Damascene contemporary, Nu'man Qasatli, read the work and declared it 'a very fine book.' Lebanese journalist and novelist Jurji Zaydan (1861–1914), who visited Mishaqa at home in 1883, consulted the text to draft Mishaqa's biography for the *Who's Who* of the nineteenth-century Orient that Zaydan published in the early twentieth century. Even today the book stands as one of the classics of nineteenth-century Arabic historical writing.[3]

Dr Mishaqa opened his narrative in the mid-eighteenth century, when his family, seafarers from the Greek island of Corfu, settled in Syria. In five chronological blocks, he meticulously traced the history of Syria and Lebanon from 1750 to 1873, often from his own eyewitness account. It is only in the fifth and final part of the book that he treated the tortured history of the Damascus Events and the subsequent efforts of the Ottoman government to rebuild the city and reintegrate the Christian community. I imagine Mishaqa reverting to his notebooks of consular reports for some of the detail, just as I have done in writing this book.

Although the facts in Dr Mishaqa's book correspond to those in his reports, the tone is markedly different. In his reports, Mishaqa lambasted Ottoman officials for their failings. As recently as January 1869, just four years before Mishaqa completed his book, the US vice-consul sounded alarms over renewed communal tensions in Damascus provoked by the Cretan uprising of 1866–1869 (discussed toward the end of Chapter 8). He had no confidence in the Ottoman government's ability to intervene and traced his doubt back to its handling of the 1860 Events: 'There is no doubt that the dreadful event which befell the Christians of Syria in 1860 was the work of the government itself, by order of the state. There are many proofs of that, and there isn't place here to list them.' Mishaqa's alarming report was a plea for foreign intervention to preserve the fragile Christian community from extermination. 'If the states of Europe don't take the decision to send soldiers,' he warned, 'there will not remain a trace of the Christians in Eastern lands, and the only ones who will be left will be those who abandon the Christian religion and become Muslim.'[4]

In his book, however, Dr Mishaqa took a remarkably different tone, placing full trust in the Ottoman government. From the out-set, in introducing his section on 'the massacre of the Christians of Damascus and the reasons therefor,' Mishaqa condemned the Christian victims rather than the Ottoman governors or the Muslim mob. 'The Christians in Syria,' he wrote, 'were the smaller and weaker portion in everything, and in all regards the Christians should have not only paid great respect to the Muslims but given total obedience to the authorities.' As a segue from these introductory musings to his narrative of events, Mishaqa continued in the same vein: 'Let us leave this talk of the conduct of the ignorant and look at what happened when the government's orders were disobeyed,' and turned to the tensions raised in 1860 by Christians refusing to pay the exemption fee sparing them from mandatory military service as a preliminary cause of the Events.[5]

In his account of the massacres, Dr Mishaqa repeated many of the accusations against the governor, Ahmad Pasha, and the Muslim notables implicated in the violence, that he first raised in his consular reports in 1860. Yet when he came to the end of his narrative, Mishaqa reverted to this new submissive tone. 'Let the reader know that by what I have written I intend no blame of the Empire for what it brought upon its subjects, be they Muslim, Christian or Druze, for everything it did was its right to do,' he asserted. 'My sole intention was to illustrate the results of disobedience to the orders of one's overlords and to explain the causes for what happened to the subjects and their leaders, for we have never yet seen a state wreak vengeance on obedient subjects.' If Mishaqa sounded as though he was once again blaming the victims, his closing argument should have left his readers in no doubt of the moral of his story: 'A rational person will be convinced by the results of opposition, which have been clearly set forth, that it is incumbent upon subjects to have no allegiance save to their rightful monarch, whose every order they should obey explicitly and implicitly.'[6]

How to explain the sudden resignation of the once-assertive Mikhayil Mishaqa? A different author might have feared criticising the government lest the book come to the attention of the Ottoman authorities. But Dr Mishaqa had never spared the authorities the full force of his views, and it seems unlikely that he feared their reaction more in retirement than he had while in active service. Perhaps retirement was the explanation—that Mishaqa was, to use his own words, a 'humble writer...well advanced in years, having reached the age of infirmity and confined to his home, well away from all work.' Yet the 381 pages of manuscript do not bear witness to humility or a dulling of the author's wits. His critical acumen and insightful analysis sparkle through each page of the text.[7]

In my view, Dr Mishaqa's newfound deference to Ottoman authority was a result of pragmatism rather than fatalism. He came to recognise that the European powers would never deliver Syrian Christians from Ottoman rule. Nor would they need to. With hindsight, his 1869 call for Western military intervention looked like hysterical overreaction. The Cretan crisis, and the communal tensions that the conflict provoked in Damascus, came and went with no consequences for Syrian Christians (tellingly, Mishaqa made no reference to the 1869 tensions in his book). The government's security measures had proved sufficient to deter Muslim mobs from acting on their threats against the Christians of Damascus. It was doubtless an uncomfortable moment for these Christians, but not life threatening. The Ottoman system of law and order put in place in the aftermath of the 1860 Events, and the common interests binding all Damascenes to the fragile gains of reconstruction, had proven sufficient to deter renewed violence.

Judging from his concluding remarks, Dr Mishaqa had come to be persuaded that Damascus's future *was* Ottoman, for Christians, Muslims, and Jews alike. It was a realisation bred of pragmatism, built over the fraught reconstruction era and encouraged in the years since the creation of the province of Syria in 1865. The injection of new funding and the infrastructural development of Damascus were, by 1873, beginning to bear fruit. Although corruption persisted, and Syrians still found much to criticise in Ottoman rule, Damascus had emerged from the economic death spiral provoked by the Events. Trade and industry were on the rise. The economy was expanding. And the benefits of growth and opportunity were shared among the different communities of Damascus, rather than divided in a zero-sum game in which one group's gain was at the expense of another's. Damascus was returning to prosperity, and this fragile recovery was reason enough to encourage universal obedience to the government in the interest of stability. At least that was Mishaqa's parting message to future generations of Damascenes as he drew the

narrative of his book to a close—the moral of the story of the Damascus Events, and the reconstruction and reconciliation that followed.

Dr Mishaqa's interpretive shift was undoubtedly influenced by
his colleague Butrus al-Bustani, a leading intellectual who headed
the translation offices of both the American Protestant missionaries in Lebanon and the US consulate in Beirut. It was al-Bustani
who translated Mishaqa's reports from Arabic to English for Consul Johnson's consumption. In the aftermath of the 1860 events,
al-Bustani penned a series of anonymous pamphlets that proved of
enduring influence in shaping a new social contract, both between
the different faith communities of Syria and between Arabs and the
Ottoman state. He called the pamphlets 'The Clarion of Syria' (*Nafir
Suriyya*) and signed each of the eleven issues simply as 'a patriot.'[8]

Al-Bustani has been celebrated by modern historians as one of
the leading lights of the late-nineteenth-century Arab intellectual
movement known as the *Nahda* ('renaissance'). His 1860 pamphlets
stand as one of his major contribution to political thought, recon-
ciling Arab citizens' position in the Ottoman state with the reality
of religious and ethnic divisions within the Arab-Ottoman world—
what historian Ussama Makdisi has dubbed 'the ecumenical frame.'
In Makdisi's view, 'The sectarian violence of 1860 became a catalyst
for a new ecumenical sensibility rooted in a diminished, but still viable, Ottoman sovereignty. This sensibility produced a modern ideal
and language of coexistence between Arabic-speaking Muslims and
Christians and Jews.' This basic ecumenical awareness permitted a
meaningful coexistence between Muslim and non-Muslim in the
post-1860 age, in which al-Bustani claimed Syrians would see how
their 'personal well-being' required that 'virtuous ties of unity and

concord exist between the different communities and among themselves individually.' As Makdisi concluded, "The events of 1860 constituted a glimpse of the apocalypse that men had it in their power to avert; but they just as obviously represented a glorious opportunity for spiritual redemption and material progress toward a liberated and civilized state."[9]

Viewed from this perspective, Dr Mishaqa's concluding remarks in his 1873 book seem less a capitulation than a conviction that a better future for all Syrians, free from sectarian conflict, would be achieved through 'concord' (al-Bustani used the Arabic word *ulfa*) with their Ottoman rulers.

The benefits of this 'concord' for Damascenes became apparent with the passing of the decades. The measures taken by the Ottoman authorities following the Damascus Events led to both reconstruction and reconciliation. But the significance of the Events and their aftermath go well beyond the city of Damascus, to reflect on the experience of reform and the advent of a new era of modernity in the Ottoman Empire as a whole.

Until 1860, the Ottoman reforms of the Tanzimat were imposed on the sultan's subjects without consultation or consent. The Sublime Porte was more concerned with European than Ottoman public opinion at that stage, coming out of the Second Egyptian Crisis in 1839 and the Crimean War in 1856. However, the attempt to overturn the old social order through measures such as legal equality between Muslims and non-Muslims, in the absence of any incentives or benefits to the majority population, was bound to generate resistance. The results were unprecedented communal violence in Syria, culminating in the Damascus Events. Europe's intervention following the Events could well have led to a partition of Ottoman domains and European colonialism in Syria. Instead, through the deft diplomacy of Fuad Pasha, the Ottomans navigated the crisis and preserved their sovereignty and territorial integrity.

The need to reform the empire was in no way diminished in the aftermath of the Damascus Events. Yet the implementation of reform was handled very differently after 1860. The government continued to impose new measures on its subjects but was more careful to balance demands with benefits, responsibilities with rights. Through reforms like the 1858 Land Law, the government came to tax its citizens more efficiently, but it also gave them title to their land that made it a much more tradeable good and collateral for borrowing. For the first time, title to property could pass from parents to children through inheritance without having to resort to complex trusts. Moreover, the enhanced tax revenues provided the government with means to invest in Ottoman society—in the road networks, in markets, in schools— just as had been done in reconstruction Damascus. Moreover, the 1864 Provincial Reform Law gave Ottoman subjects a greater role in local government, allowing Muslims, Christians, and Jews to vote and also to stand for elected office. Communal leaders and notables were quick to take advantage of the new positions in the municipal councils and courts to enhance their power and influence in their own society. Grubby politics perhaps, but the advent of elected office marked an important transition from subjects to citizens in the reformed Ottoman Empire. These gains were consolidated in 1876 with Sultan Abdülhamid II's adoption of the Ottoman Constitution.

At one level, the 1860 crisis was a direct consequence of the early Tanzimat reforms. The success of the reconstruction effort, and the later measures of the post-1860 Tanzimat, played a decisive role in the restoration of Damascus. The later Tanzimat also spelled the end of the old Ottoman order, of governors who ruled through absolute power and the legal subordination of the non-Muslim communities to the Muslim majority. Those changes ushered in the advent of the modern Middle East, based on accountable government, regular taxation, municipal development, and citizen participation. This is not to say that the Ottoman government emerged from the Tanzimat with all its problems solved. Contemporary accounts continued to lament the incompetence and venality of individual officials, with the pessimism that marks political analysis down to our times. Yet 1860 marked a turning point from an old to a new age, with the Ottoman Empire emerging, in the expression of the day, as 'the well-protected domains.'[10]

I have long contemplated the role of 1860 as a turning point between the old Ottoman order and the modern Middle East. When I took up my job in Oxford in 1991, I inherited a history course first created by the great historian Albert Hourani thirty years earlier: 'The History of the Middle East, 1860–1952.' The end date, coinciding with the Free Officers' Revolution in Egypt, was self-evident, but I always meant to ask Mr Hourani why he chose to start his survey of the modern history of the Middle East in 1860. I could think of so many other starting points for that story: the French occupation of Egypt in 1798, the rise to power of Mehmed Ali Pasha in Egypt in 1805, and the start of the Tanzimat Reforms in

1839 all seemed essential milestones in the region's modern history. Since Hourani's passing in 1993, I have been left to second-guess his reasons.

At one level, I believe that Hourani was guided in his choice of starting date by the central role the 1860 Events played in his ancestral home of Lebanon. The new governance structures crafted by the European Commission for Mount Lebanon imbedded sectarianism as a principle of public office, with a Christian governor assisted by an elected assembly with quotas for each of the major religious communities. In that sense, the 1860 Events marked the beginning of the confessional system of government that has shaped Lebanese politics down to the present day. Moreover, the whole idea of a greater Lebanon, expanding beyond the highlands of Mount Lebanon to include the coastal plain and the Bekaa Valley, was first introduced by General Beaufort and the French commissioners in 1860. Although this map was not acted upon in 1861, both the idea of Greater Lebanon and the sectarian system of government would be resurrected by the French colonial authorities when they assumed a League of Nations mandate over Syria and Lebanon in 1920.[11]

The French gerrymandered the boundaries of Greater Lebanon (which corresponds to the modern state of Lebanon) to ensure the largest land mass while still keeping a slim Christian majority, a strategy that would impose a Christian identity on the new state and benefit France's Maronite supporters. Inevitably, the system came under strain as differential birthrates gave rise to a Muslim majority in Lebanon during the interwar years. When Lebanon's confessional system of government collapsed into civil war, first in 1958 and again in 1975, historians traced the origins of sectarian conflict in Lebanon to the Events of 1860. In this sense, the modern era of Lebanese history began in 1860.

Damascus did not experience a sectarian legacy after 1860. Instead, reconstruction was accompanied by the enduring reintegration of the Christian community into the social and economic life of the city. Because Damascus was an Ottoman provincial capital, the reforms of the Tanzimat influenced its politics more directly than they did in Mount Lebanon. As such, I believe that 1860 stands as the turning point in Ottoman reforms, when new government measures marked the end of the old Ottoman order and the start of a new age of Ottoman modernity. The Damascus Events played a central role in that transformation, making 1860 the turning point between the old order and the modern Middle East.

Following reconstruction, the 1860 Events left no sectarian legacy between Muslims and Christians in Damascus. In the twentieth century, Christians and Muslims united in nationalist movements and forged a secular identity to which all Syrians might subscribe. It was only after the outbreak of civil war in Syria in 2011, and the emergence of the Islamic State in Iraq and Syria in 2014, that the country experienced sectarian conflict. Even then, the Christians were not the only or even the main target of the fighting, and no one thought to link the current civil war to the Events of 1860.

The success of Ottoman measures in healing communal divisions is all the more remarkable given the low esteem in which both the European powers and the local Christian community held the

Sublime Porte. The Ottoman minister plenipotentiary, Fuad Pasha, played a crucial role in winning the confidence of both the Europeans and the local Christians. But Fuad was in Damascus only for the first eighteen months after the Events. He left to others the difficult tasks of raising indemnities to compensate Christian losses and to oversee the reconstruction of the damaged Christian quarters. More credit is due to the men on the ground who, year by year, slowly advanced the reconstruction programme. Moreover, the success was the product of a string of governors, appointed to Damascus for two- or three-year terms, with little by way of a template to guide them. Their trials and errors provide some useful principles that might still be of value to communities recovering from deeply divisive traumas.

Fuad Pasha led the way with a forceful reimposition of the rule of law in the ghastly disorder of post-massacre Damascus. His efforts to arrest those implicated in the massacres without regard to their social standing, to put them on trial, and to execute the guilty sent a clear signal that no one was above the law. That signal was of particular importance to the scarred Christian community in need of reassurance that the state would protect their lives and property in the future, as it had failed to do in 1860. But Fuad did well to resist European pressures to bring yet more commoners and notables before the firing squad or to the gallows. Further executions would almost certainly have encouraged growing Muslim hostility against both the Christian survivors and the Ottoman state that might have led to renewed violence. The Ottoman minister seemed to strike a constructive balance by imposing enough justice to restore law and order without provoking a retaliation from the Muslim community.

So not total justice, pursuing every rioter guilty of murder, theft, or arson, but enough justice to secure respect for the law moving forward.

Similarly, the Ottoman government struck an equilibrium in its indemnity programme, taxing the Muslims of Syria to provide funding for the reconstruction of the Christian quarters. This was both a collective punishment against the Muslim community as a whole, penalising those innocent of taking part in the violence along with the guilty, and the only means to raise the funds needed to rebuild. The Ottomans probably knew from the outset that they would never raise the necessary sums to indemnify all the Christians' losses. But the punitive tax provided enough funding to enable the homeless Christians to build what at first must have been very rudimentary shelter and to secure the tools to resume their trades. The fact that most Christians probably received no more than half their claims no doubt imposed tremendous hardship on the survivors of the Events. Yet prolonging the indemnity taxes to try to honour a greater share of Christian claims would have provoked growing resentment and resistance from the Muslim majority that would have worked against the reintegration of the Christian community.

These measures alone—punishing the guilty and providing indemnities for the survivors—were essential but insufficient to rebuild Damascus and reintegrate the Christian community. Damascus needed substantial investment to generate a broader prosperity that would transcend communal interests. The expansion of the revenues of Damascus, following the introduction of the Provincial Reform Law and the creation of the super-province of Syria in 1865, was transformative in the city's history. Public spending on infrastructure, markets, and government offices created opportunities for all Damascenes—Muslims, Christians, and Jews alike. And the modernisation and expansion of the state school system provided all Damascenes equal access to well-paid government jobs. Markets, cafés, government buildings, and schools provided ever more public spaces for Damascenes of different communities to meet, work, and socialise together. As Damascenes looked to a more promising future for themselves and their children, they grew ever more willing to turn the page, consign the Damascus Events to the past, and place their trust in an Ottoman future. That, at least, seemed to have been Dr Mishaqa's conclusion in writing his book.

By 1888, when the Ottoman government decided to detach Beirut and much of the Lebanese coastline from the province of Syria, a new generation of notables had risen to prominence in Damascus. Among contemporaries of the Events, the young diarist Muhammad Abu al-Sa'ud al-Hasibi came into his own during the reconstruction era. In 1869 he was elected to the Majlis (the city council of Damascus), and upon his father's death in 1876 he assumed leadership of the Hasibi clan. He was called to Istanbul and decorated by Sultan Abdülhamid II for his services to Damascus, and in 1898 he was elected Naqib al-Ashraf: chairman of the association of the descendants of the Prophet Muhammad, an influential group of Damascene notables. He lived until 1914—the same year that Nasif Mishaqa retired as US vice-consul in Damascus—when the men of the nineteenth century in turn gave way to a younger generation that came of age in the twentieth century.[12]

The 1860 generation had long since shuffled off this mortal coil. Damascenes would have learned with mixed feelings of the passing of Fuad Pasha. To Christians he was a saviour, yet many Damascene Muslims saw Fuad as a scourge. Architect of Damascus's reconstruction, Fuad died in the French city of Nice in February 1869 at the relatively young age of fifty-five. He had accompanied Sultan Abdülaziz on a visit to Paris in 1867 and took ill, remaining in France for medical treatment. He never recovered sufficiently to return home to Istanbul.[13]

Amir 'Abd al-Qadir withdrew from Damascene society in the years following the Events. He made no effort to hide his disdain for those notables he believed played an active role in the massacre, or those he accused of failing to use their influence to prevent the violence. For their part, the Muslim elite took an increasingly jaundiced view of the Algerian freedom fighter they once had celebrated. Far from leading resistance to European encroachment in Syria as he had done in Algeria, 'Abd al-Qadir seemed all too willing to accept Western accolades as foreign consuls lined up to pin medals on his chest. It was as though he were being rewarded for betraying the very Muslim notables who had welcomed him to their ranks. The decorations were the least of the amir's rewards. The Algerian appeared to be on everyone's payroll. He, his family, and key retainers received generous stipends from both the French and the Ottoman governments while Damascene Muslims were being squeezed by indemnity taxes to finance the reconstruction of the Christian quarters. Little wonder that the Muslim notables gave 'Abd al-Qadir the cold shoulder.[14]

Ostracised in Damascus, 'Abd al-Qadir went abroad. In 1863 he returned to Mecca, a city he had last visited with his father when he was only seventeen, to perform a second pilgrimage. On his return from pilgrimage, he spent time in Egypt in 1864 before travelling to Istanbul 'to pay his respects to the Sultan.' Sultan Abdülaziz received the amir with full honours and pinned yet another medal on the Algerian's chest in May 1865. The amir later submitted claims for his expenses during his two months' stay in Istanbul totalling in excess of Pt. 65,000 for rent and suitable furnishings. Had word of his extravagance reached the Muslim notables of Damascus, it would only have fanned the flames of their resentments against him.[15]

Rather than face the hostility of the Damascenes, 'Abd al-Qadir travelled around Europe to a hero's welcome. He called on Emperor Napoleon III in Paris in 1865, where he was also embraced by a number of Masonic lodges. Freemasonry seemed to appeal to 'Abd al-Qadir's esoteric spirituality. He also subscribed to Masonic beliefs in a universal brotherhood that sought to reconcile the three monotheistic faiths. Speaking to a group of Masons, he claimed: 'In my view, any man who doesn't profess belief in masonry is incomplete. I hope that one day masonic principles will spread across the entire world. Once they do, all people will live in peace and fraternity.' The amir travelled to London, where influential figures in politics and culture celebrated the man and his accomplishments. He returned to Paris in 1867 to attend the Universal Exposition, one of the highlights in the reign of Napoleon III, and in 1869 he joined Empress Eugénie for the opening of the Suez Canal in Egypt.[16]

'Abd al-Qadir's world was turned upside down by the French loss in the Franco-Prussian War in 1870. In the decisive Battle of Sedan, the Prussians captured his patron, Napoleon III, who abdicated his throne and went to Britain in exile, where he died in

1873. The Prussians tried to turn 'Abd al-Qadir against the French with the promise of restoring him to power in his native Algeria. Although 'Abd al-Qadir declined, his son Muhyi al-Din accepted German assistance and returned to Algeria to raise an ill-fated rebellion there against the French. The Si Mokrani Revolt of 1871 would prove the century's last major Algerian insurrection against French rule. 'Abd al-Qadir declared his opposition to the revolt, despite his own son's involvement, and the French ultimately suppressed the movement as ever with great violence. Although 'Abd al-Qadir preserved French support for himself and his family in Damascus, his influence in France never recovered after the collapse of the Second Empire.

Back in Damascus, 'Abd al-Qadir attempted to return to his earlier life of Sufi mysticism and religious scholarship. He fell ill in 1873, leading several newspapers to publish premature obituaries. Yet the years began to weigh heavily on the Algerian prince. The American essayist and journalist Charles Dudley Warner called on 'Abd al-Qadir when he visited Damascus in the spring of 1875. Accompanied by the US vice-consul, Nasif Mishaqa, Warner had expected a more imposing figure: 'I had heard so much of the striking, venerable, and even magnificent appearance of this formidable desert hero, that I experienced a little disappointment in the reality.' Warner described a man of 'medium size and scarcely medium height' who was beginning to show his age 'by a little pallor, by a visible want of bodily force, and by a lack of lustre in those once fiery and untamable eyes.' Warner suspected that the amir dyed his jet-black beard. The two men talked politics, 'Abd al-Qadir expressing his hope that the Americans had put the divisions of their own civil war behind them, and raising his concerns for Syria and Egypt, where the people were 'oppressed with taxation and exactions of all sorts.' Their interview at an end, the aging amir accompanied his guests through his courtyard home to the front door to bid them farewell.[17]

'Abd al-Qadir died in his home in Damascus on 26 May 1883. His family and Algerian followers carried his body to the Umayyad Mosque for final prayers. Although we have no record of who attended the funeral, the fact that he was eulogised in the city's most illustrious mosque might have reflected a posthumous reconciliation between the Algerian and the Muslim notables of Damascus. He was buried near the tomb of his spiritual guide, the Sufi master Ibn 'Arabi, on the slopes of al-Salihiyya overlooking the city of Damascus, where he would lay in rest until 1965, when the newly independent state of Algeria exhumed his remains for reburial in a mausoleum in Algiers as a celebrated national hero.[18]

Shaykh Sa'id al-Istuwani noted 'Abd al-Qadir's funeral in his diary and probably attended the funeral himself. The former preacher of the Umayyad Mosque had received recognition and promotions in the years after the Events. In 1867 he left his beloved Damascus for a two-year posting as chief justice to the port city of Tripoli (today in northern Lebanon). He returned to Damascus in 1869 to serve as chief justice of the Sharia Court, where he worked for the next four years. He retired from the court circuit in 1873 and spent the remainder of his days teaching Islamic theology from his home in Hayy al-Sulaymaniyya. He taught until the day he died, on 30 April 1888.[19]

Despite advanced age and its infirmities, Dr Mishaqa outlived most of his generation and all of the eyewitnesses cited in this book except the young al-Hasibi. He remained active well into his eighties. Like 'Abd al-Qadir, Mishaqa attracted a regular stream of visitors, the two men becoming human tourist attractions. 'The learned Mikhayil Mishaqa is famous among the people of the east and the west and is held in the highest regard by all,' the Christian historian of Damascus, Nu'man Qasatli, wrote in the 1870s:

> All sorts of people call on him regularly to visit him. He is tall and of robust build; intelligent, courteous, a gentle man, a man of integrity and humility who welcomes each of his visitors and speaks to each in accordance with his standing and occupation. No visitor of any social rank calls on him without taking pleasure in the exchange, leaving with praise and thanks.[20]

In 1883 Dr Mishaqa received Jurji Zaydan, who echoed Qasatli's praise:

> He is a man of gravity and dignity, made venerable by his white hair. He wore a turban and long gown. He is tall in stature, a large frame, well spoken, widely knowledgeable, most welcoming of visitors as are the Damascenes generally. He showed us many of his unpublished writings, including a treatise on Arabic musical modes, works on mathematics and an almanac to calculate the days, months and years for one hundred years to give the correspondence between the Arabic, Roman, Coptic, Hebrew and Hijri calendars, and the occurrence of

solar and lunar eclipses over the breadth and width of Syria, and other works.[21]

Mikhayil Mishaqa died in Damascus on 6 July 1888 at the advanced age of 88. I imagine him on his deathbed, surrounded by his wife and children. His eldest son, Nasif, was fifty, and we know from his consular service that he lived well into the twentieth century. Mishaqa's second son, Salim, would have been forty-four and, like his father and brother before him, served in the British consulate as a dragoman. The third son, Ibrahim, would have been thirty-eight and, following in his father's footsteps, was a physician trained in the medical faculty of the American College in Beirut. His daughter, Salma, only six years old at the time of the Events, would have been thirty-four at the time of her father's passing. Iskandar, the youngest, would have been thirty-one. When he completed his book in 1873, Mishaqa already had one grandson, Nasif's boy, named Mikhayil in his grandfather's honour. No doubt by the time of his death, Mishaqa would have had several more grandchildren—a modern genealogical website records at least sixteen.[22]

Those who loved him no doubt mourned his passing, but today we can only marvel at what a remarkable life Mikhayil Mishaqa lived. In many ways, his life's trajectory of struggle and survival followed that of his adoptive home, Damascus. Growing up through the conflicts and turmoil that rocked Syria from the 1820s down to 1860, he, like Damascus, was almost destroyed by the Events. Slowly he recovered his health, just as Damascus slowly rebuilt, but both bore the scars of their ordeals. By the 1870s, Dr Mishaqa began to trust in his city's future under Ottoman rule. His children were growing up in an increasingly prosperous city and entering respectable professions. They in turn started families and had children who could look toward the future with optimism.

At the end of the nineteenth century, Damascus would soon face all the trials and tribulations that came with the twentieth century—world war, European imperialism, nationalism, autocracy. But it would do so freed from sectarian violence. As he breathed his last, Dr Mishaqa and all those of his generation who survived the Damascus Events could go to the grave confident that their children and grandchildren faced a safer and better future. One could not ask for more.

الذي محمد لسامه ركتم

معامل حسامه

محمد بن سليمان

دولة امريكا

عالم

ACKNOWLEDGEMENTS

To write this book, I withdrew from the pleasures and distractions of my Oxford community to spend a year in the magnificent city of Toulouse. Inspired during the working week by the 'pink city' of France (so called for the distinctive color of its traditional bricks), I was sustained and supported each weekend by my dear friends Claude and Henri Mollinari in their village home in nearby Palaminy. Over wonderful meals and fine wine, they had me recount the previous week's research and writing, sharpening my narrative skills in ways that definitely influenced the following week's revisions and writing. Their enthusiasm and encouragement saw me through from start to finish. I could not have written this book without them.

In more than thirty years of research, I chalked up debts to librarians and archivists across three continents. Particular thanks are due to the remarkable team in the United States National Archives, in both Washington, DC, and College Park, Maryland. It was through their determination that we were able to locate the crucial first volumes of records from the US vice-consulate in Damascus that inspired this book. I wish to record my gratitude to the staff of the Ottoman State Archives (Başbakanlık Osmanlı Arşivi) in Istanbul and to Alidost Numan for his invaluable work as my research assistant in those rich archives. I am grateful to the staff in the Jafet Library of the American University of Beirut for their help in providing microfilms of contemporary manuscripts relating to the Damascus Events. I wish to express my particular thanks to Miss Debbie Usher of the Middle East Centre Archive in St Antony's College, Oxford, for her help with both the Richard Wood Collection and nineteenth-century photographs of Damascus. My thanks to Dr Joanne Bloom, photographic resources librarian at Harvard's Fine Arts Library, for her help in securing copies of Bonfils images of Damascus, and to Karen Lawson, picture library manager for the Royal Collection Trust, for her assistance in securing copies of the remarkable Francis Bedford images of 1862 Damascus.

Dr Martin Davis, digital map curator at the Bodleian Libraries, Oxford, gave generously of his precious time and profound expertise in researching and creating the maps for this book, for which I am deeply in his debt.

Many colleagues helped me track down out-of-print and hard-to-access books. I would like to thank Matthieu Rey and Dima de Clerck for all their help in securing the wonderful edited volume that Dima coedited on the 1860 Events, then out of print. I am also indebted to Sami Moubayed for sharing his excellent new study in Arabic on the Damascus Events. Talha Çiçek provided an essential second opinion on key Ottoman documents, a tricky language in the best of times and trickier yet when the author of a document is trying to cover his tracks, as the disgraced governor of Damascus, Ahmad Pasha, did in his only report to the Sublime Porte on the Events.

I am most grateful to Catherine Clarke of Felicity Bryan Associates, and to George Lucas of Inkwell, for their advice and guidance in securing the very best possible publishers for this book. And I am delighted to have had the opportunity once again to work with Lara Heimert at Basic Books and Simon Winder at Penguin, the best possible editors in the business. My thanks to the amazing team at Basic Books who helped guide the book through production, particularly Michelle Welsh-Horst, production editor; Kristen Kim, editorial assistant; and Dr Donald Pharr for his sensitive copy-editing of the text. May those who find this book readable join me in thanking its editors.

Friends and colleagues read draft chapters and provided invaluable feedback as the manuscript took shape. Dr Peter Hill not only shared the manuscript of his own brilliant new intellectual biography of Mikhayil Mishaqa but provided detailed comments on this book that enriched the text and protected me from errors. My dear friend and colleague Leila Fawaz, whose 1994 study of the Events in Mount Lebanon and Damascus has shaped the field for the past three decades, read each chapter with insight and generosity. Joshua Landis, my graduate school roommate, joined me in Toulouse for a month of his own sabbatical and shared his deep knowledge of Syrian history in reading the first half of the manuscript. Others read individual chapters along the way, and I benefitted from the insights and criticisms of each of them: Ariel Blavatnik, Diana Darke, Sami Moubayed, Joseph Sassoon, and Dana Sajdi.

Nor was my family spared. I wish to thank my mother, Margaret Rogan, who from deep in retirement read early chapters and provided her invaluable encouragement. My daughter Isabelle and son

Richard each read early chapters and buoyed me with their enthusiasm. Most of all I wish to record my love and gratitude to my wife, Ngaire, who indulged my decision to retreat to France to write this book, whose regular visits raised my spirits to keep on writing, and whose constant publicity for the work in progress has generated remarkable prepublication interest in certain circles. For all your support, Ngaire, this one is yours.

BIBLIOGRAPHY

Archives and Manuscripts

Lebanon

American University of Beirut, Jafet Library

    Tanahudat Suriyya [The sighs of Syria], MS 956.9 T16

    Kitab al-Ahzan [The book of sorrows], MS 956.9 K62kA

Turkey

Basbakanlik Osmanli Arsivi (BOA)

Irade (Imperial decrees) 1277–1293 (1860–1876)

    Irade Dahiliye (I.Dah, internal affairs)

    Irâde Hâriciye (I.Har, foreign and minority affairs)

    Irâde Meclis-I Mahsus (I.MM, Council of Ministers)

    Irâde Meclis-I Vâlâ (I.MVL, Supreme Council of Judicial Ordinances)

    Irâde Sûra-yi Devlet (I.SD, Council of State)

United Kingdom

Middle East Centre Archive, St Antony's College, Oxford

Sir Richard Wood Collection: Letters from Hanna Misk to Sir Richard Wood, 1862–1877

Royal Collection Trust, London, England

Prince of Wales's Journal: 6 February–14 June 1862

United Kingdom National Archives, Kew, England

FO 406 10 Correspondence relating to the Affairs of Syria, 1860–1861

FO 406 11 Part II. Correspondence relating to the Affairs of Syria, January to July 1861

FO 406 12 Correspondence respecting Consul Burton's Proceedings at Damascus, 1868–1871

United States

United States National Archives and Research Administration, College Park, Maryland: Record Group 84: Department of State, Consular Correspondence.

Damascus Vice-Consulate: Correspondence vol. 1 (1859–1865), vol. 2 (1866–1870), vol. 3 (1871–1873), vol. 4 (1872–1890), vol. 5 (1890–1899).

Beirut Consulate: C8.1—Official Letters Received: vol. 42 Instructions and General Correspondence (1865); vol. 44 I & GC (1861); vol. 45 I & GC (1863); vol. 46 I & GC (1864); vol. 80 Miscellaneous Correspondence (May–December 1860). C8.2—Official Letters Sent: vol. 22 Miscellaneous Correspondence (1858–1863); vol. 24 Legation (1855–1863); vol. 35 Miscellaneous (1860–1864); vol. 36 Official correspondence (1853–1862); vol. 124 (1862).

Published Sources

Abu-Mounes, Rana. *Muslim-Christian Relations in Damascus amid the 1860 Riot*. Leiden: Brill, 2022.

Abu Shaqra, Yusif Khattar. *Al-Harakat fi Lubnan ila `ahd al-mutasarrifiyya* [The movements in Lebanon until the era of the Mutasarrifiyya]. Beirut: Matba`a al-Ittihad, 1952.

Akarli, Engin. *The Long Peace: Ottoman Lebanon, 1861–1920*. London: I.B. Tauris, 1993.

Al-Barudi, Fakhri. *Mudhakkirat al-Barudi* [Memoirs of al-Barudi]. Beirut: Dar al-Hayat, 1951.

Albert Edward, Prince of Wales. 'The Prince of Wales's Journal: 6 February–14 June 1862.' Royal Collection Trust RA/VIC/MAIN/EVIID/1862, www.rct.uk.

Al-Bitar, `Abd al-Rizaq. *Hilyat al-bashar fi tarikh al-qarn al-thalith `ashar* [The embellishment of mankind in the thirteenth century]. Damascus, 1961–1963.

Al-Bustani, Butrus. *The Clarion of Syria: A Patriot's Call against the Civil War of 1860*. Oakland: University of California Press, 2019.

Al-Haj, Badr, and Ahmad Asfahani. *Mukhbir al-qunsuliyya: Rasa'il Yuhanna Misk ila Richard Wood, 1862–1877* [Informant of the Consulate: Letters of Yuhanna Misk to Richard Wood]. Beirut: Kutub, n.d. (2009).

Al-Jaza'iri, Muhammad ibn `Abd al-Qadir. *Tuhfat al-za'ir fi tarikh al-Jaza'ir wa'l-Amir `Abd al-Qadir* [A masterful review of the history of Algeria and of the Amir `Abd al-Qadir], 2nd ed. Beirut: Dar al-Yaqiza al-`Arabiyya, 1964.

Allen, Beverly. *Rape Warfare: The Hidden Genocide in Bosnia-Herzegovina and Croatia*. Minneapolis: University of Minnesota Press, 1996.

Al-Qasimi, Zafir. *Maktab ʿAnbar: Suwar wa dhikrayat min hayatina al-thaqafiyya waʾl-siyasiyya waʾl-ijtimaʿiyya* [Maktab ʿAnbar: Images and memories from our social, political, and cultural lives]. Beirut, 1964.

Al-Ustuwani, Muhammad Saʿid, ed. *Mashahid wa ahdath dimish-qiyya fi muntasif al-qarn al-tasiʿ ʿashar, 1840–1861* [Damascene scenes and events in the mid-19th century, 1840–1861]. Damascus: Dar al-Jumhuriyya, 1994.

ʿAwwad, ʿAbd al-ʿAziz Muhammad. *Al-Idara al-ʿuthmaniyya fi wilayat suriyya, 1864–1914* [Ottoman administration in the province of Syria, 1864–1914]. Cairo: Dar al-Maʿarif, 1969.

Barbir, Karl. *Ottoman Rule in Damascus, 1708–1758*. Princeton, NJ: Princeton University Press, 1980.

Bellemare, Alexandre. *Abd-el-Kader, sa vie politique et militaire*. Paris: Hachette, 1863.

Ben-Bassat, Yuval, and Yossi Ben-Zrtzi. 'Ottoman Maps of the Empire's Arab Provinces, 1850s to the First World War.' *Imago Mundi* 70, no. 2 (2018): 199–211.

Bjornlund, Matthias. ' "A Fate Worse Than Dying": Sexual Violence During the Armenian Genocide.' In *Brutality and Desire: War and Sexuality in Europe's Twentieth Century*, edited by Dagmar Herzog, 16–58. London: Palgrave MacMillan, 2008.

Blake, Corinne. 'Training Arab-Ottoman Bureaucrats: Syrian Graduates of the Mülkiye Mektebi, 1890–1920.' PhD diss., Princeton University, 1991.

Braude, Benjamin, ed. *Christians and Jews in the Ottoman Empire.* Boulder: Lynne Rienner, 2014.

Burton, Isabel. *The Inner Life of Syria, Palestine, and the Holy Land.* London: Henry S. King, 1875.

Chevalier, Dominique. 'Western Development and Eastern Crisis in the Mid-Nineteenth Century: Syria Confronted with the European Economy.' In *Beginnings of Modernization in the Middle East: The Nineteenth Century,* edited by William R. Polk and Richard L. Chambers, 205–222. Chicago: University of Chicago Press, 1968.

Churchill, Charles Henry. *Life of Abdel Kader, Ex-Sultan of the Arabs of Algeria.* London: Chapman and Hall, 1867.

Curtis, George William. *The Howadji in Syria.* New York: Harper, 1856.

Danziger, Raphael. *Abd al-Qadir and the Algerians.* New York: Holmes and Meier, 1977.

Davison, Roderic H. *Reform in the Ottoman Empire, 1856–1876.* Princeton, NJ: Princeton University Press, 1963.

De Clerck, Dima, Carla Eddé, Naila Kaidbey, and Souad Slim, eds. *1860: Histoires et mémoires d'un conflit.* Beirut and Damascus: IFPO, 2015.

Deguilhem, Randi. 'State Civil Education in Late Ottoman Damascus: A Unifying or a Separating Force?' In *The Syrian Land: Processes of Integration and Fragmentation,* edited by Thomas Philipp and Birgit Schaebler, 221–250. Stuttgart: Franz Steiner, 1998.

Deguilhem-Scheom, Randi. 'Idées française et enseignement ottoman: L'école Maktab 'Anbar à Damas.' *Revue du Monde Musulman et de la Méditerranée* 52/53 (1989): 199–206.

Deringil, Selim. *The Well-Protected Domains: Ideology and the Legitimation of Power in the Ottoman Empire, 1876–1909*. London: I.B. Tauris, 1997.

Doumani, Beshara. *Rediscovering Palestine: Merchants and Peasants in Jabal Nablus, 1700–1900*. Berkeley: University of California Press, 1995.

Edwards, Richard. *La Syrie, 1840–1862*. Paris: Aymot, 1862.

El-Hage, Badr. *Des Photographes à Damas, 1840–1918*. Paris: Marval, 2000.

El Kenz, David, ed. *Le massacre, objet d'histoire*. Paris: Gallimard, 2005.

Étienne, Bruno. *Abdelkader*. Paris: Fayard/Pluriel, 2012.

Fahmy, Khaled. *In Quest of Justice: Islamic Law and Forensic Medicine in Modern Egypt*. Oakland: University of California Press, 2018.

Farah, Caesar E. *The Politics of Interventionism in Ottoman Lebanon 1830–1861*. London: I.B. Tauris, 2000.

Farley, J. Lewis. *The Massacres in Syria*. London: Bradbury & Evans, 1861.

Farley, J. Lewis. *Two Years in Syria*. London: Saunders and Otley, 1858.

Fawaz, Leila Tarazi. 'Amir Abd al-Qadir and the Damascus "Incident" in 1860.' In *Études sur les villes du Proche-Orient XVIe–XIXe siècles*, edited by Brigitte Marino, 263–272. Damascus: Presses de l'IFPO, 2001.

Fawaz, Leila Tarazi. 'The Beirut-Damascus Road: Connecting the Syrian Coast to the Interior in the 19th Century.' In *The Syrian Land: Processes of Integration and Fragmentation*, edited by

Thomas Philipp and Birgit Schaebler, 19–28. Stuttgart: Franz Steiner Verlag, 1998.

Fawaz, Leila Tarazi. *Merchants and Migrants in Nineteenth-Century Beirut*. Cambridge, MA: Harvard University Press, 1983.

Fawaz, Leila Tarazi. *An Occasion for War: Civil Conflict in Lebanon and Damascus in 1860*. London: I.B. Tauris, 1994.

Fortna, Benjamin C. *Imperial Classroom: Islam, the State and Education in the Late Ottoman Empire*. Oxford: Oxford University Press, 2002.

Frankel, Jonathan. *The Damascus Affair: 'Ritual Murder,' Politics, and the Jews in 1840*. Cambridge: Cambridge University Press, 1997.

Gambier, James William. 'The Life of Midhat Pasha.' *Nineteenth Century* 3 (1878): 71–96.

Ghazzal, Zouhair. *L'Économie politique de Damas durant le XIXe siècle: Structures traditionnelles et capitalisme*. Damascus: Institut Français de Damas, 1993.

Goey, Ferry de. *Consuls and the Institutions of Global Capitalism, 1783–1914*. London: Pickering & Chatto, 2014.

Gross, Jan T. *Neighbors: The Destruction of the Jewish Community in Jedwabne, Poland*. Princeton, NJ: Princeton University Press, 2001.

Gross, Max. 'Ottoman Rule in the Province of Damascus, 1860–1909.' PhD diss., Georgetown University, 1979.

Guys, Henri. *Esquisse de l'état politique et commercial de la Syrie*. Paris: Chez France, 1862.

Hakim, Carol. *The Origins of the Lebanese National Idea, 1840–1920*. Berkeley: University of California Press, 2013.

Hanna, ʿAbdullah. ʿAdwaʾ ʿala ahdath 1860 al-taʾifiyya fi Dimashq wa aryafiha [Light on the sectarian events of 1860 in Damascus and its countryside].' In *1860: Histoires et mémoires d'un conflit*, edited by Dima de Clerck, Carla Eddé, Naila Kaidbey, and Souad Slim, 234–270. Beirut: IFPO, 2015.

Hanssen, Jens. *Fin de Siècle Beirut: The Making of an Ottoman Provincial Capital*. Oxford: Oxford University Press, 2005.

Harik, Iliya F. *Politics and Change in a Traditional Society: Lebanon, 1711–1845*. Princeton, NJ: Princeton University Press, 1968.

Harris, William. *Lebanon: A History, 600–2011*. New York: Oxford University Press, 2012.

Hill, Peter. *Prophet of Reason: Science, Religion and the Origins of the Modern Middle East*. London: Oneworld Academic, 2024.

Hourani, Albert. *A History of the Arab Peoples*. Cambridge, MA: Harvard University Press, 1991.

Hourani, Albert. 'Ottoman Reform and the Politics of Notables.' In *Beginnings of Modernization in the Middle East: The Nineteenth Century*, edited by William R. Polk and Richard L. Chambers, 41–68. Chicago: University of Chicago Press, 1968.

Hurewitz, J. C. *The Middle East and North Africa in World Politics*. New Haven, CT: Yale University Press, 1975.

Ibesch, Ahmad, and Koutaiba Shihabi. *Maʿalim Dimashq al-tarikhiyya* [A Toponymical Survey of Damascus]. Damascus: Ministry of Culture, 1996.

Ismail, Adel, ed. *Documents Diplomatiques et Consulaires Relatifs à l'Histoire du Liban vol. 10 (1853–1861)*. Beirut: Éditions de Oeuvres Politiques et Historiques, 1978.

Issawi, Charles, ed. *The Economic History of the Middle East, 1800–1914*. Chicago: University of Chicago Press, 1966.

Issawi, Charles. *The Fertile Crescent 1800–1914: A Documentary Economic History*. New York: Oxford University Press, 1988.

Jessup, Henry Harris. *The Women of the Arabs*. New York: Dodd & Mead, 1873.

Kane, Eileen. *Russian Hajj: Empire and the Pilgrimage to Mecca*. Ithaca, NY: Cornell University Press, 2015.

Keenan, Brigid. *Damascus: Hidden Treasures of the Old City*. London: Thames & Hudson, 2001.

Kerr, Malcolm H. *Lebanon in the Last Years of Feudalism, 1840–1868: A Contemporary Account by Antun Dahir al-'Aqiqi and Other Documents*. Beirut: American University of Beirut Press, 1959.

Keskinkiliç, Erdogan, and Ebubekir Ceylan. 'Her Majesty's Protected Subjects: The Mishaqa Family in Ottoman Damascus.' *Middle Eastern Studies* 51 (2015): 175–194.

Khalaf, Samir. *Persistence and Change in 19th Century Lebanon*. Syracuse, NY: Syracuse University Press, 1979.

Khoury, Philip S. *Urban Notables and Arab Nationalism: The Politics of Damascus, 1860–1920*. Cambridge: Cambridge University Press, 1983.

Khuri-Makdisi, Ilham. *The Eastern Mediterranean and the Making of Global Radicalism, 1860–1914*. Berkeley: University of California Press, 2010.

Kiser, John W. *Commander of the Faithful: The Life and Times of Emir Abd el-Kader*. Rhinebeck, NY: Monkfish, 2008.

Krimsti, Feras. 'The Massacre in Damascus, July 1860.' In *Christian-Muslim Relations: A Bibliographical History*, edited by David Thomas and John Chesworth, 378–406. Leiden: Brill, 2021.

Lamartine, Alphonse de. *Travels in the East, Including a Journey in the Holy Land*. Edinburgh: William and Robert Chambers, 1839.

Lellouch, Benjamin. 'Puissance et justice retenue du sultan ottoman: Les massacres sur les fronts iranien et égyptien (1514–1517).' In *Le massacre, objet d'histoire*, edited by David El Kenz, 171–182. Paris: Gallimard, 2005.

Lewis, Bernard. *Istanbul and the Civilization of the Ottoman Empire*. Norman: University of Oklahoma Press, 1963.

Makdisi, Ussama. 'After 1860: Debating Religion, Reform, and Nationalism in the Ottoman Empire.' *International Journal of Middle Eastern Studies* 34 (2002): 601–617.

Makdisi, Ussama. *Age of Coexistence: The Ecumenical Frame and the Making of the Modern Arab World*. Oakland: University of California Press, 2019.

Makdisi, Ussama. *The Culture of Sectarianism: Community, History, and Violence in Nineteenth-Century Ottoman Lebanon*. Berkeley: University of California Press, 2000.

Ma'oz, Moshe. *Ottoman Reform in Syria and Palestine, 1840–1861: The Impact of the Tanzimat on Politics and Society*. Oxford: Oxford University Press, 1968.

Marozzi, Justin. *Islamic Empires: Fifteen Cities That Define a Civilization*. London: Penguin, 2019.

Massot, Anaïs. 'Les chrétiens de Damas face aux réformes fiscales et militaires.' In *Minorités en Méditerranée au XIXe siècle:*

Identités, identifications, circulations, edited by Valérie Assan, Bernard Heyberger, and Jakob Vogel, 177–195. Rennes: Presses Universitaires de Rennes, 2019.

Massouh, George. *'Ahdath 1860 fi mudhakkirat Dimitri Dabbas* [The 1860 Events in the Memoirs of Dimitry Dabbas].' In *1860: Histoires et mémoires d'un conflit,* edited by Dima de Clerck, Carla Eddé, Naila Kaidbey, and Souad Slim, 301–308. Beirut: IFPO, 2015.

Masters, Bruce. *Christians and Jews in the Ottoman Arab World: The Roots of Sectarianism.* Cambridge: Cambridge University Press, 2001.

Masters, Bruce. 'The 1850 Events in Aleppo: An Aftershock of Syria's Incorporation into the Capitalist World System.' *International Journal of Middle East Studies* 22 (February 1990): 3–20.

Masters, Bruce. 'The Sultan's Entrepreneurs: The *Avrupa Tuccaris* and the *Hayriye Tuccaris* in Syria.' *IJMES* 24 (1992): 579–597.

McDougall, James. *A History of Algeria.* Cambridge: Cambridge University Press, 2017.

Miller, Donald E., and Lorna T. Miller. 'Women and Children of the Armenian Genocide.' In *Armenian Genocide: History, Politics, Ethics,* edited by Richard Hovannisian, 173–207. New York: St. Martin's, 1992.

Mishaqa, Mikhayil. *Mashhad al-`iyan fi hawadith suriyya was lubnan* [Eyewitness to events in Syria and Lebanon], trans. and edited by Milhim Khalil 'Abduh and Andrawus Hanna Shakhashiri. Cairo, 1908.

Mishaqa, Mikhayil. *Muntakhabat min al-jawab `ala iqtirah al-ahbab* [Selections from the Response to the Suggestion of the Loved

Ones], edited by Assad Roustom and Soubhi Abou Chacra. Beirut, 1985.

Mishaqa, Mikhayil. *Murder, Mayhem, Pillage, and Plunder: The History of the Lebanon in the 18th and 19th Centuries.* Translated by Wheeler M. Thackston Jr. Albany: State University of New York Press, 1988.

Moubayed, Sami Marwan. *Nakbat Nasari al-Sham fi 1860* [The tragedy of Levantine Christians in 1860]. Beirut: Riad El-Rayyes, 2021.

'Nubdha mukhtasara fi hawadith Lubnan wa'l-Sham (1840–1862) [An abbreviated account of events in Lebanon and Syria].' *Al-Mashriq* 24 (1926): 801–824, 915–938.

Owen, Roger. *The Middle East in the World Economy, 1800–1914.* London: Methuen, 1981.

Ozavci, Ozan. *Dangerous Gifts: Imperialism, Security, and Civil Wars in the Levant, 1798–1864.* Oxford: Oxford University Press, 2021.

Philipp, Thomas, and Birgit Schaebler, eds. *The Syrian Land: Processes of Integration and Fragmentation.* Stuttgart: Franz Steiner Verlag, 1998.

Philipp, Thomas, and Christoph Schumann. *From the Syrian Land to the States of Syria and Lebanon.* Beirut: Orient-Institut, 2004.

Porter, J. L. *Five Years in Damascus: Including an Account of the History, Topography, and Antiquities of That City.* London: John Murray, 1855.

Porter, J. L. *The Giant Cities of Bashan and Syria's Holy Places.* New York: Thomas Nelson, 1871.

Poujoulat, Baptistin. *La Vérité sur la Syrie et l'Expédition française.* Paris: Gaume Frères et J. Duprey, 1861.

Qasatli, Nu'man. *Al-Rawdat al-ghanna' fi Dimishq al-fayha'* [The lush garden of Damascus the Fragrant]. Beirut: Dar al-Ra'id al-'Arabi, 1982 [1879].

Rafeq, Abdul-Karim. *Buhuth fi'l-tarikh al-iqtisadi wa'l-ijtima'i li-bilad al-sham fi'l-'asr al-hadith* [Research in the social and economic history of Greater Syria in the modern era]. Damascus, 1985.

Rafeq, Abdul-Karim. 'Damascus and the Pilgrim Caravan.' In *Modernity and Culture: From the Mediterranean to the Indian Ocean,* edited by Leila Fawaz and C. A. Bayly, 130–143. New York: Columbia University Press, 2002.

Rafeq, Abdul-Karim. 'New Light on the 1860 Riots in Ottoman Damascus.' *Die Welt des Islams* 28 (1998): 412–430.

Rafeq, Abdel-Karim. 'Qafilat al-hajj al-shami wa ahamiyyatuha fi'l-dawla al-'uthmaniyya [The Damascene pilgrimage caravan and its significance in the Ottoman state].' In *Buhuth fi'l-tarikh al-iqtisadi wa'l-ijtima'i li-bilad al-sham fi'l-'asr al-hadith* [Studies in the social and economic history of Greater Syria in the modern era], 193–216. Damascus, 1985.

Rodogno, Davide. *Against Massacre: Humanitarian Interventions in the Ottoman Empire 1815–1914.* Princeton, NJ: Princeton University Press, 2012.

Rogan, Eugene. *The Arabs: A History,* 2nd ed. New York: Basic Books, 2017.

Rogan, Eugene. *Frontiers of the State in the Late Ottoman Empire: Transjordan, 1850–1921.* Cambridge: Cambridge University Press, 1999.

Rogan, Eugene. 'Instant Communication: The Impact of the Telegraph in Ottoman Syria.' In *The Syrian Land: Processes of*

Integration and Fragmentation, edited by Thomas Philipp and Birgit Schaebler, 113–128. Stuttgart: Franz Steiner Verlag, 1998.

Rogan, Eugene. 'The Political Significance of an Ottoman Education: Maktab 'Anbar Revisited.' In *From the Syrian Land to the States of Syria and Lebanon*, edited by Thomas Philipp and Christoph Schumann, 77–94. Beirut: Orient-Institut der DMG Beirut, 2004.

Rogan, Eugene. 'Sectarianism and Social Conflict in Damascus: The 1860 Events Reconsidered.' *Arabica* 51, no. 4 (2004): 493–511.

Saliba, George. 'Mikha'il Mishaqa and the State of Science in Nineteenth Century Lebanon.' In *In the House of Understanding: Histories in Memory of Kamal S. Salibi*, edited by Abdul Rahim Abu Husayn, Tarif Khalidi, and Suleiman A. Mourad, 157–194. Beirut: American University of Beirut Press, 2017.

Salibi, Kamal. 'The 1860 Upheaval in Damascus as Seen by al-Sayyid Muhammad Abu'l-Su'ud al-Hasibi, Notable and Later *Naqib al-Ashraf* of the City.' In *Beginnings of Modernization in the Middle East: The Nineteenth Century*, edited by William R. Polk and Richard L. Chambers, 185–202. Chicago: University of Chicago Press, 1968.

Salibi, Kamal. '*Lamahat min tarikh Dimashq fi 'ahd al-tanzimat: Kunnash Muhammad Abu al-Sa'ud al-Hasibi* [Reflections from the history of Damascus in the age of the Tanzimat: The scrapbook of Muhammad Abu al-Sa'ud al-Hasibi].' *Al-Abhath* 21 (March 1968): 57–78; 21 (December 1968): 117–153; 22 (June 1969): 51–69.

Salibi, Kamal. *The Modern History of Lebanon*. Delmar, NY: Caravan, 1977.

Salibi, Kamal, and Yusuf K. Khoury, eds. *The Missionary Herald: Reports from Ottoman Syria, 1819–1870*. Amman: Royal Institute for Inter-Faith Studies, 1995.

Sâlnâme-yi Vilâyet-i Sûriye, 3rd ed. Damascus, 1287–1288.

Sâlnâme-yi Vilâyet-i Sûriye, 13th ed. Damascus, 1298/1881.

Sâlnâme-yi Vilâyet-i Sûriye, 23rd ed. Damascus, 1308–1309/1891–1892.

Sâlnâme-yi Vilâyet-i Sûriye, 24th ed. Damascus, 1309–1310/1892–1893.

Sarafian, Ara. 'The Absorption of Armenian Women and Children into Muslim Households as a Structural Component of the Armenian Genocide.' In *Genocide and Religion in the Twentieth Century*, edited by Omer Bartov and Mack Phylis, 209–221. Oxford: Berghahn, 2001.

Schilcher, Linda Schatkowski. *Families in Politics: Damascene Factions and Estates of the 18th and 19th Centuries*. Stuttgart: Franz Steiner Verlag, 1985.

Scott, Rachel Marion. 'Education and Arabism in Damascus at the Turn of the Twentieth Century.' *Islamic Culture* 72 (1998): 17–64.

Slim, Souad. 'Les indemnités versées aux chrétiens de Damas à la suite des massacres de 1860.' In *1860: Histoires et mémoires d'un conflit*, edited by Dima de Clerck, Carla Eddé, Naila Kaidbey, and Souad Slim, 309–324. Beirut: IFPO, 2015.

Somel, Selçuk Aksin. *The Modernisation of Public Education in the Ottoman Empire, 1839–1908: Islamization, Autocracy and Discipline*. Leiden: Brill, 2001.

Steppat, Fritz. 'Some Arabic Manuscript Sources on the Syrian Crisis of 1860.' In *Les Arabes par leurs archives*, edited by Jacques Berque and Dominique Chevalier, 183–191. Paris: CNRS, 1976.

'Tabrir al-Nasara mima nasaba ilayhim fi hawadith sanat 1860 [The vindication of the Christians from what is related of them in the Events of 1860].' *Al-Mashriq* 26 (1928): 631–644.

Toledano, Ehud. *As If Silent and Absent: Bonds of Enslavement in the Islamic Middle East*. New Haven, CT: Yale University Press, 2007.

Traboulsi, Fawwaz. *A History of Modern Lebanon*, 2nd ed. London: Pluto, 2012.

Twain, Mark (Samuel Clemens). *The Innocents Abroad*. Hartford, CT: American Publishing Company, 1869.

Wakabayashi, Hirofumi. *Syria no Hitan: Kirisuto Kyoto gyakusatsu Jiken 1860* [The tragedy of Syria: The genocide of Christians in 1860]. Tokyo: Chisen-shokan, 2019.

Walker, Annie Kendrick. *Memoirs of the Graham Family*. New York: Tobias A. Wright, n.d.

Warner, Charles. *In the Levant*. Boston: Houghton Mifflin, 1895.

Weber, Stefan. *Damascus: Ottoman Modernity and Urban Transformation 1808–1918*. Aarhus: Aarhus University Press, 2009.

Weber, Stefan. 'Reshaping Damascus: Social Change and Patterns of Architecture in Late Ottoman Times.' In *From the Syrian Land to the States of Syria and Lebanon*, edited by Thomas Philipp and Christoph Schumann, 41–58. Beirut: Orient-Institut, 2004.

Williams, James. *The South Vindicated, Being a Series of Letters Written for the American Press During the Canvass for the Presidency in 1860*. London: Longman, Green, Longman, Roberts, and Green, 1862.

Wishnitzer, Avner. *Reading Clocks, Alla Turca: Time and Society in the Late Ottoman Empire*. Chicago: University of Chicago Press, 2015.

Woerner-Powell, Tom. *Another Road to Damascus: An Integrative Approach to 'Abd al-Qadir al-Jaza'iri (1808–1883)*. Berlin: De Gruyter, 2017.

Zachs, Fruma. ''Mikha'il Mishaqa—The First Historian of Modern Syria.' *British Journal of Middle Eastern Studies* 28, no. 1 (2001): 67–87.

Zachs, Fruma. ' "Novice" or "Heaven-Born" Diplomat? Lord Dufferin's Plan for a "Province of Syria": Beirut, 1860–61.' *Middle Eastern Studies* 36, no. 3 (2000): 160–176.

Zaydan, Jurji. *Tarajim Mashahir al-sharq fi'l-qarn al-tasi' 'ashar* [Biographical dictionary of the celebrities of the East in the nineteenth century], 2nd ed. Cairo: Matba'a al-Hilal, 1911.

NOTES

Introduction: Found in the Archives

1. Mikhayil Mishaqa, *Murder, Mayhem, Pillage, and Plunder: The History of the Lebanon in the 18th and 19th Centuries*, trans. Wheeler M. Thackston Jr. (Albany: State University of New York Press, 1988).

2. NARA, RG 84, Damascus vol. 1, Dr Mishaqa to US consul J. Augustus Johnson in Beirut, 12 July 1860. The violence broke out on Monday, 9 July, so this report was written on the fourth day of the eight-day massacre.

3. On Ottoman massacres of the sixteenth century, see Benjamin Lellouch, 'Puissance et justice retenue du sultan ottoman: Les massacres sur les fronts iranien et égyptien (1514–1517),' in *Le massacre, objet d'histoire*, ed. David El Kenz (Paris: Gallimard, 2005), 171–182.

4. On massacres during the Greek War of Independence, see Davide Rodogno, *Against Massacre: Humanitarian Interventions in the Ottoman Empire 1815–1914* (Princeton, NJ: Princeton University Press, 2012), 63–90.

5. Bruce Masters, 'The 1850 Events in Aleppo: An Aftershock of Syria's Incorporation into the Capitalist World System,' *International Journal of Middle East Studies* 22 (February 1990): 3–20.

6. For scholarship on the 1860 Events, see the works of Kamal Salibi, Albert Hourani, Dominique Chevalier, Moshe Ma`oz, Abdul-Karim Rafeq, Leila Tarazi Fawaz, Samir Khalaf, Fritz Steppat, Linda Schatkowski Schilcher, Philip Khoury, and Ussama Makdisi cited in the Bibliography. More recent works include Dima de Clerck, Carla Eddé, Naila Kaidbey, and Souad Slim, eds., *1860: Histoires et mémoires d'un conflit* (Beirut: IFPO, 2015); Hirofumi Wakabayashi, *Syria no Hitan: Kirisuto Kyoto gyakusatsu Jiken 1860* [The tragedy of Syria: The genocide of Christians in 1860] (Tokyo: Chisen-shokan, 2019); Sami Marwan Moubayed, *Nakbat Nasari al-Sham fi 1860* [The tragedy of Levantine Christians in 1860] (Beirut: Riad El-Rayyes, 2021); and Rana Abu-Mounes, *Muslim-Christian Relations in Damascus amid the 1860 Riot* (Leiden: Brill, 2022).

7. For an excellent intellectual biography of Mishaqa, see Peter Hill, *Prophet of Reason: Science, Religion and the Origins of the Modern Middle East* (London: Oneworld Academic, 2024).

8. The figure on house demolition, from the Syrian Observatory for Human Rights, was quoted in the *Middle East Monitor* on 1 June 2018: www.middleeastmonitor.com /20180601-3m-homes-destroyed-in-syria-war. See also Moubayed, *Nakbat Nasari al-Sham*, 12.

Chapter 1: Dr Mishaqa Opens the US Vice-Consulate in Damascus

1. NARA RG84, Beirut, C8.2 vol. 22, J. Augustus Johnson to James Williams, Beirut, 24 July 1859, 96; 31 July 1859, 98–100; 11 August 1859, 103; 17 August 1859, 105–107.

2. The best source for the life of Mikhayil Mishaqa is his own family history, which he titled *Al-jawab `ala iqtirah al-ahbab*, or 'The response to the suggestion of the loved ones.' The manuscript was widely circulated and copied in his lifetime and was published in various editions after his death. A first edition was published in Cairo in 1908 under the title *Mashhad al-`iyan fi hawadith suriyya was lubnan* [Eyewitness to events in Syria and Lebanon], heavily edited by Milhim Khalil `Abduh and Andrawus Hanna Shakhashiri. A subsequent edition, with all sectarian conflicts expunged to avoid provoking the Lebanese censor, was published by Assad Roustom and Soubhi Abou Chacra under the title *Muntakhabat min al-jawab `ala iqtirah al-ahbab* [Selections from the Response to the Suggestion of the Loved Ones] (Beirut: St. Paul, 1985). The most complete edition, based on a surviving handwritten manuscript preserved in the American University of Beirut Library, is Wheeler Thackston's English translation, *Murder, Mayhem, Pillage, and Plunder: The History of the Lebanon in the 18th and 19th Centuries*, trans. Wheeler M. Thackston Jr. (Albany: State University of New York Press, 1988).

In addition to Mishaqa's own family history, several of his contemporaries celebrated him with biographical essays: the Damascene Nu`man Qasatli, in his 1879 history of Damascus *Al-Rawdat al-ghanna' fi Dimishq al-fayha'* [The lush garden of Damascus the Fragrant] (Beirut: Dar al-Ra'id al-`Arabi, 1982 [1879]), 150–154; and the Syrian émigré to Cairo Jurji Zaydan in his biographical dictionary of the most famous men of the Orient in the nineteenth century, *Tarajim mashahir al-sharq fi'l-qarn al-tasi` `ashar*, 2nd ed. (Cairo: Matba`a al-Hilal, 1911), 177–180. It is clear from their biographical sketches that both Qasatli and Zaydan had read Mishaqa's history, Qasatli describing it as 'a very fine book.'

The best modern source on Mishaqa's life is Peter Hill's intellectual biography, *Prophet of Reason: Science, Religion and the Origins of the Modern Middle East* (London: Oneworld Academic, 2024).

3. Mishaqa, *Murder, Mayhem*, 149.

4. Mishaqa, 167.

5. Mishaqa, 158.

6. In keeping with the social norms of his day, Mishaqa made little or no mention of his wife and the female members of his household in his book or correspondence. Peter Hill uncovered details of Elizabeth (spelled Illidabat in Arabic) Faris through his research into the Mishaqa family's private papers; see Hill, *Prophet of Reason*, Chapter 9. He cites the American missionary Henry Harris Jessup's exchange with Mishaqa from Jessup, *The Women of the Arabs* (New York: Dodd & Mead, 1873), 118. Although such child marriage strikes modern readers as inconceivable, it is worth recalling that until the 1870s in Britain and the 1880s in the United States, the legal age of consent for girls ranged from ten to twelve.

7. Khaled Fahmy, *In Quest of Justice: Islamic Law and Forensic Medicine in Modern Egypt* (Oakland: University of California Press, 2018), 39.

8. Mishaqa, *Murder, Mayhem*, 193.

9. Mishaqa, 99, 235, 236.

10. Letter from Eli Smith dated 27 January 1849, reprinted in Kamal Salibi and Yusuf K. Khoury, eds., *The Missionary Herald: Reports from Ottoman Syria, 1819–1870* (Amman: RIIFS, 1995), 4:82–83. In *Prophet of Reason*, Peter Hill traces Mishaqa's conversion to Protestantism and his clashes with the Greek Catholic patriarch.

11. British records confirm Mishaqa's claim that he was appointed dragoman and came under British protection in 1840. See Erdogan Keskinkiliç and Ebubekir Ceylan, 'Her Majesty's Protected Subjects: The Mishaqa Family in Ottoman Damascus,' *Middle Eastern Studies* 51 (2015): 175–194. See also Mishaqa, *Murder, Mayhem*, 222.

12. Salibi and Khoury, eds., *Missionary Herald*, 3:408.

13. Bruce Masters, 'The Sultan's Entrepreneurs: The *Avrupa Tuccaris* and the *Hayriye Tuccaris* in Syria,' *IJMES* 24 (1992): 586.

14. NARA, RG 84, Beirut, C8.2 vol. 22, 108–109, J. Augustus Johnson to J. Brant, HBM's Consul at Damascus, Beirut, 1 September 1859.

15. NARA, RG 84, Damascus, vol. 1, Mishaqa to Johnson, Damascus, 12 September 1859.

16. On the 'Benton outrage,' see 'Bhamdun: Letter from Mr Benton, May 24, 1859,' in Salibi and Khoury, eds., *Missionary Herald*, 4:342–344. Mishaqa named the two suspects from Zahleh as Yusif al-Zuj and Yusif Saru; see NARA RG 84, Damascus, vol. 1, Mishaqa to Johnson, Damascus, 6 September 1859.

17. NARA RG 84, Damascus, vol. 1, Mishaqa to Ahmad Pasha, Damascus, 16 September 1859.

18. NARA RG 84, Beirut, C8.2 vol. 36, Official correspondence 1853–1862, nos. 40–41, Johnson to Mishaqa, Beirut 13 and 20 October 1859.

19. Annie Kendrick Walker, *Memoirs of the Graham Family* (New York: Tobias A. Wright, n.d.), a privately printed book, includes details on Williams through his wife's family history; see 18–21 and 33–34.

20. NARA RG 84, Damascus, vol. 1, Mishaqa to Johnson, Damascus, 9 February 1860.

21. Salibi and Khoury, eds., *Missionary Herald*, 4:363.

22. Mishaqa sent notification of his accreditation to the consuls of Iran and Great Britain (and a second to Brant in his capacity as consular agent for Prussia); the vice-consuls of Holland and Belgium, Austria, and Russia; and the consular agent of Greece. NARA RG 84, Damascus, vol. 1, Mishaqa letters dated Damascus, 28 November 1859.

23. In their study of the Mishaqa family, Keskinkiliç and Ceylan cite an exchange of letters preserved in the Ottoman Archives in Istanbul (BOA HR.MKT 322/15) between Ahmad Pasha in Damascus and the Sublime Porte, dated 4 and 10 January 1860, in which the governor questioned Mishaqa's appointment and the Porte reconfirmed the appointment. 'Her Majesty's Protected Subjects,' 182–184.

24. NARA RG 84, Damascus, vol. 1, Mishaqa to Johnson, Damascus, 9 February 1860.

25. James Williams noted in the preface to his book, *The South Vindicated, Being a Series of Letters Written for the American Press During the Canvass for the Presidency in 1860* (London: Longman, Green, Longman, Roberts, and Green, 1862), that the essays 'were written at Constantinople' during his final months as ambassador. He claimed that his book was the first publication entered according to the Copyright Act of the Congress of the Confederate States of America.

Chapter 2: Damascus 'the Fragrant' at Mid-Century

1. Mark Twain, *The Innocents Abroad* (Hartford, CT: American Publishing Company, 1869), 456–457. Twain was less lyrical in his description of Damascus close up: 'It is so crooked and cramped and dirty that one can not realize that he is in the splendid city he saw from the hill-top.'

2. Damascus is mentioned regularly in the Hebrew Bible; see, for example, Genesis 14:15, 15:2; 2 Samuel 8:5–6; 1 Kings 11:24, 19:15, 20:34; 2 Kings 14:28, 16:9; Isaiah 17:1–14; Jeremiah 49:23–27; Ezekiel 38:1–39:29; and Zecharia 9:1. On Umayyad Damascus, see Justin Marozzi, *Islamic Empires: Fifteen Cities That Define a Civilization* (London: Penguin, 2019), 24–46.

3. J. L. Porter, *Five Years in Damascus* (London: John Murray, 1855), 1:33–34. On the features of Damascene houses, see Stefan Weber, *Damascus: Ottoman Modernity and Urban Transformation 1808–1918* (Aarhus: Aarhus University Press, 2009); and Brigid Keenan, *Damascus: Hidden Treasures of the Old City* (London: Thames & Hudson, 2001). The Mishaqa house, now quite run-down, is still standing. For a detailed description with floor plans and photographs of Mishaqa's house, see Weber, *Damascus*, 1:368–371.

4. The Damascene chronicler Nu'man Qasatli provides detailed figures based on Ottoman census sources showing a total population of 145,000, with roughly 120,000 Muslims, 20,000 Christians, and 5,000 Jews; *Al-Rawdat al-ghana' fi Dimishq al-fayha'* [The lush garden of Damascus the Fragrant] (Beirut: Dar al-Ra'id al-'Arabi, 1982 [1879]), 8. Porter, who had access to official Ottoman census figures in the early 1850s through a local agent, gave a total figure of 109,000, which, allowing for undercounting, he raised to 150,000. Porter, *Five Years*, 138–139. J. Lewis Farley, who lived in Beirut in the late 1850s, gave a total figure of 180,000 in Damascus, with 130,000 Muslim, 30,000 Christians, and 20,000 Jews. *The Massacres in Syria* (London: Bradbury & Evans, 1861), 82–83.

5. The sources differ on the names of the eight principal districts of Damascus. In 1850, Muhammad Sa'id al-Ustuwani listed the eight *thumns* of Damascus as al-Qaymariyya, al-'Amara, Suq Saruja, al-Shaghur, al-Qanawat, al-Suwayqa, al-Maydan, and al-Salihiyya; *Mashahid wa ahdath dimishqiyya fi muntasif al-qarn al-tasi' 'ashar, 1840–1861* [Damascene scenes and events in the mid-19th century, 1840–1861] (Damascus: Dar al-Jumhuriyya, 1994), 147. Writing in the 1870s, Nu'man Qasatli divided al-Maydan into an upper and lower thumn and listed al-'Uqayba but did not include al-Suwayqa or Suq Saruja; *Al-Rawdat al-ghana'*, 111.

6. Jonathan Frankel, *The Damascus Affair: 'Ritual Murder,' Politics, and the Jews in 1840* (Cambridge: Cambridge University Press, 1997). Mikhayil Mishaqa, *Murder, Mayhem, Pillage, and Plunder: The History of the Lebanon in the 18th and 19th Centuries*, trans. Wheeler M. Thackston Jr. (Albany: State University of New York Press, 1988), 193–200.

7. Shaykh Muhammad Sa'id al-Ustuwani recorded the Citadel fire in his diary; *Mashahid wa ahdath dimishqiyya*, 134; Porter described the Citadel in the 1850s, *Five Years*, 50–51.

8. Alphonse de Lamartine, *Travels in the East, Including a Journey in the Holy Land* (Edinburgh: William and Robert Chambers, 1839), 127.

9. Isabel Burton, *The Inner Life of Syria, Palestine, and the Holy Land* (London: Henry S. King, 1875), 1:42–43.

10. Qasatli, *Al-Rawdat al-ghana'*, 105–106.

11. Al-Ustuwani, *Mashahid wa ahdath dimishqiyya*, 136–137.

12. Albert Hourani has characterised the interplay between urban elites and the Ottoman government as 'the politics of notables.' See Hourani, 'Ottoman Reform and the Politics of Notables,' in *Beginnings of Modernization in the Middle East: The Nineteenth Century*, ed. William R. Polk and Richard L. Chambers (Chicago: University of Chicago Press, 1968), 41–68. On the role of the Majlis, see Moshe Ma'oz, *Ottoman Reform in Syria and Palestine, 1840–1861* (Oxford: Oxford University Press, 1968), 89–107; and Zouhair Ghazzal, *L'Économie politique de Damas durant le XIXe siècle: Structures traditionnelles et capitalisme* (Damascus: Institut Français de Damas, 1993), 47–68.

13. British consul Richard Burton and his wife, Isabel, lived in al-Salihiyya; she described the local view of the quarter: 'The village had the reputation of being the most lawless and unscrupulous part of Damascus...' *Inner Life of Syria*, 1:29.

14. Abdel-Karim Rafeq, 'Qafilat al-hajj al-shami wa ahamiyyatuha fi'l-dawla al-'uthmaniyya [The Damascene pilgrimage caravan and its significance in the Ottoman state],' in *Buhuth fi'l-tarikh al-iqtisadi wa'l-ijtima'i li-bilad al-sham fi'l-'asr al-hadith* [Studies in the social and economic history of Greater Syria in the modern era] (Damascus, 1985), 193–216; Karl Barbir, *Ottoman Rule in Damascus, 1708–1758* (Princeton, NJ: Princeton University Press, 1980).

15. Porter, *Five Years*, 148.

16. Abdul-Karim Rafeq, 'Damascus and the Pilgrim Caravan,' in *Modernity and Culture: From the Mediterranean to the Indian Ocean*, ed. Leila Fawaz and C. A. Bayly (New York: Columbia University Press, 2002), 130–143.

17. Isabel Burton provides a detailed description of the ceremonies surrounding the annual pilgrimage caravan from Damascus, which she witnessed in 1870; *Inner Life of Syria*, 1:54–67.

18. These examples are drawn from the diary of Muhammad Sa'id al-Ustuwani, *Mashahid wa ahdath dimishqiyya*, 142–146, 158–159, 167–168.

19. Bruce Masters, *Christians and Jews in the Ottoman Arab World: The Roots of Sectarianism* (Cambridge: Cambridge University Press, 2001); Benjamin Braude, ed., *Christians and Jews in the Ottoman Empire* (Boulder, CO: Lynne Rienner, 2014).

20. Lamartine, *Travels in the East*, 122.

21. *The Times* (London), 30 April 1834, 5, quoting 'a private letter from Damascus dated January 31.'

22. Porter, *Five Years*, 1:134–135.

23. Eileen Kane, *Russian Hajj: Empire and the Pilgrimage to Mecca* (Ithaca, NY: Cornell University Press, 2015), 35–37; on the opening of the Prussian consulate in Damascus, see Ferry de Goey, *Consuls and the Institutions of Global Capitalism, 1783–1914* (London: Pickering & Chatto, 2014).

24. *The Times*, 30 April 1834, 5.

25. By the terms of the 1838 Anglo-Turkish Commercial Convention, British merchants faced a 5 percent tariff on all goods brought into the Ottoman Empire and paid a 12 percent duty on all goods exported from Ottoman domains; Roger Owen, *The Middle East in the World Economy, 1800–1914* (London: Methuen, 1981), 91.

26. The conversion from 1839 to 2023 pounds sterling is made with the UK Consumer Price Index inflation calculator, consulted on www.in2013dollars.com/uk/inflation/1830.

27. Owen, *Middle East in the World Economy*, 85.

28. Trade figures for the 1850s from J. Lewis Farley, who served in the Ottoman Bank in Beirut. *Two Years in Syria* (London: Saunders and Otley, 1858), Appendix 1, 370–373. Porter, *Five Years*, 1:57.

29. Owen, *Middle East in the World Economy*, 93.

30. Dominique Chevalier, 'Western Development and Eastern Crisis in the Mid-Nineteenth Century: Syria Confronted with the European Economy', in *Beginnings of Modernization in the Middle East: The Nineteenth Century*, ed. William R. Polk and Richard L. Chambers (Chicago: University of Chicago Press, 1968), 220.

31. Chevalier, 'Western Development and Eastern Crisis', 205–222.

32. Henri Guys, *Esquisse de l'état politique et commercial de la Syrie* (Paris: Chez France, 1862), 213.

33. Lamartine, *Travels in the East*, 126.

34. Owen, *Middle East in the World Economy*, 88; Guys, *Esquisse de l'état*, 215–216.

35. Richard Edwards, *La Syrie, 1840–1862* (Paris: Aymot, 1862), 78–79.

36. Muhammad Abu al-Sa'ud al-Hasibi was a notable of Damascus and a member of the ashraf, or descendants of the Prophet Muhammad. Kamal Salibi, '*Lamahat min tarikh Dimashq fi 'ahd al-tanzimat: Kunnash Muhammad Abu al-Sa'ud al-Hasibi* [Reflections from the history of Damascus in the age of the Tanzimat: The scrapbook of Muhammad Abu al-Sa'ud al-Hasibi]', *Al-Abhath* 21 (December 1968): 117–118.

Chapter 3: Resistance to Ottoman Reforms

1. 'Abd al-Rizaq al-Bitar, *Hilyat al-bashar fi tarikh al-qarn al-thalith 'ashar* [The embellishment of humanity in the thirteenth century] (Damascus, 1961), 1:260.

2. Muhammad Sa'id al-Ustuwani, *Mashahid wa ahdath dimishqiyya fi muntasif al-qarn al-tasi' 'ashar, 1840–1861* [Damascene scenes and events in the mid-19th century, 1840–1861] (Damascus: Dar al-Jumhuriyya, 1994), 167–168. Taverns selling wine were introduced during the Egyptian occupation in the 1830s in order to raise taxes, but the religious authorities in Damascus strongly opposed this measure; see Sami Marwan Moubayed, *Nakbat nasari al-Sham fi 1860* [The tragedy of Levantine Christians in 1860] (Beirut: Riad El-Rayyes, 2021), 80–81. On the al-Maydan conflict and subsequent crackdown on the Aghawat, see also Moshe Ma'oz, *Ottoman Reform in Syria and Palestine, 1840–1861* (Oxford: Oxford University Press, 1968), 234. Note that Ma'oz suggests that Ahmad Pasha's full name was Ahmad 'Izzat Pasha and that he had served a prior eleven-month term as governor in 1856–1857 before assuming the dual roles of governor and commander of the Syrian garrison. However, in his diary, al-Ustuwani recorded the appointment of an 'Izzat Pasha as governor in 1857 and of Ahmad Pasha in 1859. He never suggested that they were the same person or used the name 'Ahmad 'Izzat Pasha'. Al-Bitar also names the governor simply as Ahmad Pasha, not as Ahmad 'Izzat Pasha. As such, I suspect they were different men.

3. Mikhayil Mishaqa, *Murder, Mayhem, Pillage, and Plunder: The History of the Lebanon in the 18th and 19th Centuries*, trans. Wheeler M. Thackston Jr. (Albany: State University of New York Press, 1981), 238. On Brant and Ahmad Pasha, see Ma'oz, *Ottoman*

Reform, 234; for the consular corps more generally, see Leila Tarazi Fawaz, *An Occasion for War: Civil Conflict in Lebanon and Damascus in 1860* (London: I.B. Tauris, 1994), 145–146.

4. On moneylending to secure discounted grain in late-Ottoman Syria, see Eugene Rogan, *Frontiers of the State in the Late Ottoman Empire: Transjordan, 1850–1921* (Cambridge: Cambridge University Press, 1999), 102–109. See also Beshara Doumani, *Rediscovering Palestine: Merchants and Peasants in Jabal Nablus, 1700–1900* (Berkeley: University of California Press, 1995).

5. On Ya'qub al-Islambuli's wealth, gift giving, and association with Ahmad Pasha, see the anonymous manuscript *Kitab al-Ahzan* [The book of sorrows], American University of Beirut MS 956.9 K62kA, 116–117; on extortionate interest rates charged by lenders to farmers, see 126. On the luxurious Islambuli House, see Stefan Weber, *Damascus: Ottoman Modernity and Urban Transformation 1808–1918* (Aarhus: Aarhus University Press, 2009), 2:391–392.

6. The young Muslim notable Muhammad Abu al-Sa'ud al-Hasibi passed this harsh judgement of Mustafa Bey al-Hawasli; see Kamal Salibi, "Lamahat min tarikh Dimashq fi 'ahd al-tanzimat: kunnash Muhammad Abu al-Sa'ud al-Hasibi," *Al-Abhath* 21 (March 1968): 77–78.

7. NARA, RG 84, Damascus, vol. 1, Mishaqa to Johnson, 10 and 13 October 1859; Mishaqa to the Mushir, 1 November 1859; Mishaqa to US Vice Consul Barclay in Beirut, 9 February 1860.

8. NARA, RG 84, Damascus, vol. 1, Mishaqa to the Mushir, 2 and 14 Jan 1860; Mishaqa to Barclay, 9 February 1860.

9. Al-Ustuwani, *Mashahid wa ahdath dimishqiyya*, 165, 167.

10. On the Surur Agha case, see NARA, RG 84, Damascus, vol. 1, Mishaqa to Johnson, 14 May; Mishaqa to the Mushir, 14, 15 May 1860; Mishaqa to Johnson, Mishaqa to the Mushir, 17 May 1860; Mishaqa to the Mushir, 19 May 1860; Mishaqa to Barclay, 20 May 1860. Beirut, C8.2 vol. 35, Barclay to Mishaqa, 17 May 1860.

11. NARA, RG 84, Damascus, vol. 1, Mishaqa to Barclay, 9 February 1860.

12. I addressed the origins of the Tanzimat in *The Arabs: A History*, 2nd ed. (New York: Basic Books, 2017), 120–125.

13. A translation of the 1839 Reform Decree is reproduced in J. C. Hurewitz, *The Middle East and North Africa in World Politics* (New Haven, CT: Yale University Press, 1975), 1:269–271.

14. A translation of the 1856 Reform Decree is reproduced in Hurewitz, *Middle East*, 1:315–318.

15. On the link between taxation, conscription, and communal tensions, see Anaïs Massot, 'Les chrétiens de Damas face aux réformes fiscales et militaires,' in *Minorités en Méditerranée au XIXe siècle*, ed. Valérie Assan, Bernard Heyberger, and Jakob Vogel (Rennes: Presses Universitaires de Rennes, 2019), 177–195.

16. Bruce Masters, *Christians and Jews in the Ottoman Arab World: The Roots of Sectarianism* (Cambridge: Cambridge University Press, 2001), 152–154.

17. On the link between the Crimean War and the Tanzimat, see Ozan Ozavci, *Dangerous Gifts: Imperialism, Security, and Civil Wars in the Levant, 1798–1864* (Oxford: Oxford University Press, 2021), 278–286.

18. Roderic H. Davison, *Reform in the Ottoman Empire, 1856–1876* (Princeton, NJ: Princeton University Press, 1963), 3.

19. As'ad al-Ustuwani provides a biography of Muhammad Sa'id al-Ustuwani in the introduction to the published edition of al-Ustuwani's diary; al-Ustuwani, *Mashahid wa ahdath dimishqiyya*, 49–51.

20. Al-Ustuwani, 136–137.

21. Al-Ustuwani, 153–154.

22. Al-Ustuwani, 162.

23. Masters, *Christians and Jews*, 132.

24. Kamal Salibi describes al-Hasibi and his notebook in his article 'The 1860 Upheaval in Damascus as Seen by al-Sayyid Muhammad Abu'l-Su'ud al-Hasibi, Notable and Later *Naqib al-Ashraf* of the City,' in *Beginnings of Modernization in the Middle East: The Nineteenth Century*, ed. William R. Polk and Richard L. Chambers (Chicago: University of Chicago Press, 1968), 185–187.

25. Kamal Salibi, '*Lamahat min tarikh Dimashq fi 'ahd al-tanzimat: Kunnash Muhammad Abu al-Sa'ud al-Hasibi* [Reflections from the history of Damascus in the age of the Tanzimat: The scrapbook of Muhammad Abu al-Sa'ud al-Hasibi],' *Al-Abhath* 21 (December 1968): 117.

26. Mishaqa, *Murder, Mayhem*, 244.

Chapter 4: Rivers of Blood in Mount Lebanon

1. 'Abd-el-Kader,' *New York Times*, 22 November 1852, 4.

2. Biographers were already at work in 'Abd al-Qadir's lifetime. The French civil servant and army translator Alexandre Bellemare (1818–1885) published *Abd-el-Kader, sa vie politique et militaire* (Paris: Hachette, 1863), and the British officer and diplomat Colonel Charles Henry Churchill (1807–1869) published *Life of Abdel Kader, Ex-Sultan of the Arabs of Algeria* (London: Chapman and Hall, 1867) after extensive personal contact with 'Abd al-Qadir. Modern biographies include Bruno Étienne, *Abdelkader* (Paris: Fayard/Pluriel, 2012); Raphael Danziger, *Abd al-Qadir and the Algerians* (New York: Holmes and Meier, 1977); and John W. Kiser, *Commander of the Faithful: The Life and Times of Emir Abd el-Kader* (Rhinebeck, NY: Monkfish, 2008).

3. I treat the origins of the French invasion of Algeria in *The Arabs: A History*, 2nd ed. (New York: Basic Books, 2017). For more on the French invasion of Algeria, see James McDougall, *A History of Algeria* (Cambridge: Cambridge University Press, 2017).

4. Churchill, *Life of Abdel Kader*, 304–305. Churchill first met 'Abd al-Qadir in Bursa in 1853 and invited the amir to stay with him in Mount Lebanon in 1855, where 'Abd al-Qadir consented for Churchill to write his biography. In the winter of 1859–1860, while based in Damascus, Churchill went daily to interview Amir 'Abd al-Qadir in his home to extract his life story. The quoted passages are Churchill's paraphrasing of the amir's words.

5. On the social hierarchy in Mount Lebanon under the Imara, see Kamal Salibi, *The Modern History of Lebanon* (Delmar, NY: Caravan, 1977), 8–10. For simplicity's sake, I have left out one category in the principality of Mount Lebanon. The Muqaddams were lower than the princely families but higher than the great shaykhs. The Abu'l-Lama family was promoted from muqaddam to amir in 1711, leaving the Druze Muzhir family as the sole occupants of the muqaddam category by the eighteenth century.

6. For further information on Mount Lebanon in the eighteenth and nineteenth centuries, see Salibi, *Modern History of Lebanon*; Iliya F. Harik, *Politics and Change in a Traditional Society: Lebanon, 1711–1845* (Princeton, NJ: Princeton University Press, 1968); Leila Tarazi Fawaz, *An Occasion for War: Civil Conflict in Lebanon and Damascus in 1860* (London: I.B. Tauris, 1994); and Fawwaz Traboulsi, *A History of Modern Lebanon*, 2nd ed. (London: Pluto, 2012).

7. Harik, *Politics and Change*, 242–243.

8. The anonymous Christian author of the 1860s manuscript '*Nubdha mukhtasara fi hawadith Lubnan wa'l-Sham* [An abbreviated account of events in Lebanon and Syria]' cited the 1851 register and provided figures for each district of Mount Lebanon. Only in the Druze heartland of the Shuf and in the southernmost region of Jabal al-Riyhan did the Druzes enjoy an outright majority. All other districts recorded large Christian majorities. *Al-Mashriq* 24 (1926): 802–805.

9. Churchill, *Life of Abdel Kader*, 305.

10. Churchill, 305.

11. Bellemare, *Abd-el-Kader*, 415–416.

12. Mikhayil Mishaqa, *Murder, Mayhem, Pillage, and Plunder: The History of the Lebanon in the 18th and 19th Centuries*, trans. Wheeler M. Thackston Jr. (Albany: State University of New York Press, 1988), 226.

13. On the popular challenge to notable rule in Mount Lebanon in 1858–1860, see Ussama Makdisi, *The Culture of Sectarianism: Community, History, and Violence in Nineteenth-Century Lebanon* (Berkeley: University of California Press, 2000), 96–117.

14. Adel Ismail, *Documents Diplomatiques et Consulaires Relatifs à l'Histoire du Liban vol. 10 (1853–1861)* (Beirut: Éditions de Oeuvres Politiques et Historiques, 1978), 162–163.

15. Letter from Commoners in Kisrawan to Maronite Patriarch Bulus Mas'ad dated 17 December 1859 [*sic* 1858], in Malcolm H. Kerr, *Lebanon in the Last Years of Feudalism, 1840–1868: A Contemporary Account by Antun Dahir al-'Aqiqi and Other Documents* (Beirut: American University of Beirut Press, 1959), 97–99. See also Traboulsi, *History of Modern Lebanon*, 31.

16. Kerr, *Lebanon in the Last Years of Feudalism*, 'Aqiqi quotation on 48–49; Dufferin quotation on 21–22.

17. Quotation referring to trembling peasants in letter from French Consul Bentivoglio in Beirut to Foreign Minister Walewski, 7 January 1860, in Ismail, *Documents Dipolomatiques vol. 10*, 163; Traboulsi, *History of Modern Lebanon*, 30; Salibi, *Modern History of Lebanon*, 86–90; Ottoman nonintervention from 'Aqiqi, in Kerr, *Lebanon in the Last Years of Feudalism*, 51–52.

18. 'Aqiqi in Kerr, 53–54. On the Kisrawan uprising and its republican credentials, see Caesar E. Farah, *The Politics of Interventionism in Ottoman Lebanon, 1830–1861* (London: I.B. Tauris, 2000), 531–535.

19. 'Aqiqi in Kerr, *Lebanon in the Last Years of Feudalism*, 55.

20. Salibi, *Modern History of Lebanon*, 88–90; Makdisi, *Culture of Sectarianism*, 118–145. 'Aqiqi quotes Tanyus Shahin's claim to a force of fifty thousand Christians. Kerr, *Lebanon in the Last Years of Feudalism*, 56.

21. As one Christian source from September 1860 noted, terror spread among the Christians who witnessed death, provoking flight. '*Tabrir al-Nasara mima nasaba ilayhim fi*

hawadith sanat 1860 [The vindication of the Christians from what is related of them in the Events of 1860],' *Al-Mashriq* 26 (1928): 636.

22. *Kitab al-Ahzan* [The book of sorrows], AUB Jafet Library MS 956.9 K62, 29–30.

23. Salibi, *Modern History of Lebanon*, 95–96; Fawaz, *Occasion for War*, 59–60; Traboulsi, *History of Modern Lebanon*, 34.

24. Mishaqa, *Murder, Mayhem*, 241.

25. NARA, RG 84, Damascus, vol. 1, Mishaqa to Johnson, 4 June 1860.

26. NARA, RG 84, Damascus, vol. 1, Mishaqa to Johnson, 17 June 1860, 18 June 1860.

27. *Kitab al-Ahzan*, 25.

28. Kamal Salibi, '*Lamahat min tarikh Dimashq fi `ahd al-tanzimat: Kunnash Muhammad Abu al-Sa`ud al-Hasibi* [Reflections from the history of Damascus in the age of the Tanzimat: The scrapbook of Muhammad Abu al-Sa`ud al-Hasibi],' *Al-Abhath* 21 (December 1968): 118.

29. Mishaqa wrote of 'rivers of blood'; *Murder, Mayhem*, 240. The casualty figures are from Salibi, *Modern History of Lebanon*, 106.

30. NARA, RG 84, Damascus, vol. 1, Mishaqa to Johnson, 25 and 28 June 1860.

31. NARA, RG 84, Damascus, vol. 1, Mishaqa to Johnson, 21 June, 25 June, 28 June, 2 July 1860.

32. NARA, RG 84, Damascus, vol. 1, Mishaqa to Johnson, 25 June 1860. The anonymous author of *Kitab al-Ahzan* recounted the rumours about Hums, 39–40.

33. NARA, RG 84, Damascus, vol. 1, Mishaqa to Johnson, 28 June 1860; '*Nubdha mukhtasara*,' 916.

34. Muhammad Sa`id al-Ustuwani, *Mashahid wa ahdath dimishqiyya fi muntasif al-qarn al-tasi` `ashar, 1840–1861* [Damascene scenes and events in the mid-19th century, 1840–1861] (Damascus: Dar al-Jumhuriyya, 1994), 172–173; the quotation is from the anonymous Christian author of '*Nubdha mukhtasara*,' 916.

35. '*Nubdha mukhtasara*,' 916–917.

Chapter 5: Plunder, Kill, and Burn

1. Kamal Salibi, '*Lamahat min tarikh Dimashq fi `ahd al-tanzimat: Kunnash Muhammad Abu al-Sa`ud al-Hasibi*' [Reflections from the history of Damascus in the age of the Tanzimat: The scrapbook of Muhammad Abu al-Sa`ud al-Hasibi],' *Al-Abhath* 21 (March 1968): 121. NARA, RG 84, Damascus, vol. 1, Mishaqa to the Governor, 23 June 1860. On the flooding of the houses and streets of the Christian quarters with refugees, see Muhammad Sa`id al-Ustuwani, *Mashuhid wa ahdath dimishqiyya fi muntasif al-qarn al-tasi` `ashar, 1840–1861* [Damascene scenes and events in the mid-19th century, 1840–1861] (Damascus: Dar al-Jumhuriyya, 1994), 172.

2. Salibi, '*Lamahat*,' *Al-Abhath* 21 (March 1968): 77–78. On the restoration of the Citadel's cannons, see the memoir of the anonymous Christian author, '*Nubdha mukhtasara fi hawadith Lubnan wa'l-Sham (1840–1862)* [An abbreviated account of events in Lebanon and Syria],' *Al-Mashriq* 24 (1926): 915. On the dispatch of the regular garrison to escort the pilgrimage caravan, see Sami Marwan Moubayed, *Nakbat Nasari al-Sham fi 1860* [The Tragedy of Levantine Christians in 1860] (Beirut: Riad El-Rayyes, 2021), 109; on Damascene soldiers sent to Bosnia, see Ozan Ozavci, *Dangerous Gifts: Imperialism, Security and Civil Wars in the Levant, 1798–1864* (Oxford: Oxford University Press, 2021), 300.

3. '*Nubdha mukhtasara*,' 915–916; al-Ustuwani, *Mashahid wa ahdath*, 172.

4. In al-Ustuwani's words, the Christian notables 'exposed the corruption of [the governor's] thoughts and practice' to him; see 173–174. See also '*Nubdha mukhtasara*,' 916.

5. The townspeople's cry in al-Ustuwani, *Mashahid wa ahdath*, 174; the detainees' response was recorded by al-Hasibi in Salibi, '*Lamahat*,' *Al-Abhath* 21 (December 1968): 126. Note that both sources were Muslim notables of Damascus.

6. *Kitab al-Ahzan* [The book of sorrows], AUB Jafet Library, MS 956.9 K62kA, 47.

7. Al-Hasibi, in Salibi, '*Lamahat*,' *Al-Abhath* 21 (December 1968): 127–128. He never mentions the clerk's son again, leaving readers to wonder if the young man survived or was among the dead. Al-Ustuwani claims that ten Muslims were shot dead by gunfire from soldiers and Christians in nearby houses, 'as it was said.' *Mashahid wa ahdath*, 174.

8. NARA, Beirut, RG 84, C8.1 vol. 80, 546–553, Mikhayil Mishaqa, 'Report of the attack made on me the undersigned, his family, and his house during the late outbreak at Damascus,' 23 August 1860. In his report, Dr Mishaqa listed the names of the eight people he recognised: Mustafa al-Hilu, Jawad Zalzala, Husayn al-Muhish, Husayn al-Tubl, `Abduh al-Kalish, `Ali Zahur, `Ali Mughrabiyya, and Shaykh `Umar al-Halabi.

9. The US Archives conserves a loose page from a report in English with no date or author that provides an eyewitness account of the attack on the Mishaqa house. This account, quoting a woman who 'lived near the house of the American Vice Consul,' mentioned Mishaqa's wife and how she prostrated herself. This account also recorded that the Mishaqas paid the mob fourteen thousand piastres to spare their lives. It is an important detail that Mishaqa neglected in all accounts of his ordeal, explaining why the mob stopped short of killing him and let him escape with his life. NARA, RG 84, Beirut, C8.1 vol. 80, Misc. Corr., 588.

10. Rev. Smiley Robson wrote this report on 10 July—the day after the violence broke out. He kept a running log of events from 9 through 16 July, copies of which are to be found in the US National Archives. NARA, RG 84, Beirut, C8.1 vol. 80, Misc. Corr., 589–595.

11. The formula 'to rob, kill, and burn' is repeated in virtually all of the contemporary sources in both Arabic and English to capture the nature of the violence in Damascus. Of the groups mentioned by al-Hasibi, the Nusayris are an offshoot of Islam also known as Alawites, Mitwali and Rafidi were different names for Shi`ite Muslims, and the Yazidis are a non-Muslim sect who are (wrongly) said to worship fire. Al-Hasibi, in Salibi, '*Lamahat*,' *Al-Abhath* 21 (March 1968): 76; al-Ustuwani, *Mashahid wa ahdath*, 174.

12. *Tanahudat Suriyya* [The sighs of Syria], AUB, MS 956.9 T16, 27–28.

13. For Dimitri Dabbas's experiences, see Georges Massouh, '*Ahdath 1860 fi mudhakkirat Dimitri Dabbas* [The 1860 Events in the Memoirs of Dimitry Dabbas],' in *1860: Histoires et mémoires d'un conflit*, ed. Dima de Clerck, Carla Eddé, Naila Kaidbey, and Souad Slim (Beirut: IFPO, 2015), 302–308; and Leila Tarazi Fawaz, *An Occasion for War: Civil Conflict in Lebanon and Damascus in 1860* (London: I.B. Tauris, 1994), 94–97.

14. NARA, RG 84, Beirut, C8.1 vol. 80, Mishaqa, 'Report of the attack…during the late outbreak at Damascus,' 23 August 1860. Mishaqa's son Nasif worked for the British consul and survived the massacre in the safety of the consulate. It was three days before they found his younger son Salim, who had taken refuge in a Muslim house in the al-Shaghur quarter.

15. NARA, RG 84, Beirut, C8.1 vol. 80, Misc. Corr., Smiley Robson reports, 589–595.

16. Alexandre Bellemare, *Abd-el-Kader, sa vie politique et militaire* (Paris: Hachette, 1863), 443–446. Bellemare had the advantage of interviewing ʿAbd al-Qadir, and at one point cites the amir's words in transliterated Arabic. ʿAbd al-Qadir's English biographer, Col. Charles Henry Churchill, relates a similar story and a similar exchange of words, suggesting that ʿAbd al-Qadir related this account to both men. Churchill, *Life of Abdel Kader, Ex-Sultan of the Arabs of Algeria* (London: Chapman and Hall, 1867), 313.

17. Al-Hasibi, in Salibi, 'Lamahat,' *Al-Abhath* 21 (December 1968): 131; his account is confirmed by al-Ustuwani, *Mashahid wa ahdath*, 175.

18. The anonymous author of this account was believed to be either a Greek Catholic or an Armenian Catholic priest who claimed to record only what he witnessed himself or heard from eyewitnesses. 'Nubdha mukhtasara,' 917.

19. Bellemare, *Abd-el-Kader*, 447–448.

20. Dimitri Dabbas invoked the horrors of Hasbayya, Rashayya, and Dayr al-Qamar to explain his initial resistance to leave the relative security of a Muslim notable's home for the Citadel; Massouh, 'Ahdath 1860 fi mudhakkirat Dimitri Dabbas,' 305.

21. NARA, RG 84, Beirut, vol. 80, Misc. Corr., 590–595, Smiley Robson report.

22. 'Nubdha mukhtasara,' 918–920. The anonymous Christian author of *Tanahudat Suriyya* claimed that women were abducted and raped starting on the second day of the violence; see 28–29.

23. Al-Hasibi, in Salibi, 'Lamahat,' 132; Kamal Salibi, 'The 1860 Upheaval in Damascus as Seen by al-Sayyid Muhammad Abu'l-Suʿud al-Hasibi, Notable and Later *Naqib al Ashraf* of the City,' in *Beginnings of Modernization in the Middle East: The Nineteenth Century*, ed. William R. Polk and Richard L. Chambers (Chicago: University of Chicago Press, 1968), 196. For ʿAbd al-Qadir's reaction, see FO 406 10, 132–134, interview with ʿAbd al-Qadir, Fraser to Russell, Damascus, 23 August 1860.

24. BOA, I.Dah. 30602/1, Ahmad Pasha's report on the situation in Damascus, 22 Dhu al-Hijja 1276 (12 July 1860), and cover letter dated 6 Muharram 1277 (25 July 1860). It is, to the best of my knowledge, the only report that Ahmad Pasha submitted on the Events in Damascus.

25. Al-Ustuwani, *Mashahid wa ahdath*, 175.

26. BOA, I.Meclis-i Mahsus 814 (24 Zilkâde 1276/14 June 1860) notes the appointment of Muʿammar Pasha, former governor of Izmir, to replace Ahmad Pasha as governor of Damascus weeks prior to the outbreak of the Events.

27. Al-Ustuwani, *Mashahid wa ahdath*, 175–176.

28. NARA, RG 84, Damascus, vol. 1, Mikhayil Mishaqa, 'Report on the Damascus Massacre that occurred 9 July 1860,' 27 September 1860, 54–57 (all subsequent references to Dr Mishaqa's data come from this report). Smiley Robson's report is in FO 406 10, 190–196, enclosed with Dufferin to Russell, Beirut, 23 September 1860 (again, all subsequent references to Robson are from this report).

29. The anonymous Christian author of the unpublished manuscript *Kitab al-Ahzan* [The book of sorrows] dedicated a whole chapter to forced conversion, detailing the risks of the heterogeneous crowd, mentioning the forced circumcisions, and citing anonymised examples of those who converted, reverted, or remained Muslim; see 147–155. See also the report by Smiley Robson, who noted that 'hundreds professed Mohametanism, during the massacre, in the hope of saving their lives.'

30. 'On Abduction,' in *Kitab al-Ahzan*, 128–147. See also FO 406 10, 272, Dufferin to Bulwer, Beirut, 26 October 1860, where Lord Dufferin claims 'that a great portion of the Christian girls, now living with their mothers, are discovered to be with child by those who ravished them during the late disturbances.' Scholars of the Armenian genocide have examined the role of sexual violence; see Matthias Bjornlund, '"A Fate Worse Than Dying": Sexual Violence During the Armenian Genocide,' in *Brutality and Desire: War and Sexuality in Europe's Twentieth Century*, ed. Dagmar Herzog (London: Palgrave MacMillan, 2008), 16–58. For a more recent example of sexual violence during genocide, see Beverly Allen, *Rape Warfare: The Hidden Genocide in Bosnia-Herzegovina and Croatia* (Minneapolis: University of Minnesota Press, 1996).

31. Smiley Robson made the same observation in his report: 'Children, therefore, being Moslems, it is unlawful to kill them; but it was doubtless intended to take possession of them and bring them up as Moslems.' He noted that many children restored to their parents had been circumcised as proof that their abductors had planned to raise them as Muslims. Similar arguments have been made in the context of the Armenian genocide: see Donald E. Miller and Lorna T. Miller, 'Women and Children of the Armenian Genocide,' in *Armenian Genocide: History, Politics, Ethics*, ed. Richard Hovannisian (New York: St. Martin's, 1992), 173–207; see also Ara Sarafian, 'The Absorption of Armenian Women and Children into Muslim Households as a Structural Component of the Armenian Genocide,' in *Genocide and Religion in the Twentieth Century*, ed. Omer Bartov and Mack Phylis (Oxford: Berghahn, 2001), 209–221.

32. On the protection offered Christians in the al-Maydan quarter, see Linda Schatkowski Schilcher, *Families in Politics: Damascene Factions and Estates of the 18th and 19th Centuries* (Stuttgart: Franz Steiner Verlag, 1985), 91; and Fawaz, *Occasion for War*, 134. On Muslims who sheltered Christians, see Fawaz, 98; and Sami Marwan Moubayed, *Nakbat Nasari al-Sham fi 1860* [The tragedy of Levantine Christians in 1860] (Beirut: Riad El-Rayyes, 2021), 22–23.

33. On the violence of neighbours in genocidal moments, see Jan T. Gross, *Neighbors: The Destruction of the Jewish Community in Jedwabne, Poland* (Princeton, NJ: Princeton University Press, 2001). Unlike the Jews of Jedwabne, some 85 percent of the Christians of Damascus survived to confront their neighbours after the Events.

Chapter 6: Punish the Guilty and Restore Order

1. UKNA, FO 406 10, 74–75, Graham to Moore, Damascus, 26 July 1860, described the ruins, the visible human remains, the stench of the dead, and the dogs 'still at work' one week after the massacres. The quotation is from Baptistin Poujoulat, *La Vérité sur la Syrie et l'Expédition française* (Paris: Gaume Frères et J. Duprey, 1861), 395.

2. NARA, RG 84, Damascus, vol. 1, Mishaqa to Johnson, 19 July 1860. The cries of the mob were quoted in UKNA, FO 406 10, 74–75, Graham to Moore, Damascus, 26 July 1860.

3. Al-Hasibi, in Kamal Salibi, '*Lamahat min tarikh Dimashq fi `ahd al-tanzimat: Kunnash Muhammad Abu al-Sa`ud al-Hasibi* [Reflections from the history of Damascus in the age of the Tanzimat: The scrapbook of Muhammad Abu al-Sa`ud al-Hasibi],' *Al-Abhath* 21 (December 1968): 133.

4. UKNA, FO 406 10, 74–75, Graham to Moore, Damascus, 26 July 1860, notes 'the slight confidence' after Mu`ammar Pasha's arrival 'was now fast going' and that 'the new Pasha is such a coward that he is afraid to show himself in the town.'

5. Al-Hasibi, in Salibi, 'Lamahat', Al-Abhath 21 (March 1968): 62. Mishaqa's comment is from his report to Johnson dated 19 July 1860.

6. Cited in Leila Tarazi Fawaz, An Occasion for War: Civil Conflict in Lebanon and Damascus in 1860 (London: I.B. Tauris, 1994), 105–106.

7. NARA, RG 84, Damascus vol. 1, 38, Mishaqa to Johnson, Damascus, 29 July 1860; al-Hasibi, in Salibi, 'Lamahat', Al-Abhath 21 (December 1968): 134.

8. NARA, RG 84, Damascus, vol. 1, 38, Mishaqa to Johnson, Damascus, 29 July 1860; Mishaqa to Johnson, 2 August 1860. On troop deployments, see UKNA, FO 406 10, 135–136, Summary of Fuad Pasha's dispatches presented by Ottoman Ambassador Musurus to Mr E. Hammond in the British Foreign Office, London, 8 September 1860.

9. Dr Mishaqa reproduced Fuad Pasha's words in his report to Johnson: NARA, RG 84, Damascus, vol. 1, Mishaqa to Johnson, Damascus, 2 August 1860. The Times of London reproduced a similar version of Fuad's speech on 23 August 1860, suggesting that the Ottoman minister released his text for dissemination; see Caesar E. Farah, The Politics of Interventionism in Ottoman Lebanon 1830–1861 (London: I.B. Tauris, 2000), 611.

10. NARA RG 84, vol. 1, Mishaqa to Johnson, 6 August 1860; Mishaqa to Johnson, 12 August 1860. Mishaqa noted how reluctant the notables were to discuss the meetings and his difficulty in obtaining these details. 'No one can find out what was decided,' he reported to Mr Johnson. Although he seems not to have attended the meetings, Shaykh al-Ustuwani provided some insight into what was agreed, suggesting one of those who attended confided in him; see Muhammad Sa`id Al-Ustuwani, Mashahid wa ahdath dimishqiyya fi muntasif al-qarn al-tasi` `ashar, 1840–1861 [Damascene scenes and events in the mid-19th century, 1840–1861] (Damascus: Dar al-Jumhuriyya, 1994), 178.

11. UKNA, FO 406 10, 118–119, Brant to Bulwer, Damascus, 4 August 1860; NARA, RG 84, Damascus, vol. 1, Mishaqa to Johnson, 17 August 1860.

12. UKNA, FO 406 10, 101–102, Fuad Pasha to Consul-General Moore, Damascus, 4 August 1860; NARA, RG 84, Damascus, vol. 1, Mishaqa to Johnson, 6 August 1860; al-Ustuwani recorded the discovery of the silver; see Mashahid wa ahdath, 180.

13. Al-Ustuwani, 178–180.

14. Al-Hasibi, in Salibi, 'Lamahat', Al-Abhath 21 (December 1968): 128, 134–139.

15. NARA, RG 84, Damascus, vol. 1, Mishaqa to Johnson, 9 August 1860; al-Ustuwani, Mashahid wa ahdath, 180.

16. A copy of the regulations governing the extraordinary tribunal is preserved in BOA, I. Meclis-I Mahsus 864/3.

17. The analysis of Mustafa Bey al-Hawasli's estate, along with that of his nephew Rashid Agha al-Hawasli, is provided by Abdul-Karim Rafeq, 'New Light on the 1860 Riots in Ottoman Damascus,' Die Welt des Islams 28 (1988): 421–423; al-Hasibi, in Salibi, 'Lamahat', Al-Abhath 21 (December 1968): 139–141.

18. NARA, RG 84, Damascus, vol. 1, Mishaqa to Johnson, 20 August 1860.

19. This account is based on al-Ustuwani, Mashahid wa ahdath, 183–185; and al-Hasibi, in Salibi, 'Lamahat', Al-Abhath 21 (December 1968): 141–142. According to Leila Fawaz's sources, the families of the condemned were on hand for the execution by firing squad; see Occasion for War, 140. Dr Mishaqa, in his report of 27 September,

claimed that two of the men hanged had escaped and that one of those shot by firing squad survived. Such variations are inevitable when people are reliant on hearsay for their information.

20. BOA, I. Meclis-i Mahsus 864/3, Fuad Pasha report dated 21 August 1860, names all those sentenced to death by hanging (57) and by firing squad (110), listed by their residential quarter. UKNA, FO 406 10, 111–112, Fuad Pasha to Ali Pasha, Damascus, 20 August 1860.

21. UKNA, FO 406 10, 132–134, Fraser to Russell, 23 August 1860; 165–167, Dufferin to Bulwer, Damascus, 8 September 1860.

22. Al-Ustuwani, *Mashahid wa ahdath*, 185; NARA, RG 84, Damascus, vol. 1, Mishaqa to Johnson, 22 August 1860.

23. UKNA, FO 406 10, 190–196, Dufferin to Russell, Beirut, 23 September 1860, enclosing a report by Rev. Smiley Robson.

24. Al-Ustuwani, *Mashahid wa ahdath*, 187–188. A translation of the sermon delivered in Damascene mosques on 31 August 1860 is preserved in NARA, RG 84, Beirut, vol. 80, Misc. Corr., 524–526. See also Mishaqa's report on the sermon in NARA, RG 84, Damascus, vol. 1, 47, Mishaqa to Johnson, Damascus, 27 August 1860. On Mahmud Hamza, see Linda Schatkowski Schilcher, *Families in Politics: Damascene Factions and Estates of the 18th and 19th Centuries* (Stuttgart: Franz Steiner Verlag, 1985), 55, 101.

25. NARA, RG 84, Damascus, vol. 1, Mishaqa to Johnson, 3 September 1860.

26. NARA RG 84, Damascus, vol. 1, Mishaqa to Johnson, 27 August 1860. BOA, I Meclis-i Mahsus, 864/3, list of 139 men condemned to life imprisonment with heavy labour, by their quarter; 872/1, list of 886 men conscripted for military service, by their quarter.

27. UKNA, FO 406 10, 75–76, Bulwer to Russell, Therapia, 1 August 1860. On 23 August, Fuad reported to British prime minister John Russell's envoy to Syria, Major Fraser, that Ahmad Agha's trial had ended; see 132, Fraser to Russell, 23 August 1860. See also Fawaz, *Occasion for War*, 148–149.

28. The documents establishing the military tribunal to hear Ahmad Agha's trial and the membership of the courts are preserved in BOA, I.Meclis-i Mahsus 864/3.

29. UKNA, FO 406 10, 178–180, Brant to Bulwer, Damascus, 30 August 1860; 132–134, Fraser to Russell, Damascus, 23 August 1860.

30. BOA, I. Meclis-i Mahsus 872/1, audit of Nizami soldiers under Ahmad Agha's command on 9 July 1860 (n.d.).

31. UKNA, FO 406 10, 125, Brant to Russell, Beirut, 16 August 1860; 168–169, Dufferin to Bulwer, Damascus, 8 September 1860.

32. BOA, I.Meclis-i Mahsus 872/1, 21 Safar 1277/8 September 1860, convictions handed down by the Damascus court-martial of Ahmad Agha, former governor of Damascus; Miralay Ali Bey, commanding officer in Damascus; 'Uthman Bey, district governor of Hasbayya; and Binbasi Mehmet Ali Agha, commander of Ottoman forces in Rashayya for their roles in the massacres in those towns.

33. NARA, RG 84, Damascus, vol. 1, Mishaqa to Johnson, 8 September 1860; 53–54, Mishaqa to Johnson, 27 September 1860. On public reaction following the executions, UKNA, FO 406 10, 206–208, Fraser to Russell, Damascus, 21 September 1860.

Chapter 7: Beetles and Scorpions

1. NARA, RG 84, Damascus, vol. 1, Mishaqa to Johnson, Damascus, 2 August 1860; UKNA FO 406 10, 105–107, Fraser to Russell, Beirut, 8 August 1860.

2. On the rapid growth of Beirut and for population figures, see Leila Tarazi Fawaz, *Merchants and Migrants in Nineteenth-Century Beirut* (Cambridge, MA: Harvard University Press, 1983), 30–34.

3. Al-Hasibi, in Kamal Salibi, '*Lamahat min tarikh Dimashq fi `ahd al-tanzimat: Kunnash Muhammad Abu al-Sa`ud al-Hasibi* [Reflections from the history of Damascus in the age of the Tanzimat: The scrapbook of Muhammad Abu al-Sa`ud al-Hasibi],' *Al-Abhath* 21 (December 1968): 143–144. Muhammad Sa`id al-Ustuwani, *Mashahid wa ahdath dimishqiyya fi muntasif al-qarn al-tasi` `ashar, 1840–1861* [Damascene scenes and events in the mid-19th century, 1840–1861] (Damascus: Dar al-Jumhuriyya, 1994), 183, 186–187. NARA, RG 84, Damascus, vol. 1, Mishaqa to Johnson, 17 August 1860; Mishaqa to Johnson, 27 August 1860.

4. NARA, RG 84, Damascus, vol. 1, Mishaqa to Johnson, 27 August 1860. UKNA, FO 406 10, 132–134, Fraser to Russell, 23 August 1860; 138, Brant to Russell, 25 August 1860; 140–141, Brant to Bulwer, 22 August 1860; 159, Fraser to Russell, 30 August 1860; 188–189, Brant to Russell, 20 September 1860.

5. The taunts were quoted by al-Ustuwani from a letter sent by a conscript in Beirut to his father in Damascus; al-Ustuwani, *Mashahid wa ahdath*, 194. A French observer recounted an angry confrontation between Damascene refugees and Fuad Pasha the day after his arrival in Beirut; see Baptistin Poujoulat, *La Verité sur la Syrie et l'Expédition Française* (Paris: Gaume Frères et J. Duprey, 1861), 109–110.

6. UKNA, FO 406 10, 143, Moore to Russell, 31 August 1860; 185–186, Dufferin to Bulwer, 21 September 1860, with a translation of one of Fuad Pasha's announcements to Christians dated 1 Rabi` al-Awwal 1277/17 September 1860. Dr Mishaqa forwarded an Arabic declaration dated 3 Rabi` al-Akhir 1277/18 October 1860 reiterating the call for Damascenes to return to their city. NARA, RG 84, Beirut, C8.1 vol. 80, enclosure with Dr Meshaka's dispatch of October 22, 1860.

7. 'The Massacre at Damascus,' London *Examiner*, 4 August 1860, 487–488, reproduces the 15 July 1860 dispatch published in the *Daily News*, which was based on a telegraphed dispatch dated 11 July, just three days after the start of the Damascus massacre.

8. The song, which runs to eleven stanzas in total, was set to the tune of a song called 'Village Pride,' which in itself might carry some significance, although I have been unable to locate the tune. National Library of Scotland, Crawford.EB.2165, collection of 2,300 broadside ballads, reproduced with permission from the Balcarres Heritage Trust, https://digital .nls.uk/english-ballads/archive/74893189?. The past-tense verb *massacreed* was frequently used in nineteenth-century vernacular English.

9. 'Intervention in Syria,' from the London weekly *Saturday Review* 10, no. 247 (21 July 1860): 68–69. On the European press commentary and its influence on international politics, see Davide Rodogno, *Against Massacre: Humanitarian Interventions in the Ottoman Empire 1815–1914* (Princeton, NJ: Princeton University Press, 2012), 94–95; and Ozan Ozavci, *Dangerous Gifts: Imperialism, Security, and Civil Wars in the Levant, 1798–1864* (Oxford: Oxford University Press, 2021), 302–309.

10. UKNA, FO 406 10, 160–161, 'Notes of a Conversation held with Fuad Pasha by Major Fraser, at Damascus, September 3, 1860.' On Beaufort's mission, see Leila Tarazi Fawaz, *An Occasion for War: Civil Conflict in Lebanon and Damascus in 1860* (London: I.B. Tauris, 1994), 114–126; and Caesar E. Farah, *The Politics of Interventionism in Ottoman Lebanon, 1830–1861* (London: I.B. Tauris, 2000), 647–674.

11. BOA, I.Meclis-i Mahsus 864/3, 6 Safar 1277/24 August 1860, Fuad Pasha's report on correspondence with General Beaufort; FO 406 10, 203, Dufferin to Bulwer, Beirut, 24 September 1860.

12. NARA, RG 84, Damascus, vol. 1, Mishaqa to Johnson, 19 July 1860, 2 August 1860, 17 August 1860.

13. NARA, RG 84, Beirut C8.1 vol. 80 (May–December 1860), Mishaqa to Johnson, list of property lost in attack on his Damascus home, 6 August 1860. The offer to work as a doctor in the hospital is reported in Damascus, vol. 1, Mishaqa to Johnson, 4 October 1860. The conversion rate in 1860 was 110 piastres to the pound sterling.

14. NARA, RG 84, Damascus, vol. 1, Mishaqa to Johnson, Damascus, 8 August 1860.

15. NARA, RG 84, Damascus, vol. 3, 'Commercial Report for the year August 1870—August 1871' and 'Commercial Report for 1871,' submitted in December 1872.

16. NARA, RG 84, Damascus, vol. 1, Mishaqa to Johnson, 4 October 1860.

17. For annual revenues in the province of Damascus, see UKNA, FO 406 10, 340–343, Dufferin to Bulwer, Beirut, 18 November 1860. Abro Efendi, Fuad's assistant in Beirut, reported Ottoman spending on provisions for refugees from Syria and Lebanon at the fourth meeting of the Syrian Commission, 15 October 1860; see FO 406 10, 276–279. British commissioner Lord Dufferin reported on arrears in payment of daily rations caused by the 'utter exhaustion' of Ottoman finances; FO 406 10, 287–289, Dufferin to Bulwer, Beirut, 1 November 1860.

18. On the offer to restore the Mishaqa house, see NARA, RG 84, Damascus, vol. 1, Mishaqa to Johnson, 30 August 1860. On threats against Mishaqa, see UKNA, FO 406 10, 132–134, Fraser to Russell, Damascus, 23 August 1860.

19. Al-Ustuwani, *Mashahid wa ahdath*, 197–199.

20. NARA, RG 84, Damascus, vol. 1, Mishaqa to the Welfare Council [*majlis al-i`ana*], 1 October 1860 (two documents).

21. Al-Ustuwani, *Mashahid wa ahdath*, 196. NARA, RG 84, Damascus, vol. 1, Mishaqa petition to the Wali for compensation of his claims, 23 October 1860; Mishaqa to Wali, responding to compensation offer, 12 December 1860. Ehud Toledano found references to African slaves in 1860s Damascus in court and consular records; see *As if Silent and Absent: Bonds of Enslavement in the Islamic Middle East* (New Haven, CT: Yale University Press, 2007), esp. 63–65, 86–87.

22. UKNA, FO 406 10, 221–222, Brant to Russell, notes the appearance of crosses on 'Mussulman houses inhabited by Christians' appearing on 4 October. NARA, RG 84, Damascus, vol. 1, Mishaqa to Johnson, 8 October 1860.

23. UKNA, FO 406 10, 183–184, Dufferin to Bulwer, Beirut, 14 September 1860; 198–199, Dufferin to Bulwer, Beirut, 23 September 1860.

24. UKNA, FO 406 10, 222–224, Dufferin to Bulwer, Beirut, 1 October 1860; 230–231, Dufferin to Bulwer, 5 October 1960.

25. UKNA, FO 406 10, 243–246, report of the second meeting of the Syrian Commission, 9 October 1860.

26. UKNA, FO 406 10, 279, Fuad Pasha to Abro Efendi, Damascus, 10 October 1860.

27. Copy of Fuad Pasha's proclamation to Damascene Christian refugees in Beirut calling for their return in NARA, RG 84, Beirut, C8.1 vol. 80, 3 Rabi` al-Awwal 1277/18 October 1860. On renewed refugee flows from Beirut to Damascus, see UKNA, FO 406 10, 274–276, Dufferin to Bulwer, Beirut, 26 October 1860.

28. FO 406 10, 216–218, Brant to Bulwer, Damascus, 25 September 1860. Consul Brant called for Halabi's execution as 'a measure indispensable to the public security.' FO 406 10, 262–263, Brant to Russell, Damascus, 8 October 1860. In the fourth meeting of the Syrian Commission, on 15 October, French Commissioner Béclard urged the 'resumption of justice against the guilty in Damascus.' FO 406 10, 276–279.

29. Al-Hasibi, in Salibi, 'Lamahat', Al-Abhath 21 (December 1968): 145–146.

30. On both the Halabi trial and on al-Ghazzi's outburst, see al-Ustuwani, Mashahid wa ahdath, 204, 208–210.

31. UKNA, FO 406 10, 384, Fuad Pasha to Major Fraser, Damascus, 20 October 1860. Al-Hasibi quoted the proverb when detailing the sentences of exile; see al-Hasibi, in Salibi, 'Lamahat', Al-Abhath 21 (December 1968): 148.

32. UKNA, FO 406 10, 287–289, Dufferin to Bulwer, Beirut, 1 November 1860; 307–308, Dufferin to Bulwer, Beirut, 3 November 1860.

33. UKNA, FO 406 10, 274–276, Dufferin to Bulwer, Beirut, 26 October 1860. On another of Dufferin's grand schemes for Syria, see Fruma Zachs, ' "Novice" or "Heaven-Born" Diplomat? Lord Dufferin's Plan for a "Province of Syria": Beirut, 1860–61,' Middle Eastern Studies 36, no. 3 (2000): 160–176.

34. UKNA, FO 406 10, 325–327, Protocols of the Eighth Meeting of the Syrian Commission, 2 November 1860.

35. UKNA, FO 406 10, 330–334, Protocols of the Ninth Meeting of the Syrian Commission, 10 November 1860.

36. NARA, RG 84, Damascus, vol. 1, Mishaqa to Johnson, Damascus, 2 December 1860; UKNA, FO 406 10, 399–400, Wrench to Bulwer, Damascus, 12 December 1860.

37. On the commissioners' reception by soldiers and the government, see NARA, RG 84, Damascus, vol. 1, Mishaqa to Johnson, 2 December 1860; on visits to Christian households and the priests' petition, see UKNA, FO 406 10, 403–407, Dufferin to Bulwer, Damascus, 4 December 1860.

38. FO 406 10, 132–134, Interview with `Abd al-Qadir, Fraser to Russell, Damascus, 23 August 1860.

39. FO 406 10, 340–343, Dufferin to Bulwer, Beirut, 18 November 1860, sets out a synoptic table of all schemes proposed by the European commissioners for the future governance of Syria, including 'a vice-royalty under a Muslim prince' with `Abd al-Qadir suggested for the role. On `Abd al-Qadir and the Arab kingdom proposal, see also Bruno Étienne, Abdelkader (Paris: Fayard/Pluriel, 2012), 283–306.

40. NARA, RG 84, Damascus, vol. 1, Mishaqa to Johnson, Damascus, 29 November 1860; FO 406 10, 408–409, Dufferin to Bulwer, Beirut, 11 December 1860.

41. Fawaz, *Occasion for War*, 192–217. On the Mutasarrifiyya era, see Engin Akarli, *The Long Peace: Ottoman Lebanon, 1861–1920* (London: I.B. Tauris, 1993). On the role of the Syrian Commission and the Mutasarrifiyya in shaping the modern state of Lebanon, see Carol Hakim, *The Origins of the Lebanese National Idea, 1840–1920* (Berkeley: University of California Press, 2013).

Chapter 8: Rebuilding Damascus with Money Grown on Trees

1. Shaykh Sa`id al-Ustuwani noted the opening of the telegraph office in his diary on 7 Dhu al-Hijja 1277 (15 June 1861); see Muhammad Sa`id Al-Ustuwani, *Mashahid wa ahdath dimishqiyya fi muntasif al-qarn al-tasi` `ashar, 1840–1861* [Damascene scenes and events in the mid-19th century, 1840–1861] (Damascus: Dar al-Jumhuriyya, 1994), 222.

2. NARA, RG 84, Damascus, vol. 1, Mishaqa to Johnson, 8 July 1861. It seems very likely that the event was timed to coincide with the first anniversary of the Events. The dinner was held on 5 July 1861, not quite the first anniversary by the Western calendar (which would have been 9 July), but by the lunar Hijri calendar the date was 26 Dhu al-Hijja 1277, which fell six days after the start of the Events on 20 Dhu al-Hijja, 1276.

3. NARA, RG 84, Damascus, vol. 1, Mishaqa report, n.d., appendix to Mishaqa to Johnson, Damascus, 27 September 1860. On Ottoman borrowing in the 1850s, see Roger Owen, *The Middle East in the World Economy, 1800–1914* (London: Methuen, 1981), 100–104.

4. Laila Tarazi Fawaz, *An Occasion for War: Civil Conflict in Lebanon and Damascus in 1860* (London: I.B. Tauris, 1994), 155–156.

5. For Mishaqa's estimate of total Christian losses in Damascus, see NARA, RG 84, Damascus, vol. 1, undated report appended to Mishaqa to Johnson, Damascus, 27 September 1860.

6. NARA, RG 84, Damascus, vol. 1, Mishaqa to Johnson, 8 September 1860; al-Ustuwani, *Mashahid wa ahdath*, 192, 198, 209; UKNA, FO 406 10, 263–264, Brant to Russell, Damascus, 8 October 1860.

7. NARA, RG 84, Damascus, vol. 1, Mishaqa to Johnson, 2 December 1860; al-Ustuwani, *Mashahid wa ahdath*, 211, 216.

8. Shaykh al-Ustuwani claimed that the secret committee first met on 20 April 1861, and he noted that members of the Qanawati, Tawil, Baqu, Jabri, al-Wara`, al-Qabbani, and al-Qazziha families served alongside the Ottoman officials. Al-Ustuwani, *Mashahid wa ahdath*, 220. See also Souad Slim, 'Les indemnités versées aux chrétiens de Damas à la suite des massacres de 1860,' in *1860: Histoires et mémoires d'un conflit*, ed. Dima de Clerck, Carla Eddé, Naila Kaidbey, and Souad Slim (Beirut: IFPO, 2015), 309–324.

9. Dr Mishaqa did not name any of the Muslim members of the committee but reported that members of the Jewish Shim`aya and Abu al-`Afiya families also served; NARA, RG 84, Damascus, vol. 1, Mishaqa to Johnson, 13 May 1861.

10. NARA, RG 84, Damascus, vol. 1, Mishaqa to Johnson, 13 May 1861. Fuad Pasha circulated tables providing official Ottoman figures for the revenues of the provinces of Damascus and Sidon in the Hijri year 1275 (1858–1859) to European members of the Syrian Commission. Lord Dufferin reported to British Ambassador Sir H. Bulwer that the figures

'may not be far from the truth.' UKNA, FO 406 10, 343–345, Dufferin to Bulwer, Beirut, 18 November 1860.

11. NARA, RG 84, Damascus, vol. 1, Mishaqa to Johnson, 13 June 1861.

12. NARA, RG 84, Damascus, vol. 1, Mishaqa to Johnson, 1 June 1861; UKNA, FO 406 11, Rogers to Russell, Damascus, 1 June 1861; Kamal Salibi, 'Lamahat min tarikh Dimashq fi 'ahd al-tanzimat: Kunnash Muhammad Abu al-Sa'ud al-Hasibi [Reflections from the history of Damascus in the age of the Tanzimat: The scrapbook of Muhammad Abu al-Sa'ud al-Hasibi],' Al-Abhath 21 (December 1968): 152.

13. Al-Hasibi, in Salibi, 'Lamahat,' Al-Abhath 22 (June 1969): 51. Al-Ustuwani reported on the government's expropriation of the Hasibi family's fortune, along with the wealth of other exiled notable families, in December 1860; see al-Ustuwani, Mashahid wa ahdath, 212.

14. NARA, RG 84, Damascus, vol. 1, Mishaqa to Johnson, 1 June 1861.

15. NARA, RG 84, Damascus, vol. 1, Mishaqa to Johnson, 3 June 1861.

16. Fawaz, Occasion for War, 159.

17. For the threat of revolt in Damascus, see NARA, RG 84, Damascus, vol. 1, Mishaqa to Johnson, 5 August 1861.

18. On the revolts in the Hawran and 'Ajlun, see NARA, RG 84, Damascus, vol. 1, Mishaqa to Johnson, 26 August 1861, 2 September 1861. Al-Hasibi wrote extensively on village abandonment in the province following the imposition of the indemnity tax; see al-Hasibi, in Salibi, 'Lamahat,' Al-Abhath 22 (June 1969): 51–52.

19. BOA, I. Dah. 365554, 4 Rebîyulahir 1281 (5 September 1864); see also Fawaz, Occasion for War, 158.

20. NARA, RG 84, Damascus, vol. 1, Mishaqa to Johnson, 13 June 1861. Dr Mishaqa gave details of the government's property records in his report to Johnson, 13 March 1862.

21. NARA, RG 84, Damascus, vol. 1, Mishaqa to Johnson, 5 August 1861. In his influential tract Nafir Suriyya [The Clarion on Syria], the Lebanese intellectual Butrus al-Bustani reflected on the risk of Christians inflating their claims in anticipation of government deductions in claims; see al-Bustani, The Clarion of Syria: A Patriot's Call against the Civil War of 1860 (Oakland: University of California Press, 2019), 85–91.

22. NARA, RG 84, Damascus, vol. 1, Mishaqa to Johnson, 24 June 1861.

23. NARA, RG 84, Beirut, vol. 44 (1861), records of the American-Ottoman commission reviewing indemnity claims of US protégés in Damascus, 154–156 (25 July 1861); 184–185 (22 October 1861); 186–189 (24 October 1861); 190–195 (31 October 1861); 196–199 (13 November 1861). The American representatives were Dr Van Dyck and Mr H. H. Jessup, both Protestant missionaries, and US consul Augustus Johnson; the Ottoman representatives were Fuad's deputy Abro Efendi, Constant Efendi, and a Muslim notable of Beirut, Muhiaddin Efendi Bayhum.

24. NARA, RG 84, Beirut, vol. 124 (1862), records of the American-Ottoman commission reviewing indemnity claims of US protégés in Damascus, 6–13 (8 January 1862); 14–17 (10 January 1862).

25. Dr Mishaqa noted that his indemnity award was signed by Fuad Pasha and issued on 23 November 1861 for Pt. 500,000. NARA, RG 84, Damascus, vol. 1, Mishaqa to Johnson, 26 November 1862.

26. NARA, RG 84, Damascus, vol. 1, Mishaqa to Johnson, 10 February 1862.

27. Entry for 29 April 1862, 60, 'The Prince of Wales's Journal: 6 February–14 June 1862,' Royal Collection Trust RA/VIC/MAIN/EVIID/1862, www.rct.uk.

28. NARA, RG 84, Damascus, vol. 1, Mishaqa to Johnson, 28 November 1861.

29. NARA, RG 84, Damascus, vol. 1, Mishaqa to Johnson, 13 March 1862.

30. NARA, RG 84, Damascus, vol. 1, Mishaqa to Johnson, 10 March 1862. Al-Hasibi also reported the 10 percent devaluation of Damascene currency for reparations payments; see al-Hasibi, in Salibi, 'Lamahat,' Al-Abhath 22 (June 1969): 52.

31. On reconstructing poor Damascene Christians' houses, see NARA, RG 84, Damascus, vol. 1, Mishaqa to Johnson, 11 April 1861. On the cash shortfall and the repayment of smallest claims, see Mishaqa to Johnson, 1 September 1862, 4 November 1862.

32. NARA, RG 84, Damascus, vol. 1, Mishaqa to Johnson, 17 February 1862, 24 March 1862, 19 March 1863. See also the reports of Yuhanna Misk dated 24 April 1862 in Badr al-Haj and Ahmad Asfahani, *Mukhbir al-qunsuliyya: Rasa'il Yuhanna Misk ila Richard Wood, 1862–1877* [Informant to the consulate: The letters of Yuhanna Misk to Richard Wood] (Beirut: Kutub, n.d. [2009]), 34, 40.

33. On the 19 percent discount, see NARA, RG 84, Damascus, vol. 1, Mishaqa to Johnson, 30 March 1863. On the 'consolidated' paper money [in Arabic, *awraq kunsulid*], see Mishaqa to Johnson, 4 January 1864. See also the reports of Yuhanna Misk in al-Haj and Asfahani, *Mukhbir al-qunsuliyya*, 40, 43, 52.

34. NARA, RG 84, Beirut, C8.1 vol. 047 (1866), 134–135, 'The Situation in the Province of Damascus, 1864.' Note that Dr Mishaqa submitted this annual report, along with his annual report for the year 1865, in his report dated 27 March 1866 to Mr Johnson. However, he did not make of copy of the 1864 report in his Damascus register; the copy in the Beirut consulate's register is the only surviving copy documenting the end of reconstruction.

35. NARA, RG 84, Damascus, vol. 3, Nasif Mishaqa to Mehmed Rashid Pasha, governor of Damascus, 22 March 1871.

36. For Mishaqa's assessment of security and reconstruction, see his report to Johnson, NARA, RG 84, Damascus, vol. 1, 22 October 1862.

37. NARA, RG 84, Damascus, vol. 2, Mishaqa to Johnson, 18 March 1867; Mishaqa to Johnson, 18 January 1869.

38. Al-Hasibi, in Salibi, 'Lamahat,' Al-Abhath 21 (March 1968): 70–72; on the return of al-Hasibi's father from exile, see Salibi, 'Lamahat,' Al-Abhath 22 (June 1969): 64. On the amnesty and return of Damascenes convicted in 1860 from exile, see BOA I.Dah. 37351 (23 Muharram 1282/17 June 1865). The Ottoman government provided financial assistance for the cost of exiles' travel home; see BOA I.Dah. 37522 (7 Rebîulâhir 1282/29 August 1865).

Chapter 9: Damascus Restored

1. Fuad's departure message is reproduced in Ussama Makdisi, 'After 1860: Debating Religion, Reform, and Nationalism in the Ottoman Empire,' *International Journal of Middle Eastern Studies* 34 (2002): 606.

2. James William Gambier, 'The Life of Midhat Pasha,' *Nineteenth Century* 3 (1878): 78–79.

3. Max Gross, 'Ottoman Rule in the Province of Damascus, 1860–1909' (PhD diss., Georgetown University, 1979), 102–105. In an appendix to his dissertation, Gross provides a translation of the full 1864 Vilayet Law; see 541–554.

4. Gambier, 'Life of Midhat,' 79–80.

5. On the establishment of the province of Syria, see `Abd al-`Aziz Muhammad `Awwad, *Al-Idara al-`uthmaniyya fi wilayat suriyya, 1864–1914* [Ottoman administration in the province of Syria, 1864–1914] (Cairo: Dar al-Ma`arif, 1969).

6. On the petitions campaign, see Jens Hanssen, *Fin de Siècle Beirut: The Making of an Ottoman Provincial Capital* (Oxford: Oxford University Press, 2005), 41–43. BOA I.Dah. 37280, petition from Muslim and Christian notables of Beirut to the governor of Syria, Mehmed Rushdi Pasha, 26 Dhu al-Qa`da 1281/21 April 1865. Among the signatories were Tubiyya `Awn, the Maronite patriarch, as well as the heads of the Armenian Catholics, the Naqib al-Ashraf, and members of leading merchant families.

7. BOA I.Dah. 37280, two petitions from the Muslim notables of Damascus to the governor Mehmed Rushdi Pasha, n.d. One was signed by 147 signatories, the second by 205 signatories, with a large degree of overlap in names. Muhammad Sa`id al-Ustuwani signed both, along with leading `ulama, including the Naqib al-Ashraf, a number of imams and khatibs of leading mosques, and leading Sharia scholars.

8. BOA I.Dah. 37280, two petitions from Christian notables, 1 and 3 May 1865, one signed by 116 notables and the other by 175 leading figures, including the Greek Orthodox and Greek Catholic patriarchs; the Assyrian Catholic bishop; priests of the Armenian, Roman Catholic, and other denominations; and leading merchant notables such as Mitri Shalhub, who had been prominent in various government committees.

9. On the growth of Beirut in the nineteenth century, see Leila Tarazi Fawaz, *Merchants and Migrants in Nineteenth-Century Beirut* (Cambridge, MA: Harvard University Press, 1983).

10. The revenue figure for 1860 is found in UKNA, FO 406 10, 340–343, Dufferin to Bulwer, Beirut, 18 November 1860. Dr Mishaqa's figure is provided in NARA, RG 84, Damascus, vol. 1, Mishaqa to Johnson, 27 March 1866. Mishaqa might have inflated his figures a bit. In 1871 the Ottoman government reported revenues of Pt. 67.5 million for the province of Syria; see Nu`man Qasatli, *Al-Rawdat al-ghanna' fi Dimishq al-fayha'* [The lush garden of Damascus the Fragrant] (Beirut: Dar al-Ra'id al-`Arabi, 1982 [1879]), 129–130.

11. Qasatli, *Rawdat al-ghanna'*, 96–97. The Turkish *lira*, or pound (T£), was worth Pt. 115 in 1868.

12. From Chapter 3 of the Vilayet Law, reproduced in Gross, 'Ottoman Rule in the Province of Damascus,' 545.

13. The resolutions of the General Council were summarised in a letter from Yuhanna Misk to Richard Wood, Beirut, 11 January 1868, reproduced in Badr al-Haj and Ahmad Asfahani, *Mukhbir al-qunsuliyya: rasa'il Yuhanna Misk ila Richard Wood, 1862–1877* [Informant of the consulate: The letters of Yuhanna Misk to Richard Wood] (Beirut: Kutub, n.d. [2009]), 84–88. Misk had his doubts that any of the resolutions would be acted on. See also Gross, 'Ottoman Rule,' which describes the committee as the first Syrian parliament. However, Gross found no evidence that the council ever met again after its 1867 season. Gross, 135–142.

14. BOA, A.Mkt.Um 542/86, 9 Sha`ban 1278/9 February 1862, French claims for compensation for goods and property stolen in the 1860 conflict in Mount Lebanon; I. Dah. 34294, letter from Count Edmond de Perthuis to Ahmad Pasha, governor of the province of Sidon, 4 January 1863, reporting the official inauguration of the carriage road. See also Leila Tarazi Fawaz, 'The Beirut-Damascus Road: Connecting the Syrian Coast to the Interior in the 19th Century', in *The Syrian Land: Processes of Integration and Fragmentation*, ed. Thomas Philipp and Birgit Schaebler (Stuttgart: Franz Steiner Verlag, 1998), 19–28.

15. NARA, RG 84, Beirut, C8.1 vol. 047, Dr Mishaqa's report on 'The Situation in Eyalet al-Sham, 1864,' 134–135. Charles Dudley Warner, *In the Levant* (Boston: Houghton Mifflin, 1895), 258–260.

16. On the extension of the Beirut line, see BOA, I. M. Vala 23541/1, 6 Sha`ban 1281 (4 January 1865); on the line to Muzayrib, see I. Mec. Vala 25856/1, 27 Rabi` al-thani 1284 (August 1868); on the line to Rashayya and Hasbayya, see I. Sura-yi Devlet 1471/1 12 Rabi` al-awwal 1293/7 April 1876. See also my essay 'Instant Communication: The Impact of the Telegraph in Ottoman Syria,' in *The Syrian Land: Processes of Integration and Fragmentation*, ed. Thomas Philipp and Birgit Schaebler (Stuttgart: Franz Steiner Verlag, 1998), 113–128.

17. BOA, Irade Dahiliye 36833/1 (21 Receb 1281/19 December 1864), orders for upgrading the markets of Damascus and widening commercial streets between government offices and the Umayyad Mosque. Most Damascene contemporaries noted the street widening with approval. NARA, RG 84, Beirut, C8.1 vol. 047, Dr Mishaqa's report on 'The Situation in Eyalet al-Sham, 1864,' 134–135. Kamal Salibi, '*Lamahat min tarikh Dimashq fi `ahd al-tanzimat: Kunnash Muhammad Abu al-Sa`ud al-Hasibi* [Reflections from the history of Damascus in the age of the Tanzimat: The scrapbook of Muhammad Abu al-Sa`ud al-Hasibi],' *Al-Abhath* 22 (June 1969): 58–59. See also Qasatli, *Rawdat al-ghanna'*, 100; and Stefan Weber, *Damascus: Ottoman Modernity and Urban Transformation, 1808–1918* (Aarhus: Aarhus University Press, 2009), 1:179–180.

18. Weber, *Damascus*, 1:180–182.

19. Weber, 1:185–189. See also Stefan Weber, 'Reshaping Damascus: Social Change and Patterns of Architecture in Late Ottoman Times,' in *From the Syrian Land to the States of Syria and Lebanon*, ed. Thomas Philipp and Christoph Schumann (Beirut: Orient-Institut, 2004), 41–58.

20. Khalil Sarkis, quoted in Weber, *Damascus*, 1:200.

21. Weber, 1:118–129. On the theatre in Damascus, see Ilham Khuri-Makdisi, *The Eastern Mediterranean and the Making of Global Radicalism, 1860–1914* (Berkeley: University of California Press, 2010), 83–84.

22. Qasatli, *Al-Rawdat al-ghanna'*, 117–121. On the need for state schools to provide trained manpower for the bureaucracy, see Randi Deguilhem, 'State Civil Education in Late Ottoman Damascus: A Unifying or a Separating Force?,' in *The Syrian Land: Processes of Integration and Fragmentation*, ed. Thomas Philipp and Birgit Schaebler (Stuttgart: Franz Steiner, 1998), 221–250.

23. Qasatli, *Rawdat al-ghanna'*, 119–120; Qasatli's figures tally with the provincial yearbook for 1871–1872: *Sâlnâme-yi Vilâyet-i Sûriye*, 3rd ed. (Damascus, 1287–1288), 108, 130. On Quranic schools and madrasas in the Ottoman Empire during the Tanzimat period,

see Selçuk Aksin Somel, *The Modernisation of Public Education in the Ottoman Empire, 1839–1908: Islamization, Autocracy and Discipline* (Leiden: Brill, 2001), 18–19.

24. Somel, *Modernisation of Public Education*, 71.

25. The elementary and rüshdiye school curriculum is reproduced in Somel, 299–303.

26. On the rise and fall of the Damascus Madrasat Sanayi' (the professional trades school), see NARA, RG 84, Damascus, vol. 3, Nasif Mishaqa to Mr Johnson, Commercial Report, 11 August 1870; Nasif Mishaqa to Johnson, Commercial Report, 10 August 1871. See also 'Education in Syria, 1885,' in Charles Issawi, *The Fertile Crescent 1800–1914: A Documentary Economic History* (New York: Oxford University Press, 1988), 67–70. The trades school is mentioned in the provincial yearbook for 1871–1872: *Sâlnâme-yi Vilâyet-i Sûriye*, 3rd ed. (Damascus, 1287–1288), 97.

27. Along with these state civil schools, the Ottoman authorities also established a military rüshdiye and high school to prepare young Muslims for military careers. The military school system attracted 274 students to the rüshdiye school and 72 to the new military high school. See *Sâlnâme-yi Vilâyet-i Sûriye*, 13th ed. (Damascus, 1298/1881), 125–128.

28. Quoted in Benjamin C. Fortna, *Imperial Classroom: Islam, the State and Education in the Late Ottoman Empire* (Oxford: Oxford University Press, 2002), 58–59.

29. Fakhri al-Barudi, *Mudhakkirat al-Barudi* [Memoirs of al-Barudi] (Beirut: Dar al-Hayat, 1951), 1:32. On Maktab 'Anbar, see Zafir al-Qasimi, *Maktab 'Anbar: Suwar wa dhikrayat min hayatina al-thaqafiyya wa'l-siyasiyya wa'l-ijtima'iyya* [Maktab 'Anbar: Images and memories from our social, political, and cultural lives] (Beirut, 1964); Randi Deguilhem-Scheom, 'Idées française et enseignement ottoman: L'école Maktab 'Anbar à Damas,' *Revue du Monde Musulman et de la Méditerranée* 52/53 (1989): 199–206; and Eugene Rogan, 'The Political Significance of an Ottoman Education: Maktab 'Anbar Revisited,' in *From the Syrian Land to the States of Syria and Lebanon*, ed. Thomas Philipp and Christoph Schumann (Beirut: Orient-Institut der DMG Beirut, 2004), 77–94.

30. Qasatli, *Al-Rawdat al-ghanna*', 96–97; Weber, *Damascus*, 2:128.

31. The memoirs of Salih al-Tall are an unpublished handwritten manuscript in Arabic from the 1940s shared with me by his grandson, the late Mulhim al-Tall of Jordan, in 1987–1988.

32. See Corinne Blake, 'Training Arab-Ottoman Bureaucrats: Syrian Graduates of the Mülkiye Mektebi, 1890–1920' (PhD diss., Princeton University, 1991).

33. Rachel Marion Scott, 'Education and Arabism in Damascus at the Turn of the Twentieth Century,' *Islamic Culture* 72 (1998): 17–64.

34. On the reaction in Damascus to the secession of the province of Beirut, see Gross, 'Ottoman Rule,' 392–395.

Conclusion: Dr Mishaqa Retires to Write His Memoirs

1. In NARA, RG 84, Damascus, vol. 2, Mishaqa reported he was suffering from gout in letters to Johnson dated 24 November 1865, 4 August 1868, and n.d. [December] 1869. Dr Mishaqa's letter of resignation, written by his son Nasif in English, is dated 18 March 1870.

2. On the duration of Nasif Mishaqa's tenure as US vice-consul in Damascus (he resigned on 10 February 1914), see Erdogan Keskinkiliç and Ebubekir Ceylan, 'Her Majesty's Protected Subjects: The Mishaqa Family in Ottoman Damascus,' *Middle Eastern Studies* 51 (2015): 190.

3. Nu`man Qasatli, *Al-Rawda al-ghanna' fi Dimishq al-fayha'* [The lush garden of Damascus the Fragrant] (Beirut: Dar al-Ra'd al-`Arabid, 1982 [1879]), 154; Jurji Zaydan, *Tarajim Mashahir al-sharq fi'l-qarn al-tasi`  `ashar* [Biographical dictionary of the celebrities of the East in the nineteenth century], 2nd ed. (Cairo: Matba`a al-Hilal, 1911), 177–180. See also Fruma Zachs, 'Mikha'il Mishaqa—The First Historian of Modern Syria,' *British Journal of Middle Eastern Studies* 28, no. 1 (2001): 67–87.

4. NARA, RG 84, Damascus, vol. 2, Mishaqa to Johnson, classified 'secret, not official,' 18 January 1869.

5. Mikhayil Mishaqa, *Murder, Mayhem, Pillage, and Plunder: The History of the Lebanon in the 18th and 19th Centuries,* trans. Wheeler M. Thackston Jr. (Albany: State University of New York Press, 1988), 244.

6. Mishaqa, *Murder, Mayhem,* 269–270.

7. Mishaqa follows an Arabic literary convention of self-abasement in the opening line of his manuscript, 9.

8. Butrus al-Bustani, *The Clarion of Syria: A Patriot's Call against the Civil War of 1860* (Oakland: University of California Press, 2019).

9. Ussama Makdisi, *Age of Coexistence: The Ecumenical Frame and the Making of the Modern Arab World* (Oakland: University of California Press, 2019), 6, 20, 64–65, 69, 71.

10. Selim Deringil, *The Well-Protected Domains: Ideology and the Legitimation of Power in the Ottoman Empire, 1876–1909* (London: I.B. Tauris, 1997).

11. On Beaufort's 1860 map and its role in shaping the modern state of Lebanon, see Carol Hakim, *The Origins of the Lebanese National Idea, 1840–1920* (Berkeley: University of California Press, 2013).

12. Kamal S. Salibi, 'The 1860 Upheaval in Damascus as Seen by al-Sayyid Muhammad Abu'l-Su`ud al-Hasibi, Notable and Later *Naqib al-Ashraf* of the City,' in *Beginnings of Modernization in the Middle East: The Nineteenth Century,* ed. William R. Polk and Richard L. Chambers (Chicago: University of Chicago Press, 1968), 188.

13. Yuhanna Misk reported the 'malicious joy' of Damascene Muslims at the death of Fuad Pasha 'because of his former acts [after the 1860 Events]' in his letter to Richard Wood of 19 February 1869; Badr al-Haj and Ahmad Asfahani, *Mukhbir al-qunsuliyya: Rasa'il Yuhanna Misk ila Richard Wood, 1862–1877* [Informant of the consulate: Letters of Yuhanna Misk to Richard Wood] (Beirut: Kutub, n.d. [2009]), 118–119.

14. The French government raised `Abd al-Qadir's pension after the 1860 Events from 100,000 to 150,000 francs; John W. Kiser, *Commander of the Faithful: The Life and Times of Emir Abd el-Kader* (Rhinebeck, NY: Monkfish, 2008), 314. On Ottoman stipends to `Abd al-Qadir and his family, see BOA, I.Dah. 37261 (28 Zilhicce 1281/23 May 1865); I.Meclis-i Vâlâ 25484 (12 Shevval 1283/17 February 1867); I.Meclis-i Vâlâ 25247 (9 Cemaziulevvel 1283/19 September 1866); I.M.Mahsus 1487 (28 Cemaziyelâhir 1285/15 October 1868); I.Dah. 42195 (20 Shevval 1286/23 January 1870).

15. `Abd al-Qadir's petition to visit Istanbul, BOA, I.Dah. 36491 (4 Rebiyulevvel 1281/6 August 1864); award of the Nishan-i Ali-i Osmani, First Class, to coincide with `Abd al-Qadir's visit to Istanbul, I.Hariciye 12335 (24 Zilhicce 1281/19 May 1865); `Abd al-Qadir's letter of thanks to the sultan, I.Dah. 37298 (4 Muharrem 1282/29 May 1865); and his expense claims for rent (Pt. 37,200) and furnishings (Pt. 28,590), I.Dah. 37653 (19 Cemaziyulevvel 1282/10 Oct 1865).

16. For `Abd al-Qadir's views on Freemasonry, see Bruno Étienne, *Abdelkader* (Paris: Fayard/Pluriel, 2021), 370. Étienne discusses `Abd al-Qadir's travels to Paris, London, and the opening of the Suez Canal, 311–373, 374–411.

17. `Abd al-Qadir's premature obituaries appeared in the *New York Times* on 12 November 1873 and again on 12 November 1879. Charles Dudley Warner, *In the Levant* (Boston: Houghton Mifflin, 1895), 299–301.

18. Muhammad Sa`id al-Istuwani recorded Amir `Abd al-Qadir's death in one of the final entries to his diary. Muhammad Sa`id al-Ustuwani, *Mashahid wa ahdath dimishqiyya fi muntasif al-qarn al-tasi` `ashar, 1840–1861* [Damascene scenes and events in the mid-19th century, 1840–1861] (Damascus: Dar al-Jumhuriyya, 1994), 225.

19. Al-Ustuwani, *Mashahid wa ahdath*, 49–51.

20. Qasatli, *Al-Rawda al-ghanna'*, 153.

21. Zaydan, *Tarajim Mashahir al-sharq*, 2:177–80.

22. Mishaqa, *Murder, Mayhem*, 270. See also the Mishaqa family tree in Peter Hill, *Prophet of Reason: Science, Religion and the Origins of the Modern Middle East* (London: Oneworld Academic, 2024). Members of the Mishaqa family (who spell their name Mechaka) have posted photos and details of their family tree on the genealogical website Geni.com; see www.geni.com/people/Khanum-Mechaka/6000000012963857656?through =6000000020732782494, accessed 19 March 2023. The same website confirmed that Nasif's oldest son's name was Mikhayil and recorded that Nasif had five children, Salim had two children, Ibrahim had four children, and Iskandar had five children. There is no record on Geni.com of Salma having had any children.

INDEX